GETTING WISER TO TEENS

More insights into marketing to teenagers

GETTING WISER TO TEENS

More insights into marketing to teenagers

by Peter Zollo

New Strategist Publications, Inc.
Ithaca, New York

539 83743

New Strategist Publications, Inc.
P.O. Box 242, Ithaca, New York 14851
800 / 848-0842
607 / 273-0913
www.newstrategist.com

HF
5415.32
.Z65
2004

ISBN 1-885070-54-3

Printed in the United States of America

To Debbie, Ben, Sarah, and Jimmy

Table of Contents

Tables

Chapter 7. Teens and Friends

Chapter 8. Teen Lifestyle

Chapter 9. Teens and Brands

Chapter 10. Teens and Media

Chapter 11. Marketing and Advertising to Teens

Author's Note

This book likely would not have been written—or, at the very least, not written as well or as soon—if not for my colleague Rob Callender. *Getting Wiser to Teens* represents a true collaborative effort: Rob drafted half the chapters.

Rob is TRU's writer-in-residence; his talent is perhaps best displayed to our clients in *TRU View*, our twice-monthly teen trend report. But Rob's contribution doesn't stop there: Almost all of our creative client communications in some way bear Rob's distinctive stamp of humor and intelligence.

Rob joined TRU four years ago as a somewhat frustrated journalist with a penchant to use his skills to do something different. I don't think he really knew what he was getting into when he decided to join a market research firm, which was probably a good thing for both of us. For a former journalist who had covered Caribbean heads of states, U.S. governors, and—by freak accident—the tour bus driver for REO Speedwagon, the idea of concentrating solely on youth marketing was, to say the least, "off career course."

As it turns out, Rob was just what TRU needed and I think in many ways TRU was what Rob needed. Not only has he quickly grown his teen-marketing acumen to the level of expertise, Rob has taken many of our "deliverables" to creative heights not typically associated with marketing research.

Collaborating on a book was a new challenge for Rob, one I know he appreciated and—for the most part—even enjoyed. Fitting this writing into his already full workload meant longer days, of course (and nights). But when we finally finished drafting, editing, and then proofing the more than 400 pages that compose this book, Rob characteristically asked me if he could read them just one more time.

Rob, I thank you.

Acknowledgements

There are many people to thank—both for their help in writing this book and for their encouragement over the years. Just as teens know that family provides the foundation for all they do and hope to accomplish (see Chapter 6!), I know that the past two-plus decades of living a traveling, frenetic life would not have been possible or worthwhile without the unflappable support of the four people I live with. Debbie, you're my most trusted advisor and the foundation of our family. Ben, Nini, and Jimmy: When I wrote the first edition, none of you had reached your teen years. As I finish this one—to use TRU parlance—one of you has "aged out" and the other two are close behind. What I've learned from the three of you could fill more pages than those that follow.

Mom, thank you as always for your unbridled pride and constant interest. Dad, in the first edition I wrote, " . . . the only book I look more forward to seeing published than this one is the first Burt Zollo novel." What an inspiration you are to us not only for persisting and succeeding but doing so with such passion, determination, and joy. Now, I look forward to novels two, three, and four.

Thank you to my brother, Paul Zollo, an author himself of many books and a writer of many more songs, for his constant support and interest.

Now, to TRU staff, who truly made this book a reality. Michael Wood, you're the primary impetus for this third edition. As you know, the very thought of putting the necessary time and effort into this project nearly kept me from beginning. But you pushed Rob and me to new heights—which is characteristic of what you do for TRU on a daily basis.

Dan Drath, without your taking over the custom side of our business and personally handling more projects than any human should, it would have been impossible for me to have taken on and completed this task. Your energy, skill, and dedication continue to amaze.

Thank you, Kate Danaj, for continuing the TRU tradition of relocating to the West coast without really moving away. Your contribution to almost everything we do is unmistakable and makes us that much better. Thank you as well for drafting the final chapter of this book.

Jill Klein, thank you for your more than a decade of service to TRU—for growing with us, for always looking for new ways to contribute, and for keeping me on task.

TRU's staff has never been stronger, more skilled, or more enthusiastic. Rob Callender (see "Author's Note"), Casey Sloan, Keith Navratil, Susan Chaggaris, Meghan Corcoran, Shannon Smiley, Maureen Woods, Shelly Denton, Melissa Robold, Kristen Beaulieu, Kit Nordmark, Casey Hess, Jason German, Michelle Trayne, Amy Brooklier, your efforts and your talent are greatly appreciated. Thank you as well to so many past staffers whose contributions to TRU live on.

I also want to thank four close friends who have been indispensable sounding boards to me during the past many years: Bobby Fisher, for convincing me to buy TRU 16 years ago and allowing me to work on the "business" that's closest to my heart; Steve Elrod, for your enthusiastic interest and insightful counsel; Steve Goodman, for your wisdom and never-ending concern; and Jay Silverman, for keeping me laughing no matter what. Thank you as well to Bill Ewing (for the best cover design yet and much more), Rick Greenswag, Dean Goldberg, Kelly Hyman, Marla Grossberg, Scott Kohn, and Hal Roseth.

I've been fortunate to have had a few mentors in my professional life. Ann and Paul Krouse, Burleigh Gardner, and Ben Kartman: I'll always remember what you gave me and what I learned from you.

Thank you to my publisher and editor, Penelope Wickham and Cheryl Russell, for keeping after me and never saying "no."

Finally, both this book as well as TRU as an organization owe everything to two key constituencies. Thank you to TRU's clients through the years for the privilege of working with you on your brands, your campaigns, and your causes, as well as for sharing and enjoying together what we do on a daily basis.

At last count, TRU has interviewed more than half a million teens—many of whom (particularly those on our Trendwatch Panel) we've been fortunate to get to know quite well. How lucky I am to have a career that's dedicated to the group that is the most enlightening, fascinating, and inspiring.

Chapter 1

Why Teens Are Important Consumers

What's the biggest change in teen marketing in the past 20 years? The easy answer—and arguably the most accurate—is that companies have become more sophisticated in their understanding of teens and in their approaches to marketing and advertising to them. In fact, marketers' new-found teen savvy may be less a matter of enlightenment than of self-preservation: teens themselves are more marketing-savvy than ever before. So, just as marketers have moved to the next level in their teen-marketing acumen, teens have evolved as marketing targets, becoming increasingly adept at detecting and processing branding messages. This parallel growth in both brand managers' and teens' marketing intelligence allows teens to maintain their status as an always-challenging target: it's almost as if teens evolve simply to defend themselves against marketers' growing cunning and zeal. And, it's just that kind of resourcefulness and flexibility that we love about teens!

At Teenage Research Unlimited (TRU), we talk about this phenomenon as Teen 201 and 301. Most (but not all) marketers have now graduated past the remedial lessons of Teen 101, but generally not without making a few inevitable wrong turns along the way. How quickly the art and science of marketing to teens has developed since we founded our company more than 20 years ago. At that time, many brands that should have been targeting teens simply ignored them. Why? Well, for one, the U.S. teen population was shrinking from its baby-boom high in 1975. But, beyond that, many brand managers simply gave up before they began. They didn't feel they could be sufficiently successful to warrant the investment, so they simply didn't try. When I recount some of these stories to our junior staff, who have experienced nothing but the teen marketing boom, they are incredulous that brands in some of the most naturally teen-appropriate categories (we're talking soft drinks, jeans, and record companies!) didn't target teens just a decade or two ago. Today it seems beyond belief that these types of companies would be devoid of teen-specific efforts. But, whether they were talking to each other or reading the same trade-journal articles, they all shared a similar contention: teens were dangerously fickle and too elusive to risk targeting them. Teen fickleness, according to these 1980s marketers, prevented the development of a message or overall branding strategy that would stand the test of time (with time being the operative term—for some, it was only a couple of years, and for others it meant much longer). Similarly, these marketers felt teens were simply too difficult to find, too hard to reach, and almost impossible to connect with. (Even 20 years ago, we vehemently disagreed with these characterizations: teens then and now are neither overly fickle nor elusive. Instead, marketers were unprepared; most hadn't even begun to learn the lessons of Teen 101.)

What, then, convinced so many companies to change their tune? For some, it was simply the recognition that their business could profit from teens *today*. For others, it was a long-term commitment to develop a relationship with teens now for future payoff. In both cases, we found that it took a real hero within an organization—an internal teen-marketing advocate, so to speak—to get his or her company on the teen track. These were the real pioneers of teen marketing, who literally blazed the trail through trial and error, but always through innovative thinking, planning, and implementing. At TRU, we've been privileged to have worked closely with many of these individuals during their formative years, to have learned shared lessons (and benefited from them), and to continue to work with many of these same clients today.

The opportunities apparent in marketing to teens are greater than ever: the coming of age of the large Millennial generation, the biggest population cohort since the Boomers, is almost reason enough to warrant a teen initiative. But, that's only the beginning.

There are two keys to unlocking the teen market: first, acknowledge the importance of teenage consumers; second, recognize their uniqueness.

Advertising and marketing efforts that work with adults often will not work with teens. And advertising and marketing geared to children are almost always inappropriate for teens. Teenagers not only like ownership, they demand it. They want media and products they can call their own. They typically respond most positively to advertising and marketing messages and tactics that are particularly age-appropriate. This characteristic guides the strategies needed to target teens. But there's a fine line between what works and what doesn't in marketing to teens. If teens regard a marketing message as blatantly pandering or too obvious in its attempt to be cool, they will quickly reject not only the message but also the messenger. The harder you press the cool button, the more teens will push back.

Teens' increasing marketing savvy not only manifests itself in their growing scrutiny of your offerings, but also in their lexicon. I wish we had kept count of the number of times we've heard teens in qualitative-research sessions use terms like "targeting," "viral marketing," "demographics," and even "product attributes" in discussing the issues at hand. And no wonder. Teens are marketed to like never before, and many are receiving consumer education in school. Just when more companies wised up to the potential of teens for their business, teens wised up to marketing tactics.

It's fair to say that many teens understand marketing better than many marketers understand teens. This scenario strikes fear in the hearts of some of the bravest marketers, and it's another reason why many continue to shy away from the teen market. Clearly, for some brands, teens remain a high-risk proposition. But they also promise high reward. If you're able to reach and communicate with them effectively, the payoff likely will be worth the effort. On the other hand, if you take the conservative path and steer clear of the teen market, you minimize the short-term risks of misstepping with teens but endanger the overall growth of your business. So, what to do? Here's a shocking recommendation from a researcher: do your homework! Conduct exploratory research to figure out what you mean to teens—what your brand currently offers them and what it could provide in the future. If you approach the research smartly, you'll likely uncover opportunities—whether it's developing a new product line for teens, optimizing current concepts with a particular teen bent, or simply improving the way you advertise or market current products or services to teens.

Over the past several years, two misconceptions about marketing to teens have finally been erased, and rightfully so: one, teens are too elusive to reach because, as a target, they move too fast to hit them with any precision; and two, they are simply too fickle. As media vehicles for youth proliferated in the 1980s and 1990s—from MTV to Channel One, from *Teen People* and *Cosmogirl* to countless Web sites, from local radio stations to a plethora of sponsored events—teens have become more reachable. Getting your message in front of the audience is only one step toward getting teens to listen to you, but it's an essential step. The second obstacle—the concern that teens are fickle to the point of being dangerous—has been overcome. This has occurred not only because of companies like ours, but also because of champions at the client level: typically, brand managers or marketing VPs (but also researchers) who pushed to target teens, seeing the pot of gold ahead. Did teens suddenly become less fickle? There has been no fundamental change among teens in this respect; in fact, teens continue to be attracted as much as ever to The Next Big Thing. Instead, the change is among marketers, who recognize that teens can be approached like any other demographic target, albeit with unique challenges. So, as more youth marketers laid these two obstacles aside, new teen-targeted products, advertising, promotions, events, and total marketing programs followed. These pioneering companies eventually became teen-market converts, even recognizing that teens' penchant for trends could be an opportunity rather than an obstacle. More about that later.

In time, most of our clients graduated to Teen 202. Many did so enthusiastically, becoming explorers in their own right, learning how to connect with teens by developing relevant product or branding propositions. Others were reluctant to the point of being obstinate, requiring more than a modicum of convincing. For some, the size of the teen market—compounded by the favorable population trend that still exists, convinced them. For others, it was a combination of factors—including the ability to reach teens through media, the availability of proper research methods, and the importance of teens as influencers within the family.

Just how viable is the teen market? An interesting perspective comes from comparing teens and adults on a few core market measures. First, in the past few years, teen population growth has outstripped that of adults: specifically, the number of 12-to-19-year-olds grew by 7.3 percent between 1997 and 2003, compared to a 5.6 percent increase among adults. But the more telling story comes from examining spending figures, which demonstrate the synergistic effect of population and spending growth that fuels interest in this market. According to TRU data, teen spending has increased by 38 percent since 1997, compared to a 14 percent increase for adults. TRU also estimates that 85 percent of teen income is discretionary, meaning teens can—and do—blow 85 cents of every dollar on impulse or other non-mandated purchases. Adults, saddled with the fixed costs of living (mortgages or rent, utilities, food, etc.), average only 10 percent of their income for discretionary spending.

Teens not only have the numbers and the dollars, they also have the confidence. TRU's teen consumer-confidence measure finds that even in the midst of a stumbling economy, 77 percent of teens are optimistic, meaning that they believe they'll spend the same amount or more in the coming year as they did in the past year. Government consumer-confidence measures, which focus on adults, find only 40 percent to be consumer-confident, just half the percentage among teens. And why shouldn't teens be consumer-confident? After all, they have a more stable income than most adults. Whereas 80 percent of adults rely on a single income source (namely, their paycheck), 80 percent of teens boast two or more income sources,

Teen Spending Outlook

Many teens plan to spend more money in the next year.

*(percent distribution of teenagers by spending outlook
for the next 12 months and gender)*

	total	female	male
Spend more	37%	34%	39%
Spend less	21	21	21
Spend same amount	40	42	37

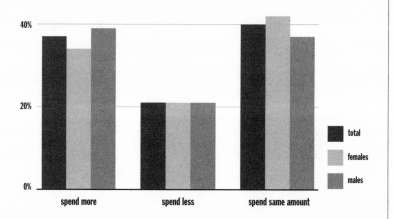

Source: The TRU Study, Teenage Research Unlimited, Inc.

7

Getting Wiser to Teens

boosting not only their confidence but also providing a more protected means of spending.

The big question is no longer why a growing number of marketers are wising up to the teen market's potential. Rather, the new question is why those still reluctant to engage teens are willing to be left behind. If the comparative teen–adult demographic and economic measures aren't sufficiently convincing, a more detailed look is warranted. Here are the Six Big Reasons to target teens:

1. Teens are important because of their discretionary spending power. How much teens spend probably continues to be the subject of more media stories than all other teen-market topics combined. Their annual spending—now approaching the $200 billion mark—is staggering, astounding reporters and entrancing marketers. Our firm probably gets at least two dozen media calls a week on teen-specific subjects running the gamut from high-tech gadgets to low-rise jeans. But probably half the questions concern what we've come to refer to as "the teen market story."

I must admit we enjoy these interviews least of all, because reporters generally want to know only the same basics: how much money teens spend and earn. Though we've recited these figures more times than any of us cares to admit, there's no escaping just how compelling they are. Combined with the growing teen population, the numbers have convinced quite a few marketers to get serious about teens.

In the 1980s, we came up with an effective (if rather lame) acronym to announce that teen consumers had arrived: skippies (School Kids with Income and Purchasing Power). Back then, we at TRU found ourselves spending as much time trying to convince companies of the viability of the teen market as helping them understand teens. These days, it feels as if companies are coming out of the woodwork to market to teens, thankfully saving us from ever again needing to utter the term "skippies" and allowing us instead to concentrate on the business of researching teens. So, on with the numbers.

In 2002, teens spent $109 billion of their own money and an additional $61 billion of their parents' cash, according to TRU estimates. These numbers alone add up to more than the gross domestic product of countries such as Finland, Norway, Portugal, Denmark, and Greece. And that's without counting how much parents spend on teens. Even the terrorist attacks of September 11, 2001, failed to change teens' proclivity to spend. It's as if cash really burns that proverbial hole in their pockets.

Teens aren't totally immune from the occasional economic dip that makes adults' stomachs turn, but teen spending declines are delayed because they are somewhat insulated from cyclical ups and downs (for which they can thank their parents!).

Part of the reason for teens' indifference to economic factors is self-imposed ignorance: despite daily reports of an ailing economy, teens tend to tune out the bad news. It's not just that they're tired of hearing about it—they simply can't relate! TRU's Trendwatch[1] panelists attribute teens' sunny spending outlook to three factors: first, parents pay most, if not all, of their bills; second, prices haven't increased noticeably for the items they buy; and third, as they look ahead, they're a year older. Teen reasoning says that the older you get, the more money you earn—and ultimately spend.

Bear in mind, too, that until recently today's teens have witnessed only economic expansion. Coupled with the fact that most teens don't feel the pinch of economic downturns until family conditions are truly desperate, it's easy to understand why they just don't get it. Perhaps that's why, even during the dark days of the recent economic downturn, more than one-third of teens assumed they would spend *more* over the next 12

---

[1] *Trendwatch is a panel comprised of teen members of the two trend-leading Teen/Types: Influencers and Edge teens. The teens on the panel live in the leading style markets, including Los Angeles, New York, Miami, Seattle, San Francisco, and Chicago. TRU and its clients employ Trendwatch for early reads on teen interest in or acceptance of a variety of lifestyle trends.*

Teens' Weekly Spending

The average teen spends more than $100 per week.

*(average weekly spending by teenagers of their own money and
their parents' money, by gender and age)*

	total	female	male	12 to 15	16 to 17	18 to 19
Total spending	$118	$119	$117	$92	$125	$163
Parents' money	38	41	35	42	36	34
Own money	80	78	82	50	89	129

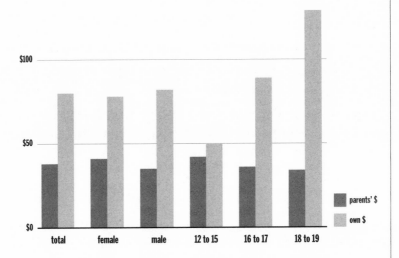

Source: The TRU Study, Teenage Research Unlimited, Inc.

months. Another one-third believed they would spend the same as the year before. Significantly more younger than older teens held this view. Not coincidentally, these youngest teens, most of whom aren't of legal working age, are more monetarily reliant on their parents than older teens are and less concerned about being laid off. A mere 16 percent of teens figured they would spend less in the current year. Notably, the oldest teens (18- and 19-year-olds) are the least optimistic. The closer teens get to the age of self-reliance, the more conservative (i.e., realistic) their economic outlook becomes.

So, nearly 80 percent of teens believe they will spend either more or the same in the coming year. Their spending reflects their confidence: despite tough times, we're seeing only slight drops in teen spending. This fact hints at the hyper-optimism that's historically been a teen hallmark. Unlike adults, teens don't panic at the threat of dreary financial forecasts. What's more, nearly all of teens' spending money is discretionary, so they can (and will) continue to make impulse buys. The lesson here is that ongoing relationships with teens, rather than large transactions, are what will keep your business in good company with this age group throughout the economy's ups and downs.

Teens' financial optimism allows youth marketers to breathe a slight sigh of relief. Clearly, teens don't view economic developments in the same way their parents do, so don't underestimate teens' consumer confidence in light of bad economic news. Not only do few teens actually set a budget for themselves, most won't even consider belt-tightening until tougher economic times prompt a family crisis that finally ties the purse strings shut.

Teen spending has changed over the past few years, however. Although teens continue to spend the bulk of their money on typical youth products such as snack foods, makeup, and clothes, they are spending growing amounts on family groceries, cell phone bills, and books.

Teen Purchases in the Past Three Months

Most teens regularly buy soft drinks, jeans, movie tickets, snacks, and CDs.

(percent of teens purchasing item or whose parents purchased item for them in the past three months)

Soft drink	71%
Jeans	69
Movie ticket	69
Potato chips	68
Chocolate candy	62
CD	61
Casual shoes	49
DVD movie	49
Breath mints	49
Cookies	47
Bubble gum	45
Video game	40
Book	37
Athletic wear	36
Disposable camera	29
Camera film	28
Concert ticket	19
Energy drink	15

Source: The TRU Study, Teenage Research Unlimited, Inc.

Teen expenditures mirror teen interests and needs. It's helpful to think of teen spending as falling into three categories: small purchases (CDs, snacks and beverages, other impulse buys, and gasoline); mid-level purchases (clothes, school club dues, and other expenditures related to hobbies and interests); and big-ticket purchases (cars and consumer electronics such as cell phones, video-game systems, and stereo equipment). Teens spend the most on what costs least—51 percent of teens' weekly purchases are for items costing less than $25, and 86 percent are for items costing less than $100. But, as the adage goes, little things add up in a big way!

Teenage boys spend an average of $82 a week of their own money, while girls average of $78. Although boys spend somewhat more of *their own* money (and historically always have), girls spend a noteworthy $6 more of *their family's* money each week ($41 of family money spent by girls versus $35 spent by boys).

This spending pattern has never ceased to intrigue us. Why do teen guys spend more of their own money while girls spend more of the family money? For one, despite being in the 21st century, guys still tend to pick up the check for girls in a formal dating situation (although there has been a big drop-off in traditional dating). Also, guys are faced with more car expenses because parents often pick up the tab for a daughter's car repairs, gasoline, and even the car itself. Although both genders are more likely to drive a car bought used than new, girls are driving around in later models. Interviews with parents (as well as with girls themselves) have revealed that parents are willing to buy the peace of mind that comes with a newer car for daughters, figuring boys are better able to deal with the maintenance and breakdowns that often accompany used cars. Think of it this way: parents would prefer to have their son rather than their daughter stranded if a used car breaks down. Another reason girls spend more family money than boys is that parents simply trust their daughters more with family funds.

Teen Ownership of Big-Ticket Items

The majority of teens own a computer.

(percent of teens owning big-ticket items)

Home stereo	82%
TV	82
Backpack	79
Computer	76
VCR	74
Portable stereo	74
Wristwatch	68
Home video game system	63
Bicycle	61
Camera (nondigital)	59
Sunglasses	59
School yearbook	58
DVD player	56
Cell phone	45
Portable video game system	45
CD burner	44
Musical instrument	42
Car stereo	41
In-line skates	35
Video camera	30
Used car (bought used)	25
Digital camera	24
Contact lenses	24
MP3 player	14

Source: The TRU Study, Teenage Research Unlimited, Inc.

Now that we have a grip on how much money teens spend, the next logical question becomes: where does all the money come from? The answer to this question—perhaps more than any other single data point—explains just how strong a market teens represent. Teens get their money from a variety of sources, including allowances, gifts, and jobs. In fact, we like to think of teens as having a more diversified income portfolio than most adults. As stated earlier, the vast majority of adults rely on a single income source (their job), while teens have several. Because of this diversification, teen income is more stable than that of adults.

Although teens think they are protected from national economic trends, teen income rises and falls with the economy. But we've discovered a lag effect: teen spending downturns are delayed. Why? The largest single source of teen income is their parents, and many parents contend that if they're suffering financially, they'll make sure the children will be the last to feel it. For most parents, when it comes to making tough decisions on where to cut back, their children are at the bottom of the list—whether it's spending money for their kids or funding teen activities and interests. But when the economy dips, teen income eventually and inevitably drops (although to a lesser degree), because so much of it comes from parents. Similarly, when the economy is on the upswing, teen income rises.

Interestingly, teens benefit more from as-needed handouts than from regular allowances. More than half of all teens—55 percent—report receiving as-needed money from parents, and this number is strong among all age segments: 59 percent of the youngest and 45 percent of the oldest teens report getting a little cash from mom and dad. In fact, rather than as-needed funds being doled out in proportion to age, it's a gender story. Here again, it pays to be female (literally): 61 percent of girls compared to only 50 percent of boys receive parental financial handouts. But guys get some semblance of revenge when it comes to allowance. While parents are more liberal in handing out cash to daughters, a larger proportion of boys enjoy a traditional allowance. Twenty-six percent of boys vs. 23 percent of

Teen Income Sources

Most teens get money from their parents, but only one in four gets an allowance.

(percent of teens receiving money from selected sources)

	total	female	male	12 to 15	16 to 17	18 to 19
Parents	55%	61%	50%	59%	59%	45%
Gifts	45	49	41	53	42	31
Odd jobs	29	26	32	30	31	25
Part-time job	29	29	28	11	39	54
Allowance	24	23	26	33	23	9
Full-time job	5	5	6	1	2	17
Own business	2	1	3	2	3	1
Other	25	29	20	27	19	25

Source: The TRU Study, Teenage Research Unlimited, Inc.

16

girls receive a weekly allowance. When it comes to allowance, age is key: 33 percent of the youngest teens receive a regular, structured stipend, compared to only 9 percent of the oldest.

It's no surprise, then, that older teens are more self-reliant when it comes to finance. More than 50 percent of teens aged 16 or older work. Among 18- and 19-year-olds, 54 percent work part-time and 17 percent work full-time. Only 11 percent of teens under age 16 report having a part-time job.

A few years ago, we asked teens in our ongoing quantitative study, "If you had an extra $100 to spend, what would you spend it on?" This proved to be a revealing question because the number-one answer was that they wouldn't spend the $100 at all—they would save it. At first look, we were impressed with the financial restraint teens showed. It appeared that either their parents or our educational system were effective at teaching teens the value of saving. But when we probed the issue, we found something else: teens would save the $100 *because* they wanted to accumulate enough cash to spend it on something that cost even more! Thinking beyond teens' predilection for spending the most on the least-expensive items, the truly enticing purchases are often well beyond the $100 price point—coordinated outfits, video-game systems, the latest cell phone, MP3 players, digital cameras, a car, etc. Still, perhaps parents and schools should feel validated that their savings lessons are not all in vain. After all, most adults also save for a rainy day. Teens, perhaps, are just more proactive about it, looking for the weather to change even more quickly.

Teens' financial acumen continues to impress us. An example occurred during a fashion/lifestyle project we did for Levi's a few years ago, which included spending time in a Johnny Rockets restaurant with several Levi's panelists from Orange County, California. As I sat across the table from a fashion-forward 13-year-old middle-school boy waiting to be served cheeseburgers and malts, he quizzed me about the stock market. Then he

What Teens Would Spend An Extra $100 on First

If teens had an extra $100, the very first thing they would do with their money is . . . save it!

(percent distribution of teens by the first thing they would do with an extra $100)

Save it	33%
Buy clothes	24
Buy CDs or tapes	11
Buy something else	9
Pay a bill	7
Buy athletic shoes	5
Spend it on entertainment	4
Buy other shoes	2
Buy collectables	2
Buy computer software or games	2
Buy food	2
Spend it on a party	2
Buy video games	2
Buy books	1
Buy makeup	1
Buy jewelry	1

Source: The TRU Study, Teenage Research Unlimited, Inc.

began a long, knowledgeable discourse about how to pick out a stock, bond, or mutual fund. He eventually revealed the remarkable success he'd had in trading. TRU found similar teens in a quantitative study we conducted a number of years ago for *Money* magazine. Although we know that the financial whiz kid is the exception rather than the rule, there is a quantifiable segment of teens (about one-fifth of all those in the *Money* study), who are especially interested—and well-versed—in personal finance.

For teens, the basic financial tool—really, the training wheels of investment options—is the simple passbook account, held by nearly two-thirds of teens. In fact, by the time they get their driver's license, most teens will have been receiving bank statements for years. Not surprisingly, once they master the passbook, most teens are eager to accelerate their fiscal control, steering toward more grown-up financial tools including checks, debit cards, and credit cards. Although today's teens have a wealth of banking options, traditional savings accounts continue to accrue most of teens' interest. More teens (62 percent) report having savings accounts than any other banking or investment option. Checking accounts follow at a distant 23 percent. Nearly one-quarter of teens enjoy access to a credit card—either their own or a parent's. An inverse relationship exists between teens who want their own credit card and teens who already have one (or access to parental plastic). The older the teen, the greater their access to credit and the lower their reported interest in obtaining another card.

Having a credit card in their name doesn't hold the same appeal to today's teens as it once did. As recently as 1998, 39 percent of teens wanted their own credit card, compared to just 17 percent today. This figure has declined steadily each year. So, what's going on? A number of things, including increased consumer credit awareness, the proliferation of debit cards, and the trend in retail toward issuing preferred customer cards—all of which appear to have detracted from the novelty and prestige plastic once enjoyed among teens. Importantly, many teens and parents fear that the convenience of credit could lead to overspending and debt. With teens

Teen Banking and Investing

Twenty-nine percent of 18-to-19-year-olds own a credit card.

(percent of teens with selected financial accounts, by gender and age)

	total	female	male	12 to 15	16 to 17	18 to 19
Saving account	62%	61%	63%	62%	60%	65%
Checking account	23	25	21	5	18	64
Debit card	20	23	17	4	16	57
Stocks or bonds	19	20	18	21	18	15
Interested in getting a credit card	17	19	15	16	21	16
Own credit card	10	11	8	2	6	29
Access to parents' credit card	10	10	9	5	13	16
Certificate of deposit	8	8	8	9	8	8
Mutual funds	7	7	8	8	7	6

Source: The TRU Study, Teenage Research Unlimited, Inc.

increasingly perceiving such cards as potentially dangerous, marketers across the board—particularly those who offer plastic—should communicate their understanding of these fears and assuage concerns by offering an educational component or campaign with their products.

2. Teens are important because they spend family money. Lifestyles have changed, and teens have met the challenge. Most teens live in households with two working parents or a single parent who works. Whether they like it or not, these latchkey kids are assuming greater responsibility for household shopping than did teens in the past. It's almost as if they've been forced to shop, getting a crash course in real-life consumer education. Simply put, teens are often the only family members who have time to stand in line at the grocery store.

Fully half of teens—57 percent of girls and 43 percent of guys—do some food shopping each week for their family. These percentages are higher than for more traditional teen activities, such as dating, going to sports events, and attending a religious or youth-group meeting. In fact, more teens grocery shop for their family weekly than download music (finally some good news for the record companies)! Most teen grocery shoppers are doing fill-in buying, but some are responsible for the major portion of household food shopping.

What an opportunity for food marketers! When teens stroll the grocery aisles, not only are they exposed to thousands of products and hundreds of brands, they are also sorting out all those brands and products and making decisions and purchases on behalf of their household. Food marketers who still think they need to target only the female head of household will undoubtedly miss out on huge teen opportunities. These companies should be catering their promotions and offerings to teens, especially on weekends and after school on weekdays. Teens aren't going to get excited about a free oven mitt as a premium. Instead, how about a compilation CD, a DVD, or even smaller-sized packages of their favorite snack and drink brands? Similarly, food retailers should offer samplings of popular teen foods during teen dayparts.

Because teens are in their infancy as grocery shoppers, it's important to think of these as their formative food-shopping years, when teens are beginning to develop buying habits, patterns, and loyalties that will stay with them for a long time. Although teens make many of the buying decisions at retail, typically they still do so under the guidance or instructions of a parent. Specifically, when going to the store to shop for the family, teens are outfitted with a list prepared by mom. Importantly, though, the list is usually generic. Instead of specifying Hellmann's, for example, it simply says mayonnaise. In this scenario, teens are empowered to make the choice. And most do end up choosing the same brand that usually resides in their refrigerator or cupboard for two reasons: 1) they're accustomed to the brand and personally prefer it; and 2) it's an easy, quick decision (and, teens are all about simplicity at the grocery store). But for a smaller segment of teens, a more rebellious nature emerges—even in the mundane setting of a grocery store. These teens seem to say, mom buys Hellmann's . . . hell if I'm going to! They choose another brand—or even another condiment altogether.

TRU estimates that teens spent $61 billion of their family's money in 2002. Notably, this figure does not include the family spending *influenced* by teenagers, which is likely more than triple this figure. Consequently, the total economic impact of teenagers far exceeds the $170 billion of their own and family money spent by teens in 2002.

3. Teens are important because they influence their parents' spending. Teens influence their parents' purchases in four all-too-familiar ways. First, when teenagers (or children) accompany their parents to the store, their parents often let them add some gimmes to the cart: either the teen convinces the parent to buy something, or the teen grabs something from the shelf without much protest from mom or dad. (In qualitative research, teens have told us about a variety of seemingly devious tactics they use to get what they want, such as sneaking items into the grocery cart while simultaneously diverting their parent's attention or handing an item directly to the cashier, quickly bypassing their parent's eyes.) Most parents understand that when their teenage children suggest that they keep them company during a grocery-store excursion, it is not because the teen is seizing the opportunity to spend quality time with them. Instead, teens know there is something in it for them. As much as they may request that mom or dad buy them a certain product or brand, teens know the odds of getting *exactly* what they want increase if they make the trip themselves. They also recognize that—like adults—they often don't know what they want until they see it on the shelves or sample it in the aisles. When asked why they voluntarily partake in the seemingly uninteresting activity of grocery shopping, teens quickly explain that there's just no substitute for being there. Although most teens say their mom (more so than dad) is adept at getting the food they want, teens say it's worth their time to go to the store and fill up the cart with their favorite snacks and beverages and then have their parents pay.

Second, teenagers influence their parents' purchase decisions even when they are not with them. There's the direct approach, when the teen specifically asks the parent to buy a particular item. Parents wryly note how teens who appear utterly oblivious to other goings-on around the house can suddenly and mysteriously sense when a parent is grocery-store-bound. After all, a parent with cash at hand is not only an appealing target for teens but also an easy mark; many parents will even seek out requests, and teens are only too happy to oblige them. There's also the indirect influence of teens on parent purchases, borne of parental observation. Countless teens we've interviewed claimed that their parents (again, primarily mom) just know what they want. Interviews with moms validate this assertion, with mothers explaining that if they don't buy exactly what the teen wants, the purchase might go to waste. So, there's something in it for mom: she doesn't want to spend money on an item she knows her teens don't like and won't use. And, unlike with younger children, parents of teens typically have thrown in the towel when it comes to trying to change teen eating habits and preferences.

Third, teens influence adult purchases when parents actively seek their counsel. Teens often know more about certain products than their parents do—cell phones, computers, and even clothes. Many parents consult with their in-house expert before buying these and other items. Mothers have told us in focus groups that part of the deal for buying clothes for their teen is that she (this seems to apply to daughters only) must accompany mom to the store to lend advice on mom's clothing purchases. Don't forget that today's parents—although not necessarily younger in years than those of a generation ago—are younger in attitude and fashion sensibility. They want to dress accordingly, and who better to keep them in fashion than their own teenager?

Fourth, teens influence parent purchasing of gifts. Teens typically receive big gifts on birthdays and Christmas or Chanukah, and they're quite eager to point a stymied parent in the right direction. Members of TRU's Trendwatch Panel recently shared their wish lists with us, and the results ran the gamut from the outrageously optimistic—a new SUV or a Jacuzzi—to the pleasantly practical—savings bonds for college and a computer for homework (and, no doubt, entertainment!). What's more, teens will be the first to tell parents that giving knows no season, and they're rarely shy about asking for interim gifts "just for being loved," as one of our panelists explained.

For many retailers and fashion marketers, the *real* teen Christmas season arrives in late summer: the back-to-school season. In fact, parents spend more on their teenaged children in preparation for the new school year than on any other occasion.

4. Teens are important because they are societal trendsetters. Not only are teens prewired to seek out The Next Big Thing, they are watched closely by our youth-obsessed culture for the latest trends. There's no age group more involved with fads or doing more to fuel the greater population's interest in trends than teens. The big irony, however, is that teens won't 'fess up to it. No matter whether the teen is a verifiable trendsetter (a member of TRU's Edge or Influencer Teen/Types) or a trend follower (a Conformer, the most common Teen/Type), teens tell us they personally don't follow trends. But, they do—and they do so adeptly and ardently. Teens are also quick to point to their peers as being trend followers, even though they insist they are not. I've grown so accustomed to teens rejecting the very notion that they personally adopt whatever's the latest and greatest that I found it remarkably refreshing one day when one of my closest friends (a highly successful attorney and community leader) enthused, "I admit it: I love trends!" And he does—sorting out the trends that interest him from all the rest. The moral of the story: 1) adults are more secure than teens and are willing to acknowledge a penchant for trends; and 2) adults follow young America's lead.

In fact, corporate America has turned the pursuit of teen trends into an obsession. Industry-wide, a phenomenal amount of time, effort, and money goes into developing products, advertising, and promotions that capitalize on teen trends. Often the marketer who gets there first wins. Much of the work we do at TRU is centered on uncovering teen trends and communicating them on a timely basis to our clients. (More on this in Chapter 4 on Teen Types, Trends, and Music.) We've developed a twice-monthly teen trend report, called TRU View, that focuses on the latest in teen trends and how marketers can tie into them. It's nearly impossible to overstate not only the importance of trends in teen lives and in marketing to teens, but also teens' role as trend ambassadors to the greater population.

The teen role as broadcaster of what's hot was driven home to us during a college project we did a number of years ago in which we visited a few of the country's top spring break destinations (I know—a tough assignment). After talking to hundreds of college students over the course of many days, we discovered that the use of mainstream fashion to secure their position in society was far less important to them than to high school students. College students are less stratified socially and less affected by peer pressure (to them, that's *so* high school), two factors that produce teens' perceived need to be fashionably in vogue. Further, when we asked college students how they find out about the latest fashions, several said they learn about what's current from their younger teenaged siblings.

Younger children, being aspirational, look up to teens and often adopt the latest in teen fashion. That's why we guide marketers to typically err on the older side when it comes to youth marketing. If you want to know what tweens care about—or, more importantly, what they're going to get into next—keep your eye on teens: tweens do. Whether it's their older brothers and sisters, older kids in the neighborhood and school, or teens depicted in popular media, tweens can't wait to be older. Of course, once teens see little kids following their lead by wearing what they're wearing, you can write the obituary for that trend! That's what makes marketing to teens challenging and studying them so fascinating.

What's worse than their little brothers and sisters adopting their styles and labels? When their parents do it! My lawyer friend wasn't unique in his trend involvement—perhaps just more honest than most adults. Even adults who are not parents of teens look to teenagers to see what's in. In fact, one factor that hurt Nike (a brand which at present is rebounding strongly with teens) was that soccer moms (and grandmothers!) could be found in every mall in America wearing the ubiquitous swoosh. Talk about taking the edge out of a brand's image. Teens want things that are especially for them—or, at the least, they need to feel that a specific part of the brand is one they can claim as their own. Nike—through newer product offerings and more teen-specific marketing and retailing—is winning teens back.

Teenage influence extends beyond fashion and popular culture, affecting the nation's economy in a big way. A few years ago, a reporter for a leading financial newsletter called our office. Assuming it was another case of a writer looking for the teen market story, I was prepared to recite the latest figures on teen earnings and spending. Then the writer explained his different, more innovative angle. Recognizing the enormous economic power of the teen market and teens' trend-setting ability, he asked me which products or brands would be popular in the coming year, so he could advise his readers to buy the stocks of those companies. We've developed a measure, known as the TRU Hit List, that combines past-year purchase of key durable items with purchase intent for the same categories. This index has proven reliable for predicting the next hot teen product. As of this writing, the list is populated not only with what's new in high-tech (MP3 players, digital cameras, DVD players, CD burners), but also includes teen staples (used cars, school yearbooks, class rings). Arming oneself with this information is important not only to the manufacturers of these items but also to teen marketers at large, who should think about how they can leverage the appeal of high-scoring Hit List items—even if their company would never market them. Marketers should consider featuring these hot products in advertising or programming or giving them away in promotions.

More than a few of our clients also closely watch TRU's Coolest Brand Meter, which measures the relative appeal of hundreds of brands on arguably the ultimate teen criterion, to get stock-purchase ideas of their own. What's key to using the Coolest Brand Meter is not to focus on the Total column but to take a look at what's on the move with Edge and Influencer teens. (More on this in Chapters 4 and 9.)

5. Teens are important because of the money they will spend in the future. If you sell acne medicine, video games, jeans, or soft drinks, marketing to teens is a no-brainer. If you sell credit cards, automobiles, or newspapers, targeting teens is a less obvious but perhaps bolder move. It's the most forward-thinking of companies that are actively developing a relationship with teens for their adult brands. These are the companies

TRU's Hit List

For teens, these are the hottest items—the big-ticket items with the greatest sales potential.

(items with the highest Potentential Purchase Score)

	potential purchase score
School yearbook	41
Cell phone	33
DVD player	31
Used car	26
CD burner	24
Digital camera	24
Contact lenses	24
Portable stereo	23
Sunglasses	23
MP3 player	22
Wristwatch	22
Backpack	22
Car stereo	21
Class ring	20
Home video game system	19
Computer	19
Video camera	16
Home stereo	16

Note: The Potential Purchase Score is derived by adding the percentage of teens who intend to purchase the item during the next 12 months to the percentage who purchased the item during the past 12 months.
Source: The TRU Study, Teenage Research Unlimited, Inc.

that are future-spending based on an understanding of the size and power of the current teen cohort. There's no time like the present to get teens to begin to think about you and like you.

We have worked with a number of companies in building awareness and positive attitudes for their adult brands among teens. A number of years ago we conducted both qualitative and quantitative research to assist Discover Card in developing and monitoring its youth-marketing program. This research included a magazine educating teens about the importance of personal finance, which was distributed in schools, as well as with college scholarships, and during special events. Since that time, other credit card companies have followed, realizing that young consumers not only have a need for credit, but that they're sorting out brands well before they're eligible to sign on the dotted line.

We helped General Motors and its publishing partner, General Learning, increase the appeal of a magazine GM distributed in high school driver education classes. Although teens aren't buying many new cars themselves, that didn't stop GM. The automaker understands that American consumers buy an average of only seven cars during their lifetime, and many stay with a specific make over the course of many years. In another GM project, we conducted a series of focus groups with teens and parents to gauge the appeal and enhance the concept of a parent-teen partnership in driver's education known as Partners in Safety. Designed to promote safety and ease a stressful situation (teaching teens to drive), this type of program builds goodwill among both teens and parents. Although overt marketing messages are muted in these efforts, the subtleness typically benefits the sponsoring brands.

Our Kids Research Unlimited division worked with the *Chicago Tribune* in developing *KidNews*, a weekly newspaper within the newspaper for tweens (8-to-14-year-olds) that has become the prototype for children's newspaper supplements nationwide. Former *Tribune* senior editor Cokie Dishon, who developed the editorial concept, was not only committed to creating a quality newspaper for this age group but also dedicated to the idea of promoting the Tribune brand. Although clearly on the editorial side, Cokie is an astute brand marketer who thinks in the long term. She was determined to get children and young teens accustomed to reading a real newspaper (and the *Trib* in particular). Despite much debate to the contrary (including selectively ignoring some qualitative research about what kids themselves said they wanted to read), she smartly insisted that hard news constitute a major section in each issue. She also decided not to shrink the paper to fit smaller hands, believing that by familiarizing young readers with a full-sized newspaper, they would more naturally graduate to the adult version once they were ready.

In discussing adult brands that have been successfully marketed to teens, I would be remiss not to include those in the tobacco business. After all, more than 80 percent of adult smokers began during their teen years, and tobacco companies are finding themselves facing a shrinking customer base (some quit, but many more die from the product itself). Although underaged smokers are supposed to be hands-off, tobacco industry documentation tells another story. American cigarette companies aren't the only ones that have targeted teens. In fact, former Food and Drug Administration commissioner David Kessler contacted TRU a few years ago to have us replicate two studies conducted by Imperial Tobacco of Canada. Dr. Kessler was determined to use the findings to shed light on how to reduce the prevalence of teenage smoking, rather than to encourage it. One of the Imperial studies was titled Project 16 (a reference to the age of the company's target). The other was known as Project Plus or Minus, reflecting the conundrum that tobacco companies face: customers die every day (i.e., the minus) and need to be replaced (yep, the plus). Camel remains probably the most notorious example of an adult brand that has courted teenagers—and successfully so. It has been accused of developing a character, Joe Camel, who distinctly appeals to youth. Unfortunately, cigarette companies, which are in many ways among the most savvy of marketers, recognize the importance of teens as a future market better than most other package-good companies. In fact, I think other adult brands can learn from their example. After all, cigarette brands—to the great detriment of our children—understand how to effectively integrate all aspects of brand marketing to teens—coordinating relevant, image-oriented advertising with promotion, product-placement (especially in movies), point-of-purchase displays, sampling, distribution, and merchandising (Marlboro and Camel gear, in particular).

Perhaps the only good thing that has come of tobacco companies' youth-directed marketing is that it has provided fodder for antitobacco efforts. These efforts have pointed out the industry manipulation of teens, which is probably the most effective youth-directed, antitobacco message platform. When presented compellingly (as done not only by the American Legacy Foundation's national Truth campaign, but also by some of the leading state campaigns including those in Florida, Iowa, and Minnesota), teens get really pissed off. Better yet, fewer of them are smoking!

Although Camel and other tobacco brands have denied—despite documentation to the contrary—having gone directly after an underage market, other, more upstanding adult brands are openly and actively developing relationships with teens, convinced that this effort will pay off as teens enter adulthood.

6. Teens are important because the large Millennial generation now fills their ranks. In 1963, there were 18 million teens in the U.S. population. Forty years later, today's 33 million American 12-to-19-year-olds account for a larger population than that of 193 of the world's 227 countries!

When TRU's founders—Paul Krouse, Dr. Burleigh Gardner, my father Burt Zollo, and I—first contemplated launching a teen-research firm in 1982, like all reasonably intelligent marketers, we checked out the associated demographics. When we looked at trends in the U.S. teen population, we discovered the segment was projected to decline for at least a decade.

The Teen Population
Is Expanding

The teen population will grow by another 1 million during this decade.

(number of people aged 12 to 19, 1990–2010; in millions)

1990	27.8
2000	32.4
2010	33.5

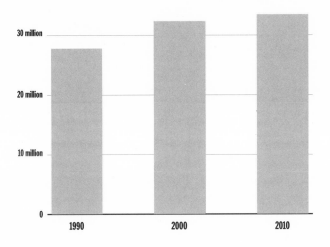

Source: U.S. Bureau of the Census and projections by New Strategist Publications

Heeding the notion that it's all in how you interpret the numbers, we figured if we could survive the first 10 years, it would be smooth sailing thereafter. Fortunately, we guessed well. Corporate America now recognizes the huge opportunity teens present. We no longer need to sell the merits of the market and can concentrate instead on helping our clients profit from it.

In the early 1990s, the long-awaited "echo boom"—the children of the baby-boom generation, otherwise known as Millennials—finally hit its teen years. In just the past decade alone, the U.S. teen population has grown by 17 percent. This teen growth spurt is still in full force as Millennials continue to enter the age group. By 2010, the population aged 12-to-19 should have expanded by another 1.1 million. Because of teens' increased spending, the teen population boom creates a powerful synergy: more teens spending more money. No wonder so many marketers now vie for teenage attention and favor. But be mindful: although it's tempting to view all 33 million teens as belonging to the same lifestage, the teen market is anything but homogenous. First, the cognitive and experiential differences between those at the youngest stage (think prepubescent middle school students) and the oldest (college students or high school grads with full-time jobs) are enormous. And, as much as today's teens embrace racial and ethnic diversity, TRU data reveals distinct differences in the preferences of teens by race and ethnicity. Fortunately, the commonalties that bind teens are stronger than the differences among segments.

Chapter 2

Teen Psyche

If you learn one thing from this book, it should be this: teens are not as simple as the one-dimensional portrayals many marketers favor. The teen years are daunting, exciting, and utterly confusing, but rarely ever clear-cut.

Occasionally, a prospective client will approach TRU asking us to simply list the things teens like and don't like. We don't consider this an entirely useful goal, because in order to be successful in marketing to teens, a deeper understanding is essential. Rather than simply knowing teens' tastes, marketers need to understand their deeper motivations—the things that prompt them to do what they do and like what they like. So, we prefer to enlighten rather than list—providing clients not only with the information but, more important, the rich insight needed to understand teens. Although more effective, this task can be tougher than it seems.

Although every adult once viewed the world through the eyes of a teen, most work aggressively to distance themselves from their teen years as they grow older. Once an individual has passed through this lifestage, it seems he or she would just as soon not revisit it. This developed distaste for the teen years has a side effect that comes back to haunt those who deal with teens: TRU has found that, as time goes by, many adults lose sight of (and empathy for) the trials and tribulations of their own adolescence. Many people call this a generation gap. We believe it's a case of selective memory.

As traditionally interpreted, the term "generation gap" describes the conflict between two distinct cohorts (typically those of parent and child) whose social, political, and cultural experiences are so different that they find it difficult to comprehend the other's worldview. This gap was perhaps best exemplified in this country during the late 1960s, when a generation that had banded together to win World War II looked on in shock and dismay at a younger generation that so mistrusted the government's policies in Vietnam that some renounced their U.S. citizenship and moved to Canada.

Today's teens and their parents are much closer ideologically than that teen-parent cohort. Baby Boomers won the philosophical battle of the late 1960s, and as they reworked society and popular culture, they established a more progressive tone. Theirs was a democracy of ideas where "different" didn't necessarily mean "wrong." Although some rue the era's moral relativism, the fact remains that by embracing and exploring so many ideas considered "different," society dramatically reduced the number of ideas considered "radical." It has been argued—and convincingly so—that nothing did more to bring the counterculture into the mainstream (and therefore to neutralize the counterculture) than the success of the counterculture itself.

Most of today's teens were born to Baby Boomers (although some of the youngest were born to Generation Xers). They have grown up in a world colored by the philosophies of inclusion and acceptance, and they have absorbed those lessons even more readily than did the generation that made these beliefs its mantra. In short, today's teen values are so similar to those of their parents that there simply isn't enough conflict for a deep, ideologically driven generation gap.

To the contrary, much of TRU's research suggests that the mis-understandings between today's parents and teens are differences in perspective, not core values. These are the inherent differences that always exist between parent and child. The squabbles arise because teens—lacking adults' first-hand experience—often go with their heart or instinct when making decisions, while adults tend to abandon ideology in favor of practicality, a tactic that often rankles teens.

Still, we've found that teens enjoy spending quality time with their families (as long as they don't feel they're missing out on a "better offer" with their friends). And, in a finding sure to surprise many adults, teens

37

The Opinions Teens Value

When asked, "Which one person's opinion, beside your own, matters to you most overall?" the largest share of teens say it is the opinion of both mother and father.

(percent distribution of teens by the person whose opinion matters most to them, by gender)

	female	male
Both mother and father	27%	30%
Mother	21	12
Friend	15	12
Boyfriend/girlfriend	9	9
Father	3	11
Brother/sister	5	4
Peers	3	5
Grandparent	2	2
Priest/rabbi/clergy	1	1

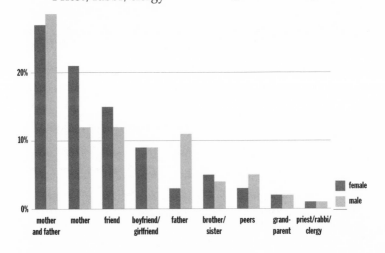

Source: The TRU Study, Teenage Research Unlimited, Inc.

even place great value in their family's opinions. In fact, when it comes to value-based decisions, teens weigh their parents' counsel more heavily than anyone else's. So, those expecting to find a generation of surly, contrary, argumentative loners are often surprised to learn that more than half of teens claim one or both parents as the person whose opinion they value most. In contrast, only 18 percent mention a friend, significant other, or peer. Notably, though, teens are still teens and aren't overly fond of authority figures outside the family. Fewer than 2 percent of teens named a clergy member, teacher, coach, or school counselor as being the most influential person in their life.

All this sounds like good news for families, right? It is, but it doesn't negate the fact that teens still fight with their parents. More often than not the sources of animosity are familiar: their "attitude" (20 percent), chores (18 percent), and grades (12 percent). Matters of independence—such as curfew, money, boyfriends/girlfriends, and how they spend their free time—also figure prominently. Few people would be surprised to learn that teens resist doing things that aren't much fun—notably, homework, chores, and cleaning their room. But the fact that the most frequent argument between teens and parents revolves around a teen's attitude is a testament both to teen rebellion and to adults' tunnel vision. Most parents tend to forget that a few decades ago they probably were making the same point their child is making now (and feeling the same persecution that their teen now claims). Whether adults choose to remember it or not, as teens they probably weren't any more delicate in their dealings with their elders! Unfortunately, when adults forget how they felt when they were young, they lose sight of where today's teens are coming from.

How do adults avoid the sort of communication breakdown that leads to so many arguments with teens? We are the first to admit it's not easy. After all, adults rely on their own (heavily edited) history of personal experience—one that teens can't understand and generally don't accept as valid. Independence-minded teens tend to see their life as a blank slate,

What Teens and Parents Fight About

Teens' "attitude" is the number one issue over which teens and parents fight.

(percent distribution of teens by the "one fight teens keep having over and over with their parents")

	total	female	male
Your attitude	20%	23%	17%
Responsibilities around the house	17	18	17
Grades / school	12	9	15
Cleaning your room	10	10	10
Curfew	8	8	8
Money	5	4	6
Your boyfriend or girlfriend	4	6	3
Your future	4	3	5
How you spend your free time	4	3	6
Your friend(s)	4	3	4
How you look or dress	3	3	4
Driving	3	3	3
The music you listen to	2	1	3
Cigarettes, drugs, or alcohol	2	1	3
Your job	2	1	2
Your parents' friend(s)	0	0	1
Something else	12	11	12

Source: The TRU Study, Teenage Research Unlimited, Inc.

and relying on someone else's preconceived notions doesn't appeal to them in the least.

By the same token, the teenage thought process tends to grow more foreign and mysterious to adults with each passing birthday. But if parents are sometimes at a loss to explain why their offspring act or think the way they do, they may be somewhat consoled to know that teens themselves sometimes have only the vaguest understanding of their own actions, thoughts, and feelings. The reality of the situation is that teens are driven by an ever-changing mix of motivations—some physiological, some psychological, and some social. The one common factor: all are heavily influenced by emotions.

The physiological shifts required to turn a child into an adult are truly profound. Teens experience physical changes more dramatic than anything they have encountered in their lives, and probably more dramatic than what they will ever again face.

In the midst of these physical changes, each teen is also faced with the daunting prospect of finding his or her own identity. After years of shelter and protection, teens find themselves increasingly responsible for their own wellbeing. And after a lifetime of being regarded principally as someone's son or daughter, they suddenly feel compelled to establish an identity of their own. What's more, they have to do all this without any kind of road map. Sure, they get advice (lots of it!), but they almost never seem to appreciate unsolicited input. When they want advice, they'll ask for it. And, although they respect their parents' opinions, they're still more likely to go to friends for advice if the subject is one they're not sure their parents will understand—or want to hear.

As rudderless as the teen years sometimes seem to an outsider, we have identified several drivers of teen behavior that are based on teens' fundamental needs, many of which are unique to this lifestage. These need-states are important to consider when crafting effective messages. To be relevant to teens, it's essential that you address—or perhaps even offer a solution to—teens' needs. Let's take a look at the needs one by one. In doing so, ask yourself whether your company or brand strategy hits one or more of the teen need-states.

Teen Need: Fun

Perhaps the most obvious teen need-state, fun is synonymous with youth. Teens are keen observers, and they understand that although adulthood means greater freedom, it also means greater responsibilities and obligations. All in all, most teens seem to view adulthood as a rather unholy tradeoff—older people have more money and independence, but they're often so hamstrung by work, bills, and family obligations that they can't take advantage of them. This was brought home to me when a group of teens explained quite seriously why fun is so important, contrasting their lifestage with that of adults. They closely watch their parents and other adults, they told me, and have come to the conclusion that older folks just don't have a whole lot of fun. Teens know that at some point in their lives they, too, will be saddled with adult responsibilities and sensibilities, and fun will become less of a priority. Therefore, they reason, they should concentrate on having as much fun as possible now—in a sense, get it while the getting is good. Consequently, most teens consider having fun their most pressing job for the time being. And they take it quite seriously!

The teen appetite for entertainment and socialization has always been insatiable. Especially today, when teen lives are increasingly overscheduled, they make sure to carve out lots of time for fun with their friends. When TRU asked more than 2,000 teens which attitudes best describe their generation, 21 percent said they have too much to do and too little time in which to do it. Another 17 percent said they are overly stressed, and 13 percent said they feel too much pressure to succeed. Still, the response that garnered the most support was, "we're all about fun." And, just as fun and youth are synonymous, teens say fun and friends are too—almost anything can be fun if it includes their friends! Much more on that later.

What Best Describes This Teen Generation?

Half of teens say their generation is about having fun.

*(percent of teens citing characteristic as one of three
that best describes their generation)*

We're about fun	50%
High-tech is so much a part of our lives	41
We're living in dangerous times	25
We're open to new ideas	24
We have too much to do and too little time to do it	21
Our world moves faster than it has for other generations at our age	21
We're about individualism	18
We're overly stressed out	17
We'll have great opportunities as adults	13
We're accepting of differences	13
There's too much pressure to succeed	13
We're focused on our own goals	11

Source: The TRU Study, Teenage Research Unlimited, Inc.

Interestingly, teens know life isn't all fun and games. Many tell us the world sometimes seems more dangerous than ever before. One-fourth say they are "living in dangerous times." Still, most teens don't hole themselves up in their room and adopt a bunker mentality. Rather, they explain that if the world truly is dangerous and the future uncertain, that's all the more reason to have fun now!

Teen Need: Independence

TRU's qualitative research finds that although teens generally speak lovingly of their families, they harbor some major points of contention with parents. One of the most common complaints is that parents won't mind their own business. Some examples of parental intrusion, of course, seem wholly justified to everyone but the teen. These include calling friends' parents to make sure the kids are where they said they would be or simply asking how a student's day went. Other examples, such as searching a teen's room without cause or provocation, could spur reasonable debate (especially within teen circles).

It's best to keep in mind that, as prickly and unpredictable as a teen's behavior may seem, a young person most assuredly believes that the rest of the world is being equally unreasonable. That point may be debatable, but understanding the underlying reason behind the tirade may make it marginally easier to bear.

In a few short years, teens are driven to demonstrate more independence than they have ever been expected—or allowed—to show before. They have the freedom to associate with whomever they choose (at least during school hours). Thanks to the prominence of cars in teen culture, they have the opportunity to venture to places they've never been before (at least not without adult supervision). They are faced with difficult choices, including whether to become sexually active and whether to experiment with tobacco, alcohol, drugs, and other high-risk behaviors.

They are expected to keep on top of their studies, decide whether and where to go to college, and determine what career path they will take. In a few short years, and with precious little experience to guide them, they are expected (or at least they believe they are) to map out the rest of their lives.

And yet, adults constantly treat them like children. Thinking about it from their perspective, you've got to admit it would be maddening.

Luckily, relief comes midway through the teen years in the form of a driver's license. It's difficult to overstate the importance of this moment in a teen's life: TRU's syndicated research begins with 12-year-olds, and by that time most of these respondents are already restlessly awaiting their 16th (or 17th, for those in some of the Eastern states) birthday. The obvious appeal of a driver's license is the freedom it bestows, the feeling of independence it brings. With that officially sanctioned piece of plastic, teens gain the ability to flee the family when things get too confining. Still more important, a driver's license dramatically improves teens' social life. Not only can they more easily meet their friends, they can do so without parental interference. And, those teens lucky enough to be the first one in his or her peer group to attain a driver's license can usually expect a significant boost in social standing. After all, even if the new driver doesn't become the peer group's de facto leader, he or she certainly wields a great deal of veto power!

Beyond the functional aspect of getting away when they want to, teen drivers no longer need to rely on adults to haul them where they want to go. This is just one step toward full independence, but it's a major milestone in a process that teens almost uniformly want to hurry along.

During the past year, we did some qualitative research with new drivers and asked them how it felt to have their license—to have moved to a new stage in their young lives. The look on their faces told it all (nonverbal cues often are more telling than verbal ones where teens are concerned). Teens simply lit up when describing their newfound mobility. The emotional benefit of obtaining a driver's license clearly transcends the functional. It means much more than simply having wheels; the independence symbolized by a driver's license gives teens a huge emotional lift. We advise our clients to look for other milestones that have as much power and meaning to teens as a driver's license. Or, better yet, think about how your brand can deliver the same sort of payoff—a symbol to which teens can zealously aspire.

Teen Need: Indi-Filiation

Lacking experience that could prepare them for the task of growing up, most teens rely on their gut instincts. And, true to form, these instincts pull them in opposing directions.

On the one hand, most teens feel an intense desire to give voice to their personality and to stand out among their friends (in short, to be cool). But occupying such a high-visibility position opens up the typically awkward, self-conscious teen to the kind of public ridicule few have developed the mental armor to tolerate. The feat of expressing their own voice without alienating their peers is a tightrope teens walk daily.

The practical result is that most teens will loudly, proudly profess their individuality. But they tend to cluster into cliques, surrounding themselves with a group of like-minded, generally similar people who will acknowledge and celebrate the relatively minor things that make them different.

TRU has coined the term "indi-filiation" to describe this seemingly conflicting set of needs. A hybrid of two teen need-states, individuality and affiliation, the phrase is TRU shorthand for the way many teens long to stand out from the crowd just enough to be recognized as unique, but not enough to be targeted as a social outcast or even markedly different. To put it into teenspeak, "I want to be an individual as long as that's what my friends are doing." This apparent contradiction offers important implications for marketers: give teens something that lets them belong to

Teen Value Monitor

Most teens think they will always be successful.

*(percent of teens agreeing "strongly" or "somewhat"
with each statement, by gender)*

	total	female	male
I'll always be successful	71%	70%	71%
I always try to have as much fun as possible	69	73	65
I really like to do things with my family	66	68	64
I think I'm pretty normal	62	66	58
My religion/faith is one of the most important parts of my life	59	61	57
It's very important for me to get involved in things that help others	58	65	52
Most people who know me or just see me think I'm cool	53	55	51
It's important to me to fit in	51	52	50
I'm often the first one to try something new	49	52	46
Success means making a lot of money	47	41	52
I wish I were more popular	26	27	25

Source: The TRU Study, Teenage Research Unlimited, Inc.

the norm but also allows them to customize just enough to stand out in their own (relatively innocuous) way. Old Navy, for one, does an outstanding job of offering 25 different colors of the same t-shirt, while cell phone manufacturers capitalize on this need-state by providing interchangeable face plates for their phones.

(Of course, for every sweeping generalization there are plenty of exceptions. In Chapter 4, which describes the four Teen/Types, we will examine teens who don't put as much stock in indi-filiation.)

Teen Need: Experimentation

The experimentation need-state is closely linked to fun, independence, and indi-filiation. Experimenting and broadening one's horizons is what the teen years are all about, although the exact nature of the experimentation depends heavily on the nature of the teen. The term "experimentation" brings alcohol, tobacco, and drugs to mind (especially among parents), and indeed these are typically the years when first encounters with illegal or illicit substances take place. However, most of the experimentation teens undertake is of a less serious nature.

TRU research reveals that an impressive 50 percent of teens claim they are "often the first one to try something new." Simple logic casts doubt upon this claim, and TRU's qualitative research shows that many teens who claim they are "first" are pointing to rather conservative fashion trends that have already gained a secure foothold. Still, the fact that so many claim to drive the bandwagon demonstrates how important it is for teens to discover new things (or at least get credit for it!).

As for more ominous experimentation (drugs, alcohol, tobacco), parental opinions do count—to an extent. Most teens recognize that their parents have gained insight over the years. Most actually listen to what parents have to say (even if it's not immediately evident during conversations). Still, teens are extraordinarily sensitive to criticism from authority, and they hate it when parents advise them against repeating the mistakes of their elders, especially if they suspect those "mistakes" were fun! Most teens are curious by nature, and they're perfectly happy to rack up their own list of mistakes in the name of "life experience."

When it comes to social marketing, we believe it's critical that there be a dual target: teens and parents. As it happens, the current national anti-drug campaign probably does a better job of targeting parents than teens, encouraging adults to monitor their teens' behavior and to talk to their kids about the benefits of not doing drugs.

Teens' natural inclination to experiment has other marketing implications as well. First, for most product categories, the goal is to not only gain teen trial but, tougher yet, to get their repeat business. Smart teen marketing can get them to try you out, but the quality of your product and the image of your brand is what will gain their loyalty. So, get teens when they're young—when they're first experimenting with brands in your particular product category. But never rest on your laurels! You must remind teens not only of why they chose you in the first place, but more important why they should stick with you. And remember, the reasons include both the rational (think product attributes, and don't be afraid to adjust) and the emotional (imagery, which needs to evolve).

Teen Need: Aspiration

The more you talk to teens, the more you realize the life they live in their heads is often different from where their feet are planted. To know teens is to understand that they are thinking, dreaming, and even planning a few years ahead. And it's no wonder. Much of the popular media and culture they devour is geared to people a few years older. All this begs the question: do teens really enjoy being teen?

We asked them, and the response was overwhelmingly positive. Nine out of 10 tell us they are enjoying this lifestage. Ironically though, many younger teens would skip most of their teen years given the opportunity. When we ask teens how old they would like to be, 12- and 13-year-olds

Age Aspiration

If teens could be any age, on average they would choose to be 19.

(age teens aspire to be, by age)

Actual age	Aspired age
12	17
13	17
14	18
15	18
16	19
17	20
18	20
19	20

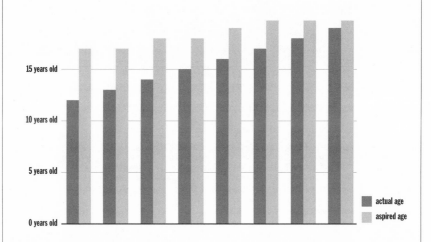

Source: The TRU Study, Teenage Research Unlimited, Inc.

uniformly answer 17. Who can blame them? The early teen years can be an ordeal. The hormones flow like water, the body goes berserk, and the process takes a terrible toll on voice and complexion. To add insult to injury, young teens are still nowhere near driving age!

The gap between how old teens are and how old they would like to be narrows steadily as they age. The age aspiration difference is only two or three years for those in their mid-teens, and just one or two years for the oldest. This illustrates the fact that older teens, equipped with more freedom, are generally happier than they were at age 12. Their responsibilities are few, but they have a lot of independence. It's not a bad life, and 18- and 19-year-olds are in no hurry to move into the high-pressure, responsibility-laden world of adulthood.

The implications of what we've learned about age aspiration are huge—and strategically convenient. Because 17 and 18 are the ages that most younger and mid-age teens aspire to, it's also the bulls-eye age to target in advertising and promotions in terms of talent, themes, and tonality. The younger end of the target will feel respected by the older nature of your appeal, while older teens will relate to your message and tactics. The caveat here is that younger teens need to clearly understand your message. Although they aspire to be older, cognitively and experientially they are still young. Do your homework: conduct qualitative research to make sure those at the younger end of the target get your main message.

But aspiration isn't just about age. Most teens aspire to be like the images of the "perfect" teens they see in the media (and they're accustomed to seeing actors who meet these lofty requirements on television and in print ads). We'd never discourage the use of a diverse cast of characters in your marketing messages. In fact, depending on the point you're trying to make, this might be the wisest course of action. But if you're selling a product that appeals to teen aspirations, a working familiarity with the characteristics to which they most aspire is helpful. We've quantified teens' aspirations in terms of appearance, talents, and personality traits. The

Physical and Personality Aspirations

Brown hair and a funny personality are popular among teens.

(characteristics to which teens aspire, by gender, 2003)

	females	males
Height	5'7"	6'2"
Body type	shapely and toned	muscular
Hair color	brown	brown
Eye color	blue	blue
Personality	funny	funny
Skill/talent	singing	athletic

Source: The TRU Study, Teenage Research Unlimited, Inc.

insights provide a picture of the type of teen to depict in advertising. For guys this means tall, but not abnormally so—most think 6'2" is just the right height. In fact, there's something downright magical about this height—boys from ages 12 to 19 want to be exactly 6'2". Guys also want to be muscular, athletic, and funny. No surprises there.

Girls, on the other hand, would opt for a more average height—the consensus is that 5'7" is the female ideal. Girls would rather be shapely and toned than thin, reflecting an orientation toward athletics and fitness. And, like guys, they say they would prefer to be funny. Girls also mention singing as a talent they would like to possess. If you can find an athlete who can belt out a tune, you'll likely grab the attention of teen girls!

What Makes a Teen Cool?

The pursuit of "cool" is an activity central to most teens' lives, and it extends to clothes, cars, music, and friends. But by what yardstick is coolness judged?

It's a testament to the concept's enduring appeal that teens are still using "cool" at all. When the word entered the national consciousness in the late 1950s, it was mostly thanks to the beatniks, a counterculture group with extremely limited appeal to today's teens. Given this fact, and the fluid nature of teen trends, it's downright amazing that the 45-year-old slang term is still in common use. (You dig?)

Cool means different things to different teens, but no matter how it's interpreted, it's overwhelmingly positive. The concept of cool can convey any number of desirable traits, including style, confidence, friendliness, and open-mindedness.

Most teens want others to consider them cool, a fact that owes much to the word's flexibility. After all, even teens who reject the reigning social cliques are likely to have a few close friends with whom they disparage their more popular peers. Typically, these members of the counterculture consider themselves every bit as cool as—if not cooler than—the people they bristle against.

If cool is hard to define, it's no easier to achieve, especially in the teen years. Whereas young adults may equate coolness with quirky individuality, most teens see coolness as doing what everyone else is doing, only doing it first or better.

Many decisions people make during their teen years are based—consciously or not—on what friends, peers, and potential romantic interests are doing. Teens become involved in sports, academic clubs, social causes, and youth groups in part because their peer group is involved in these activities or looks up to those who are. Friday night destinations usually are carefully chosen to provide the opportunity to socialize with the coolest

What Makes a Person Very Cool?

When asked what makes somebody their age "very cool," the largest shares of teens say being funny and good looking.

(percent of teens citing characteristic as one that makes somebody their age "very cool")

Funny	49%
Good looking	49
Outgoing personality	45
Has lots of friends	38
Popular with opposite sex	34
Smart	28
Good athlete	26
How they dress	25
Independent	20
Big "partier"	17
Owns "cool" stuff	13
Rebellious	8

Source: The TRU Study, Teenage Research Unlimited, Inc.

people possible. Admittedly, none of this is particularly surprising. But it begs the question: What makes a teen "cool"?

To find out, we quantified how teens describe a cool peer. One of the top answers may disappoint idealists, but it won't surprise anyone. Being good-looking is a key component of teen popularity (and it doesn't hurt adult popularity, either!). This fixation on physical appearance explains not only the monthly avalanche of cosmetic and beauty-aid advertisements in magazines targeted at teen girls, but also the recent flurry of similar (if slightly more macho) products geared toward teen boys. Marketers have begun to realize that guys are at least as interested in "dating and relating" as girls are, so many cosmetics companies are starting to capitalize on guys' desire for sex appeal in a way no one has ever bothered to do before. Early results suggest that younger boys—who have grown up in an open-minded society in which formerly rigid gender roles are relaxing—aren't particularly concerned that others might call their masculinity into question for using such products.

The fact that many teen respondents say a teen can get through high school on looks alone should come as little surprise to anyone who remembers his or her own high school experience. For those who have blocked out their teen years entirely, may we suggest a trip to your next high school reunion? We expect you'll find a couple of former lookers (probably also Mr. and Ms. Popularity) who have failed to accomplish much (to the great pleasure of many of their former classmates). Try to be kind, even if they weren't. They only had four years of glory (okay, maybe five) and that was a long time ago.

There's another equally important benefit to being attractive: confidence. This trait typically is in short supply in the teen years. The dramatic physical changes teens experience, combined with the hormonal revolution raging within their bodies, mean that most operate in a near-constant state of awkwardness. They're always on the defensive for the next challenge, and it's typically never far away.

It's an unfair (but nonetheless well-documented) fact that people display more interest, enthusiasm, and patience with attractive people than with their plainer counterparts. Teens on the receiving end of this validation quickly realize that they don't need to spend an inordinate amount of time preoccupied with whether others find them attractive. Thus, they are better able to focus their energies on other areas—most notably, socialization.

The other major factor in determining popularity is a good sense of humor. Simply put, if you're not good looking you better be funny! Teens deem this trait just as vital to a healthy social life as being attractive. And although relatively few teens would classify the two characteristics as equivalent (most say they would still rather be drop-dead gorgeous), a sense of humor is particularly useful because it can be cultivated to a much greater extent than physical appearance. In fact, many teens use humor as a "great equalizer," allowing them to climb into the popular crowd's rarified social strata even without the aid of a perfect body or a model's face.

If They Could Change Themselves

With physical appearance so important in teen life, it should come as no surprise that more teens wish they could change their appearance than any other attribute. When asked what three things they would change about themselves if they could, more than one-third said they would like to be "better looking" (as in, closer to the "perfect" teen). This umbrella response covers a huge number of insecurities. Although teens of both genders often interpret the phrase to mean more appealing facial features, it also holds gender-specific meanings for girls and boys. More girls than guys consider weight to be inextricably linked to beauty, and their consensus is that smaller is better. Meanwhile, boys are more concerned with height and build.

Other top responses to this question are also revealing because they illustrate the extent to which teens covet high school popularity. Some 24 percent say they wish they were more confident, and 19 percent say they would like to be more outgoing—both key attributes to popularity. Another 24 percent wish they were better athletes. Remarkably, more than one-fifth admit they would make themselves more popular if they knew how—a result that belies the common teen claim that they're not interested in what others think of them.

Teens' willingness to subvert their own personalities in order to fit in with the popular crowd instills a sense of dread in many parents who lie

What Teens Would Change About Themselves

When asked to name three things they would change about themselves, the largest share of guys and girls say they would like to be better looking.

(percent of teens citing characteristic as one of three they would most like to change about themselves, by gender)

	female	male
Better looking	36%	31%
Better student	24	28
More confident	28	20
Better athlete	21	26
Have a boyfriend or girlfriend	23	23
More popular	19	22
Harder worker	17	21
More outgoing	20	17
Get along better with brother or sister	17	14
More talented	14	15
Get along better with parents	15	10
More outspoken	13	11
Get into less trouble	9	13
More laid back	7	6
Get along better with friends	5	3
Nothing	9	8

Source: The TRU Study, Teenage Research Unlimited, Inc.

awake at night envisioning dark alleys filled with menacing young punks waiting to turn good children bad. But teens routinely reject the assertion that this kind of peer pressure holds sway over their lives. This claim, repeated over and over throughout TRU's research, puzzled us at first. Were teens suggesting they're immune from peer pressure? We felt certain that young people had to know that their friends and peers influence their thinking at some level. After all, what age group doesn't worry about peer pressure? (Don't believe it? Watch your colleague's face light up when you compliment her car or his new suit.) The difference between teens and adults is that teens are always getting lectured on the subject.

As it turns out, teens fully accept the fact that they sometimes alter their behavior because of their friends. In fact, their initial denial is another communication breakdown because, when adults talk about peer pressure, they tend to get it wrong. As teens wearily explain to us, the classic adult perception of peer pressure—an overbearing, perhaps even hostile peer who all but forces an innocent child into a moment (or a lifetime) of loose morals and crime—is outdated, if it ever existed at all. The peer pressure teens face is an internal phenomenon. A plurality of teen respondents (45 percent) believes that peer pressure is a personal desire to "fit in." When added to the 15 percent who believe an individual's need to experiment lies at peer pressure's core, a full 60 percent of teens indicate that real peer pressure is internal. Only 36 percent believe that peer pressure can be explained as an external pressure from friends.

TRU has done a lot of antismoking work over the years, seeking to uncover teens' motivations for tobacco initiation in the belief that such a revelation would provide insight into crafting relevant messages to encourage teens to abstain. In our work, we have discovered the erroneous assumptions adults make about peer pressure. Here's the scene: a group of teens are strategically gathered just off school grounds, lighting up before class. A nonsmoking classmate saunters in and is offered a cigarette, with the admonishment, "Do it, you'll be cool!" The good news is that scenes

What "Peer Pressure" Really Means

For most teens, peer pressure stems from internal desires rather than external pressures from friends.

(percent of teens agreeing with statements about peer pressure)

The desire to "fit in" influences somebody's decision to join in	45%
Constant pressure from friends influences somebody's decision to join in	36
Curiosity and the desire to experiment influences somebody's decision to join in	15

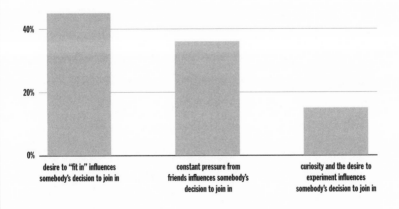

Source: The TRU Study, Teenage Research Unlimited, Inc.

like this don't really happen in the teen world. The only time the words, "Do it, you'll be cool!" are uttered is when teens are mocking antismoking ads. The bad news is that adults stubbornly persist in believing otherwise. Teens don't experience the "in-your-face" external pressure to partake that many adults imagine. Instead, a more realistic scenario is this: a teen wanders into the same scene and notices that some friends or other students he or she really likes are smoking. By asking to bum a cigarette, the non-smoker has found a way in—a relatively easy way to meld into a desirable group. Why would a smoker push a cigarette on a nonsmoker? There's nothing in it for the smoker—in fact, the opposite is true. Cigarettes aren't cheap these days and teens, on limited funds, are not eager to hand out anything for free! So, understand that peer pressure is real, but that it primarily comes from within.

Adults, generally more comfortable in their own skins, often see teens' acute need for acceptance as silly and superficial. They can scold and scoff as much as they wish, but the fact remains that teens derive a great deal of their self-image from the opinions of the people around them. That's why experts insist it's important for young people to be surrounded by attentive, supportive adults—especially during the teen years, when peers can be notoriously fickle.

Despite their tendency to get caught up in the seemingly petty concerns of youth, teens display a strong interest in their future. When asked what three things they would most like to change about themselves, 26 percent said they wish they were better students. This response, in fact, was the second most common after changing one's looks. Nearly 20 percent said they would like to work harder, and 15 percent said they wished they were more talented.

Most teens regard the future with a curious mix of anxiety and optimism. On the one hand, it's such a vague concept that many have a hard time imagining how their mundane daily activities (such as homework or a summer job) could possibly influence it. To many of these young people, the future seems less like the culmination of countless actions and decisions than it does a giant, unstoppable force almost beyond their control.

On the other hand, most teens are pretty sure it will turn out okay.

Such is this generation's penchant for optimism in the face of the unknown. Even the most motivated students sometimes have a difficult time imagining how the pieces of the puzzle will fit into place. Frequently, these teens study because their parents have taught them that education and hard work is the road to success, and their parents have a fairly good track record on such matters. But they take it on faith that, as long as they fulfill their obligations and stay out of trouble (big trouble that is—mischief's okay), everything will be fine.

Today's teens are the product of a more progressive time, and thus are more comfortable with diversity, than any previous generation. Interestingly, however, today's teens also appear more open to "traditional family values" than their recent predecessors. Please note that, for most teens, the term "traditional family values" holds no political subtext. It isn't code for intolerance or a way to dismiss someone else's lifestyle. It's the way they describe the life they expect and want for themselves. It includes religion, marriage, homeownership, and a fulfilling family life.

When TRU asked teens what they expect their life to look like when they reach 30 (adulthood by almost any teen standard), more than 70 percent predicted they would be married. Some 46 percent said that they would have kids, and 42 percent said they would own their own home. Similarly, 55 percent said that they would have a successful career, although this finding may be less "traditional" owing to the fact that more girls than guys predict success in the occupation of their choice.

Interestingly, most respondents said the odds of achieving more ambitious or exotic goals were relatively low. Some 14 percent said they expected to be famous by age 30. The same percentage of teens anticipated owning a business or traveling all over the world. Another 13 percent said

Teen Expectations
Of Life at 30

Most teens expect to be married and have a successful career by age 30.

(percent of teens who expect to do selected activities by age 30, by gender)

	female	male
Get married	75%	70%
Have a successful career	59	52
Have kids	52	41
Own my own home	39	45
Travel all over the world	15	12
Become famous	13	15
Have my own business	11	16
Have a million dollars	8	17
Have many romantic relationships	8	10
Switch jobs many times	2	3
Get divorced	3	3
Lose a lot of money	2	3
Spend time in jail	1	2
Get fired from a good job	1	2

Source: The TRU Study, Teenage Research Unlimited, Inc.

they would make a million dollars by their 30th birthday, and 9 percent predicted they would have had "many romantic relationships." Fewer than 3 percent of teens said they would switch jobs repeatedly, get divorced, lose a lot of money, spend time in jail, or get fired.

In short, today's teens—perhaps even more than their parents— believe in the American Dream.

What Stresses Teens Out and How They Cope

The path toward the American dream, however, causes teens no small amount of stress. As mentioned earlier, 21 percent of teens say they have too much to do and not enough time. An equal share say the world they live in moves faster than it did for other generations at their age. And 17 percent of teens say they are overly stressed. With the traditional teen focus on fun, it's easy to forget that today's teens are exposed to more things at an earlier age than any generation before them. The typical family now has two working parents or a single parent who's employed full-time, meaning that older children frequently need to pull more weight around the house, including watching younger siblings and running errands. Outside the home, the growth of after-school programs, sports, and clubs means that just about anyone who wants to find an extracurricular activity can do so. And despite these social obligations, today's teens are much more likely to work than they were in past decades.

Most teens say their stress is the culmination of hundreds of different challenges, but we wanted to know the specifics. We asked them how they would prioritize their biggest stressors. Not surprisingly, the top responses were issues they face on a daily basis. School is the single biggest contributor to teen stress: 23 percent say grades stress them out—the question's top response. Fully 91 percent of teens identify grades, tests, or homework as a stress factor. That's an amazing consensus for such a diverse group!

Family is a leading source of stress as well. At 19 percent, parents rank just behind grades in this measure. Another 13 percent of teens say

How Teens Cope with Stress

Listening to music is the number-one way teen guys and girls get relief from stress.

(percent of teens saying they cope with stress by doing selected activities, by gender)

	total	female	male
Listen to music	87%	90%	84%
Hang in your room	66	75	58
Watch TV	58	56	60
Sleep	58	63	52
Hang with your friends	51	54	48
Talk on the phone	45	62	30
Exercise/work out	39	40	38
Go for a run/walk	36	40	31
Spend time with your pet	33	36	30
Eat	32	37	27
Play sports	32	22	41
Read	31	39	24
Go on the computer	24	21	28
Play video games	24	8	38
Go shopping	23	35	11
Go for a drive	22	22	22
Write in a journal	20	35	6
Go to a movie	18	20	17
Go rollerblading/skateboarding	17	17	17
Play a musical instrument	17	15	19
Something illegal	8	7	9

Source: The TRU Study, Teenage Research Unlimited, Inc.

their siblings stress them out, and 10 percent worry about a family member's health.

Teens think a great deal about their responsibilities to themselves as well. Fifteen percent say they're stressed about the future, and 12 percent are worried about getting into the right college.

Conversely, only 4 percent of teens say that friends stress them out (although more than double that percentage say a boyfriend or girlfriend causes them anxiety). In fact, it's a testament to the importance of teen socialization that more than half of respondents reported hanging out with friends as one of the best ways to let off steam. Similarly, 45 percent say they unwind by talking on the phone (although it's worth noting that this is much more popular with girls than with guys). Other popular methods of stress relief involve listening to music (named by an impressive 87 percent of teens) and hanging out in their room (two-thirds lock themselves away from time to time). Watching TV and sleeping each garnered responses from 58 percent of teens.

Many adults discount teen stress, an attitude we at TRU strongly discourage. For one thing, most adults base their opinion on their often selective and rapidly fading memories of their own teen years. Today's teen experience bears only a passing resemblance to that encountered by baby boomers. Anyone born before 1965 should look to his or her own teen years as a rough guide to adolescence, not a detailed map. And whether a marketer believes teens are under stress is irrelevant. Teens believe they are, and their motivations will reflect this belief.

When we try to put a finger on the cause of teen stress, much of it comes from teens being overscheduled and overreaching. First, most teens aged 16 and up have a part-time job. Second, teen athletes are scheduled five, six, and sometimes seven days a week during their sport's season, and many of these sports have off-season training regimens and other competitions. Nonathletes (as well as particularly determined athletes) pursue other interests, hobbies, and passions—all of which cut into the day. Of course, all teens are time-pressured due to the demands of school and family. How much time does this leave teens for having fun? Not enough. No wonder teens want to make the most of what little downtime they have—whether chilling at a friend's home, spending time with a romantic interest, pursuing a hobby, or simply goofing around and causing a little trouble. This is precious time—time they need and desire, and for many, time that's way too rare. Simply juggling so many competing factors is an onerous task that causes great stress for many of today's teens.

Teen Psyche in a Nutshell

So far in this chapter you've learned that the current generation of young people is more accepting of differences, even though they're still obsessed with physical appearance. They value family input, but bristle at getting unsolicited advice. They're all about fun, but they feel more stress than previous generations did. They enjoy spending quality time with their families, but they can't wait to get out of the house. They love the thrill of discovery, but often wait until new trends are tested and accepted before committing to them. You've scratched the surface of teens' complexity, but you haven't yet determined one of the most important, overarching questions about teen life: Are they happy? We asked them, and we're pleased to report that, for the most part, they are.

In a remarkable show of unity, 93 percent of teens say they're having fun (48 percent say they're having fun "most of the time" and another 45 percent say they're having fun "some of the time"). Nearly as many say they're happy most or some of the time, with 55 percent saying they're happy "most of the time."

On the other hand, while 52 percent admit to feeling bored sometimes, only 14 percent say they feel this way most of the time. And, although one-third of teens report feeling depressed occasionally, only 7 percent say depression is a frequent problem for them. It's not likely that these teens are using the clinical definition of depression, but they evidently distinguish depression from simple boredom. Given the radical changes that teens face—social, emotional, and physiological—it's probably not surprising that only 12 percent of teens say they're never depressed.

In fact, the vast majority of teens are more than willing to take the bad with the good. When we asked respondents whether they're happy being a teenager (a separate question from whether they're happy in general), 88 percent said "yes," while only 10 percent said "no." The confusion, self-doubt, and angst are apparently a small price to pay for the sense of independence, growth, and boundless opportunity of the teen years.

Marketers, you're faced with a daunting challenge when courting teens. On the one hand, it's your job to understand the teen experience enough to accurately recreate it in your advertising messages. On the other hand, capitalizing on teen insecurities simply for the sake of differentiating your product is not only morally questionable, it's also a tactic teens are likely to see through instantly. And it won't earn your brand many style points, either!

Teens are media and marketing savvy. They view advertisements that boast miracle cures for the socially inept in much the same way they look at supermarket tabloid headlines—amusing, but insulting to their intelligence and not worth their money or time.

Chapter 3

Teen Attitudes

The previous chapter dealt with the teen psyche—the subconscious collection of thoughts, convictions, assessments, and psychological biases that influence how teens behave on a day-to-day basis. This chapter explores a closely related topic: teens' attitudes about their current life stage. If the psyche is the foundation of teen behavior, attitudes are the outward manifestation. Forests have been leveled to produce books explaining the adolescent psyche to puzzled adult observers. But we think far too little attention is paid to what teens say about themselves. After all, knowing who teens think they are can be as enlightening as learning from psychologists the roots of teen behavior.

To determine what teens believe their defining characteristics are, we conduct qualitative and quantitative research that guides us in fine-tuning our own lines of inquiry, including our syndicated TRU Study. The initial work begins months before each new wave of The TRU Study, when staff members brainstorm new questions that will serve as a sort of teen-attitude barometer for the upcoming new release. Answers to these questions frequently provide some of the study's most compelling information. After we draft the initial questions—often in the form of value statements to which teens are asked to agree or disagree—we conduct several rounds of qualitative research during which we solicit teen input on the value statements. We adjust our statements according to their suggestions and then, in another round of qualitative research, we ask a new set of teens to help us select and optimize a dozen or so of the most important statements. We place these in The TRU Study, which polls a nationally representative sample of more than 2,000 teens across the country twice each year.

Still, as carefully as we orchestrate the whole process, it's important to tread with care. Although teens often will deliver surprisingly candid personal insights (and often even more useful interpretations of their peers' behavior), they tend to be reluctant to give the unvarnished truth if they feel it may portray them in a negative light. That's why we always walk clients through teens' responses, pointing out possible mitigating factors as we find them. We'll attempt to do the same in this chapter.

Teen Attitudes Toward the Teen Years

Being teen is anything but carefree: hormonal turmoil, social insecurity, and all manner of stresses from the outside world combine to make the teen years genuinely harried. But ever-optimistic teens, when asked to weigh the good against the bad, see the bright side. It takes them only a few seconds to decide that the fun parts of the teen years more than compensate for the constant state of low-grade anxiety and the occasional teen crisis.

When we ask teens to tell us what they like best about this time of their life, their answers aren't surprising. Some 32 percent list close friends (a figure significantly higher among girls than guys). Another 25 percent say it's their boyfriend or girlfriend. These responses showcase the importance teens place upon their social relationships. In fact, two other responses that facilitate meeting friends or significant others—freedom and partying—tie for third place with 24 percent of the response. The ability to drive is another important factor in teen life: 17 percent list this rite of passage as their favorite aspect of being teen, although the figure skews strongly male.

Other highly rated responses include "doing something you're not supposed to do and not getting caught." Some 19 percent of teens claim this is one of the best things about the teen years. And if this sounds like your typical teen party-guy statement, it may come as a surprise that significantly more girls than guys say this statement describes them personally!

What Teens Like About Being Teen

Ninety percent of teens like being a teenager, with the largest share saying close friends are the best thing about being teen.

(percent of teenagers citing what they like most about being teen)

Close friends	32%
Boyfriend/girlfriend	25
Freedom	24
Partying	24
Not getting caught	19
Able to drive	17
No adult responsibility	14
Dating	14
School events	13
Going to school	9
Few worries	8
Few expectations	6

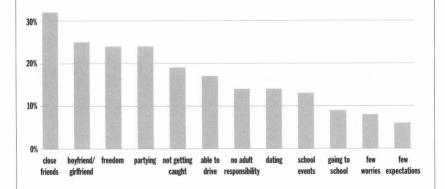

Source: The TRU Study, Teenage Research Unlimited, Inc.

Interestingly, more younger than older teens say they enjoy getting away with prohibited behavior. This difference is likely due to two factors. First, older teens have gotten away with all manner of mischief for years; the novelty and drama of their little rebellions is wearing off. Second, younger teens operate under more restrictions than their older counterparts. Simply put, more of the things young teens want to do are off-limits because of their age, so it's exceedingly easy for them to wind up breaking the rules.

Teen Attitudes Toward Fun and Responsibility

Certain images seem custom-made for certain age groups: just as aging Boomers are busily preparing for retirement and maturing Gen-Xers are concentrating on family-building, teens are going about the business of being teen. To them, that means having fun.

Most teens realize there is a family and a 401k in their future, but few regard those symbols of adulthood as fun or sexy. To their way of thinking, these things will eventually—and somewhat mysteriously—come to pass, just as they did for the generation before them. They have a difficult time envisioning the changes in store that will transform them from awkward but eager teens into confident, responsible adults.

But, if they can't quite imagine what lies in store for them, they still see no reason to waste their youth worrying about it. When given the opportunity to focus on a future they can neither control nor fully comprehend, or a youth that is quickly slipping away, they nearly always choose to celebrate the present.

Indeed, as discussed in Chapter 2, teens say the credo that best describes the overall teen experience is "We're all about fun." Younger teens particularly embrace this image, claiming their primary interest is living for the moment and enjoying their youth to the fullest. And why not? Children learn and develop better when they have ample opportunities for play. Teens are certainly more mature than children, and their idea of fun is (generally) more mature as well. But the same concept holds true.

What Teens Most Look Forward To

Teens look forward to different events, depending on their age.

(percent of teens who most look forward to selected events, by age)

	12-to-15-year-olds
Getting driver's license	35%
Graduating	30
Summer	27
Getting a job	20
College acceptance	19
Vacation/travel	18
Going to college	16
Having more freedom	16
Starting career	11
Moving out	9

	16-to-17-year-olds
Graduating	40%
Summer	25
Going to college	25
College acceptance	21
Getting a job	17
Getting driver's license	16
Having more freedom	15
Moving out	12
Vacation/travel	11
Starting career	11

	18-to-19-year-olds
Starting career	27%
Going to college	26
Moving out	20
Summer	18
Graduating	17
Getting a job	16
Vacation/travel	16
Having more freedom	9
College acceptance	4
Getting driver's license	3

Source: The TRU Study, Teenage Research Unlimited, Inc.

Teens use fun to learn valuable lessons about how to interact with the world around them. And, more important to the teen's way of thinking, they have a blast doing it.

What's more, teens are at a unique point in their lives. Despite the fact that they're still every bit as interested in "play" as their younger counterparts, most have much greater levels of freedom and aren't saddled with parents who constantly monitor their every move. With a healthy appetite for leisure pursuits and the wherewithal to satisfy it, why wouldn't they want to chase fun wherever it might lead?

As teens age they slowly abandon the *carpe diem* mentality, although boys seem to hang onto it longer than girls. Among the youngest age group, roughly equal numbers of boys and girls say their generation is "all about fun." But a dramatic shift takes place among 18- and 19-year-olds: 52 percent of guys this age still cling to that motto, but only 30 percent of girls do. This difference is partly attributable to the fact that girls mature faster than boys. But TRU qualitative research also suggests many older girls know someone who is either pregnant or raising a child, often without much help from the father. We've heard many of today's girls vowing never to put themselves in such a vulnerable position.

Although teens gravitate toward the "all-about-fun" value statement in quantitative research (when their choices are limited), qualitative research reveals that many are uncomfortable with the all-out bacchanalian portrait the statement paints. In face-to-face conversations, most teens—even some of the hardest partiers—want it known that they do have real responsibilities. Fun may be one of the most important aspects of their lives, but they insist that being "all" about fun shouldn't be construed as being free of any real responsibilities.

Asked what their responsibilities are, teens point to obligations from school assignments to studying for exams, part-time jobs, involvement with religious or other groups, chores around the house, and taking care of family members.

Parental pressure—generally inextricably linked to issues of control and autonomy—is also a matter of constant concern for teens. However, it's worth noting that twice as many teens say they like the teen years because they don't have adult responsibilities as say they dislike the period because their responsibilities are too great.

We asked teens whether the freedom from adult obligations is one of the things they enjoy about their lifestage, but their response isn't particularly impassioned.

In fact, this aspect of the teen years seems to be of secondary importance compared to the more immediate, tangible benefits, such as friends and fun. Clearly, they're better able to enjoy their youth than they would be if bound by mortgage payments and vet bills. Still, this freedom is not enough to elicit strong reactions on its own, and just 14 percent of teens cite "no adult responsibility" as the best thing about the teen years. Further, teens flatly reject two related choices—"few worries" and "few expectations." These not only fail to capture the teen imagination, but most young people consider them wildly inaccurate. They're trying to satisfy expectations from all sides, and they worry about it all the time!

Teen Attitudes Toward the Future

When we ask our national sample what future events they look forward to, their tendency toward short-term thinking really shines through! Graduation is the most frequently cited event, followed by summer, getting a driver's license, going to college, and getting a job. Teens are most excited about milestones quickly approaching because it's easier for them to visualize an event close to them than one more distant. The closer in age a teenager is to an event, the more eagerly he or she awaits it.

The results of this measure are not useful for broadly targeted marketing applications. Because 14-year-olds look forward to different events than 19-year-olds, it is essential to view results of this measure by age group. Still, the findings reveal relevant events and lifestage experiences that can be incorporated into advertising or promotions that appeal to each teenage segment. The event most imminent in the target segment's life is likely to prove the most motivating.

To get teens to think about the long-term future, we've found we need to narrowly focus our questions. Once respondents understand where our interests lie, they're better able to provide us with a great deal of interesting information.

As might be expected from an optimistic cohort such as this, teens generally report holding high expectations for themselves. Although society's self-appointed watchdogs continue to fret about the state of teens today (as they have since time immemorial), we've found that most teens actively subscribe to a strong work ethic. They don't know how the future will turn out, but they believe the opportunities for success are there; they just need to make the right decisions to capitalize upon them.

Teen Hopes and Expectations

Teens expect to own a home and go to college, but they hope for world travel and fame.

(percent of teens saying they expect an event will actually happen and percent who hope an event will happen in their adult life)

	expect	hope
Owning a home	85%	35%
Going to college	82	32
Having a successful career	72	48
Getting married	72	41
Having children	65	41
Earning a lot of money	52	61
Owning a nice car	51	54
World travel	25	70
Fame	15	65

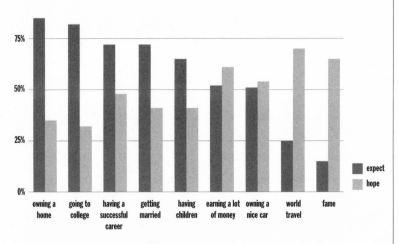

Source: The TRU Study, Teenage Research Unlimited, Inc.

In fact, TRU's Teen Value Monitor paints a picture of a population so optimistic about its future prospects that it borders on cocky. Fully 71 percent of teens agree with the statement "I'll always be successful"—an even higher level of agreement than they award to the competing claim, "I always try to have as much fun as possible." There's clearly a lesson to be learned from any value statement that overshadows the teen appetite for fun! Perhaps thanks to their optimism, most teens eagerly anticipate reaching adulthood. But because so many different milestones take place during the late teens and early twenties, it can be tricky to determine exactly when the transition to adulthood finally occurs. So, TRU asked teens themselves. Responsibility and self-determination play huge (and equal) roles, with 35 percent of teens claiming adulthood begins when they're given responsibility and when they're able to solve problems on their own. Slightly fewer (31 percent) believe adulthood comes when they move out of their parents' house. Similarly, 28 percent listed going to college as the onset of the adult years. Other significant—if less popular—responses include getting married, landing a first job, and having a child.

In a departure from previous generations, today's teens take for granted that they will achieve the main components of the American Dream. When TRU asked which goals teens *hope* to realize and which they simply *expect* will be a stage of their lives, 85 percent said they expect to own a home, and 82 percent expect to go to college. An additional 72 percent believe they will have a successful career, and the same percentage anticipate getting married. Almost two-thirds (65 percent) expect to have children, but this response ranks only in the middle of the list, trailing success-oriented responses by a considerable margin. This illustrates just how far the average teen believes he or she is from raising a family—many aren't even sure they want children. (Note that these results are in no way connected to the previously discussed results of "Teen Expectations by Age 30.")

Teens may be optimistic, but they're still fairly realistic. Although 52 percent believe they are destined to make a lot of money, and 51 percent say they expect to own a nice car, only 25 percent foresee world travel in their future, and just 15 percent expect they will be famous. The expectation of fame is much higher among younger teens, many of whom tell us they fully expect to become rock stars or professional athletes.

Still, a look at teen hopes reveals an interesting pattern: teens hope most for the things they expect least. A healthy 70 percent say they dream of becoming world travelers in their adult years, while 65 percent say they would like to be famous. Another 61 percent say they would like to earn a lot of money, and 54 percent hope to drive a really nice car. Conversely (and in a testament to just how routine college has become), fewer than one-third of teens (32 percent) list going to college as something they hope they will be able to do. Most teens today not only think of college as something they're going to do, but as one more thing their parents can harass them about.

By now, you've likely picked up on a recurring theme in teen life—teens don't like being told what to do, even if their marching orders coincide precisely with what they were going to do anyway! In fact, many teens bristle at the idea that others (whether parents, teachers, coaches, or religious leaders) should even play a role in setting personal expectations. These teens think each individual is responsible for setting his or her own expectations and others should butt out.

Nevertheless, many teens admit they are unlikely to ever test this ideal: authority figures of all stripes, especially parents, exert heavy influence over their lives almost every day. While parental involvement (or, as some might describe it, nagging) is often a source of anxiety, the fact that someone cares for them is also a point of pride and comfort. But some teens reject the expectations others set for them, choosing their own, less ambitious goals. Few of these teens look at this decision as taking the easy way out. Rather, they see their own lower expectations as more realistic than the goals set by others.

Teen stress is real, no doubt. But it's vital to keep such complaints in perspective. Although teens claim high expectations stress them out, relatively few say they truly feel overwhelmed. Indeed, most say they have a good handle on the pressures they face. And young people even see a silver lining in their stress levels: they tend to believe that if their world is stressful, it is simply a byproduct of the times. According to The TRU Study, 41 percent of teens believe one of the most important facets of their generation is their comfort with technology. Another 21 percent believe the world moves much faster today than it did when previous generations were teens. And they acknowledge advantages to their fast-moving, high-pressure environment: 13 percent say they believe they will have great opportunities as adults. Granted, 13 percent doesn't seem like a lot, but the way the question is phrased dampens the response. When asking teens what statement best defines their generation, a statement wholly focused on a distant, unknowable future isn't as likely to grab their attention as one that describes the here and now.

It's not surprising that success is an important goal for teens. So we probed the meaning of success more deeply, employing both qualitative and quantitative research to do so. Although only 47 percent of teens responding to TRU's syndicated study agree with the bluntly worded assertion that "success means making a lot of money," most of our panelists mentioned money when asked to describe the success they hope to achieve one day. The divergent results didn't surprise us. Teens frequently display a strong sense of idealism, even if this sensibility is just for show. When faced with a flatly materialistic statement and not required to defend their answer, many teens will reject it outright. But in face-to-face interviews teens acknowledge the importance they place on money.

In interviews, teens sometimes give lofty speeches about how their definition of success requires them to remain true to their ideals, not just settle for the typical "2.5 children and 3.4 dogs," as one New York teen explained. But tellingly, these same teens repeatedly show images of material wealth in collages they design to illustrate their hopes and dreams. Their collages include items such as dollar signs, piles of money, luxury vehicles, and labels such as "Master of the Universe." Despite these consumer-oriented images, respondents stubbornly cling to their assertion that success means happiness, not monetary wealth.

Younger and older teens display somewhat different perspectives on success, thanks in part to their different experiences in both life and work. Younger teens—their careers still safely in the distance—tend to describe success as a collection of adventures or the pursuit of happiness rather than the accumulation of wealth. These teens claim they don't give much consideration to long-term planning—other than simply being "happy" in the future. Older teens still shy away from placing great emphasis on money, but they are more likely to say that success is being "comfortable," "having what you need," or "not having to worry about living from paycheck to paycheck."

It's puzzling that teens talk so casually about their future finances when they are so preoccupied with money at present. More than 20 percent of teens say their chronic lack of money is what they dislike most about the teen years. In fact, the lack of money is one of teens' top-three complaints— a fact which forever shatters the myth that adults and teens share nothing in common.

Teen Attitudes Toward Peer Pressure and Authenticity

As difficult as the lack of money may be for teens, it still lags well behind the ultimate scourge of teen life: peer pressure. One-third of respondents say peer pressure is their least favorite aspect of youth, which struck us as interesting because teens in focus groups regularly downplay the influence of peer pressure.

What Teens Dislike About Being Teen

Peer pressure is the number-one thing teenagers dislike about being teen.

(percent of teenagers citing what they dislike most about being teen)

Peer pressure	33%
Not taken seriously	23
Not enough money	21
Age restrictions	19
Parent pressures	19
Lack of respect	17
Grades	15
Curfew	14
Going to school	13
Parent hassles	12
Physical changes	11
Worrying, fitting in	11
Standardized tests	9
Too much responsibility	7
Trends change too fast	8
Treated badly in stores	5

Source: The TRU Study, Teenage Research Unlimited, Inc.

Teens discount the influence of peer pressure probably because they associate the term with adult warnings of peril. Peer pressure's reality is much more insidious: teens regularly adjust their behavior based upon the way they want their friends to perceive them. Young people know this goes on all the time, and it bothers them: after all, these are the same people who grandly pronounce that nothing is as important as creativity, individuality, and being true to oneself. The knowledge that they aren't following through on this belief is a hard pill to swallow.

It's tempting to say that peer pressure takes many forms, from the banal (what soft drink to buy, what jeans to wear) to the serious (whether to join a gang or experiment with drugs). But it's more accurate to describe the phenomenon as a force of nature in the teen world. Rather like gravity, peer pressure is everywhere, and it sometimes takes a good deal of effort to overcome.

Younger teens seem more sensitive to peer pressure than their older counterparts. Older teens are further along in their physical and mental maturity, and as such, they are more comfortable in their own skins. They don't need as much outside reassurance and acceptance as teens just entering puberty. Perhaps just as important, older teens have more experience in dealing with peer pressure.

The constant struggle with peer pressure may influence—and conflict with—teen feelings about expressing their individuality. As noted previously, teens say it's impossible to overstate the importance they place on "being themselves." Similarly, honesty and genuineness are characteristics they say they most prize, both in close friends and in themselves.

Teens talk about the importance of saying what they mean and meaning what they say, and of staying true to themselves, not "posing" in front of friends and peers. The importance of being perceived as authentic and honest shows up repeatedly in teen culture. The term "keep it real" is a prime example.

The antithesis of this, of course, is "being fake." Any number of behaviors may fall under this umbrella, but most teens profess to look upon each and every one with scorn. Teens repeatedly claim misrepresenting oneself for the benefit of others is nothing more than a form of lying, not only to others but to oneself. Additionally, respondents frequently note that "poseurs" (their label for people who misrepresent who they are by acting, saying, or wearing something they normally wouldn't to gain social acceptance) are the most annoying of "fakes."

The strong feelings surrounding this subject present a paradox that teens can't easily escape. When asked, most teens claim to be straightforward in their daily interactions with others, adding that they expect the same honesty in return. But most complain that many of their peers either don't have enough confidence to be who they really are or simply misrepresent themselves in an attempt to advance socially. The fact that nearly all teens denounce "fake" people indicates that this outlook is held even by those whose peers consider them poseurs.

It's worth noting that most teens aren't actually delusional about this point: in thoughtful moments, or if they think no one is going to judge them, they admit their own complicity. One of our favorite quotes on this topic came from a Miami teen who explained to us: "You hate seeing guys acting fake in front of a girl you like, but you do it yourself so you know why the guy does it."

As much as teens say they look down upon those who aren't true to themselves, many routinely explain that being different "just to prove a point" isn't any better. Many teens say that making too much of an effort to stand out is equally unappealing—in fact, they explain it's the very essence of the term "poseur." Said one Atlanta girl, "I really hate to see people at the edge of the spectrum just trying to be different...you'll have a reputation as a goober if you do things too different." Admittedly, this attitude is likely to be much more prevalent among Conformers than any other of TRU's four Teen/Types. But then, Conformers make up roughly 50 percent of the teen population, so discounting their opinions could prove unwise.

As with so many other topics, teen attitudes regarding authenticity seem to transform as teens mature and gain more first-hand experience with the world. Younger individuals, bombarded with so many signals about who they should be and how they should act, stress the unequivocal importance of "being real," perhaps as a response to what they see as rampant "posing" among their peers. These teens usually maintain a firm, idealistic "authentic at any cost" attitude, even if their personal actions sometimes fall short of their lofty ideal.

Although still insisting on the importance of "being real" and maintaining one's authenticity, older teens take a somewhat more pragmatic approach. They are far less concerned about peer pressure, explaining that they have already been through those battles, have the scars, and are ready to move on. Rather than reciting what they consider clichéd sound bites about "being yourself," many teens nearing college prefer to look at their personal behavior in a broader context. In fact, while older teens often say that honesty gets paid a lot of lip service, they add that the "honest" approach conveniently overlooks the "white lies" that are the necessities of everyday life. Strict authenticity, they suggest, is impractical when trying to make the best of a bad situation, calm a group of squabbling friends, or survive in a work environment. As one Ohio teen explained to us, "Honesty is overrated . . . everyone pretends to be something they're not sometimes."

Teen Attitudes Toward Parents and Authority Figures

Young people constantly complain that they are not being taken seriously, and 23 percent of teens say society doesn't give them the credit they deserve. This problem is especially prevalent in—and especially galling to—18- and 19-year-olds. If it were up to them, many would gladly give up their remaining time as a teen and jump straight into proper adulthood. As often as not, these teens prefer to think of themselves as adults, and they become frustrated when the rest of the world (including marketers) lumps them into the same age class as their 14-year-old siblings.

Notably, 27 percent of 18- and 19-year-olds say age restrictions are the thing they most dislike about the teen years. Given that they have already reached every legal milestone except one, it seems obvious that they are annoyed about not being allowed to drink alcohol. Indeed, TRU qualitative research confirms that many 18- and 19-year-olds are frustrated by their in-between status: old enough to vote for the president and die in his wars, but not old enough to have a legal beer with friends. Adding insult to injury, older teens are convinced that they would show more responsible drinking behavior than their parents, whether because they are better educated about alcohol and its dangers through omnipresent school campaigns or simply because alcohol consumption is so routine for their parents that it's treated carelessly.

In addition to the 23 percent of teens who claim they are not being taken seriously, 17 percent say they are treated with a lack of respect, and 12 percent say their parents hassle them too much. Teens frequently tell us that their parents scoff at the idea that they might have any responsibility, belittling what they feel are legitimate pressures. Although teens acknowledge that their issues (peer pressure, dating, getting good grades, the quest for popularity) are not on a par with "adult" responsibilities, they nonetheless resent adult insensitivity to their concerns.

In a separate study, we asked, "What don't adults get about teens?" We listed 16 choices and invited teens to select up to three (although we suspect many would have been quite happy to choose more). A sizable 28 percent said that adults don't realize how serious teen problems can be, and 15 percent said, "We're smart and responsible—we just look young."

Part of the process of maturing is dealing with the world as an adult. Teens are eager to initiate this process (although they can be selective in demonstrating their maturity). It's a source of enormous irritation to teens that parents aren't ready to grant them the respect commanded by an adult.

What Adults Don't Get About Teens

Adults don't understand that teens need the freedom to make their own mistakes, say teens.

(percent of teens citing factor as one of three things "adults don't get about people your age," by gender)

	total	female	male
We need freedom to make our own mistakes	38%	45%	32%
How serious the problems we face are	28	30	25
Sometimes we need space from parents	27	30	24
When they were our age, they did some of the same things	25	27	23
We've grown up faster than they did	20	20	20
The music we listen to	20	15	24
We just want to have fun	19	17	21
There's more diversity now than when they were teens	17	17	17
We're smart and responsible— we just look young	15	15	14
How we dress	14	11	16
We want to be different from other generations	12	12	13
The language we use	12	9	15
We're not trying to rebel	12	12	12
Our friends	10	10	10
We don't need a curfew	6	6	7
We don't have the obligations they do, so we can be more carefree	4	3	5

Source: The TRU Study, Teenage Research Unlimited, Inc.

It's also an irony of the teen years that the more they encounter such lack of respect, the more teens complain, sulk, or lash out. This, in turn, convinces adults that they aren't ready for full adult responsibilities.

On a closely related subject, teens frequently accept input, advice, and (when necessary) orders from adults who claim to be looking out for their best interests. It's important to note that although they may accept it, they rarely enjoy it. In fact, the most common teen answer to the question of what adults don't get about teens is that young people "need the freedom to make [their] own mistakes." Fully 38 percent chose this response.

Several different schools of thought converge to make this the number-one answer. First, most teens are interested in experiences. Although they are unlikely to phrase it in quite this way, many are on a quest to learn about life. They have been sheltered most of their lives, and they want to see what's out there. Clearly, the extent to which they experiment varies depending upon personality and upbringing, but it's exceedingly rare to find a teenager completely free of curiosity. Most take a dim view of adults who shield teens from experiences, no matter how pure the motive.

Second, many teens are rather cynical about adult intentions and suspect adults are holding out on them when it comes to fun. This attitude is especially prevalent among the edgier, more experimental types, who seem certain that parents, school administrators, and government policymakers are on a quest to sterilize life. To their way of thinking, adults already had their fun and are now trying to ensure no one else does. In fact, asked what adults don't get about teens, 25 percent of respondents answered, "When they were our age, they did some of the same things."

It's hardly news that teens react to advice with volatility. In qualitative research, teens wholeheartedly embrace the statement, "I hate when people tell me what to do—I want to make my own decisions." Respondents are drawn to this statement's defiant tone and the implied quest for self. Still, most teens admit that it's a better idea than a practice. Underneath their rebellious exteriors (and despite their sneaking suspicion that adults are trying to withhold fun), teens appear to have a grudging appreciation for guidance and direction. They admit that others—particularly parents and teachers—may have sound advice or experience that will help them make more informed decisions. In fact, it's often a source of great interest (and amusement) to hear teens tell us how much they hate people telling them what to do, even as they admit that their way is wrong. However, while some teens claim to respect experience and the wisdom that comes from it, many are quick to point out that the quality of advice is contingent on the quality or stature of the person rendering it. In other words, they will suffer the advice of parents, but drunk Uncle Clyde should probably keep his opinions to himself.

Despite their bluster, teens acknowledge that their rejection of authority bears little in common with the reality of their lives. Teens repeatedly speak of how their parents stand in the way of the teen's own decision-making, and even Uncle Clyde often gets more of a say than they feel he should. As mentioned before, older teens have more mature views of most subjects, and taking advice is no exception. Being "seasoned" by the lessons of past mistakes, older teens acknowledge that input from a greater variety of sources strengthens the quality of decisions. Importantly, they also exhibit a greater sense of self-confidence and purpose that enables them to accept advice than younger teens whose insecurity causes them to interpret advice as a challenge.

It must be trying to have so many conflicting feelings about adults. At any given time, teens may see adults as 1) humorless taskmasters intent upon crushing any hope of fun, 2) concerned authority figures trying to guide their loved ones through life's minefields or 3) arrogant blowhards who think they have all the answers but don't have a clue. No wonder 27 percent of teens claim "sometimes we need space from parents."

Another way to gain insight into teens' view of adults is to monitor the professions teens admire. By and large, teens prefer two types of careers: those that serve others and those that express creativity and individuality.

Most-Admired Professions

Girls admire doctors the most, while boys admire athletes.

(percent of teens citing profession as one of the four they admire the most, by gender)

	total	female	male
Doctor	52%	63%	42%
Teacher	40	54	27
Athlete	36	25	47
Actor	33	38	28
Artist/writer	27	30	23
Police officer	26	23	28
Military	23	17	29
Lawyer	23	27	19
Firefighter	21	22	21
Business executive	18	16	19
Veterinarian	17	25	9
Software developer	16	7	24
Clergy member (priest, rabbi)	12	11	12
Farmer	8	5	10
Mechanic/carpenter	8	3	13
Advertising executive	6	7	5
Politician	5	4	5
Car dealer	3	1	4
Insurance salesperson	2	2	1

Source: The TRU Study, Teenage Research Unlimited, Inc.

Professions that advance a greater good are the most popular with teens. Far and away the most popular occupation is that of doctor—more than half of teens list physician among the most-admired careers. Surprisingly, teens also think highly of occupations that sometimes rankle their rebellious nature, including teachers, police officers, members of the military, and lawyers. All of these professions perform a valuable and much-needed service to society (yes, even lawyers), and teens look up to them because of this fact. But why do teens think more highly of lawyers than adults appear to? The answer is likely rooted in dollars and cents. As teens look toward the not-too-distant future of career choices, they regard especially highly those that require extra schooling and yield higher earnings. Note that TRU last collected this data before September 11, 2001. At that time, firefighters were somewhat less highly regarded than attorneys—a choice we highly doubt would be duplicated today, especially with the bravery of New York's firefighters still fresh in the national consciousness.

Also popular are jobs that allow people to use their talents to stand out from the crowd. Included among these ranks are athletes, actors, artists, and writers.

The occupations teens like the least are those they consider dishonest or that center around selling. Included in this category are mechanics, car dealers, insurance salespeople, politicians, and advertising executives. (We didn't include marketers on the list, but we expect teens wouldn't discriminate between ad execs and the broader marketing field.) Teens can tell when they're being manipulated, and they don't like it. As we've said before, it's fine to explain why your product is useful, but don't expect a clever jingle or a high-pressure sales pitch to win teens' hearts.

Teen Attitudes toward Safety and Vulnerability

Most cohorts have had a "defining moment" in their youth, an event so powerful, so memorable that it helped define a generation. The Great De-

Teen Fear of Terrorism

Teen guys feel safer from terrorism than girls, and older teens feel safer than younger ones.

(mean score when teens are asked, "How safe do you feel from terrorist attacks, where '1' is not at all safe and '10' is extremely safe?" by gender, age, race, and Hispanic origin)

Total	6.07
Female	5.71
Male	6.41
Aged 12 to 15	5.99
Aged 16 to 17	6.11
Aged 18 to 19	6.20
Black	5.46
Hispanic	5.95
Non-Hispanic white	6.23

Source: The TRU Study, Teenage Research Unlimited, Inc.

pression, World War II, the Civil Rights movement, JFK's assassination, and the Vietnam War—each of these events stunned the nation and found itself seared into the public consciousness. Each event is indelibly linked to a specific era, as well as to a specific cohort of Americans, whose lives and attitudes permanently changed as a result.

Several years ago, we set out to find the defining moment of today's teens. We invited members of our Trendwatch panel to discuss which big stories defined their generation. There wasn't much consensus. Panelists rejected the fall of the Berlin Wall: good news, they said, but of no particular significance to them personally. They felt the same way about the deaths of grunge rocker Kurt Cobain and Princess Diana, whose departures were tragic but perhaps not historically significant.

Several panelists lobbied for the O.J. Simpson trial. It had everything, they said: celebrities, sex, intrigue, a car chase, crooked cops, race relations, a flashy lawyer, and a made-for-TV trial. It even sparked its own riot. But in the end, most dismissed even this "trial of the century" as a media-fueled spectacle with little long-term significance.

The only event that came close to unifying the majority of panelists was the April 1999 massacre at Columbine High School in Littleton, Colorado (although even this event failed to inspire much consensus). Many teens keenly identified with the victims—middle-class suburban kids— and they believed the same thing could happen just about anywhere. After all, disaffected youths populate every school district in America, and many of them even wear black trench coats.

We conducted this qualitative research more than a year before September 11, 2001. Nevertheless, we believe Columbine stirred the same feelings in teens that adults felt on the day the World Trade Center fell. To adults, the attacks on the massive office buildings in the U.S. financial capital sent an unmistakable message: no one in the American capitalist system is safe. Likewise, to teens, the massacre at a typical suburban high school was a chilling reminder that even in the "safest" school district, safety can't be guaranteed.

TRU research shows teens recovered from the shock of the terrorist attacks remarkably fast—so fast, in fact, that outsiders might be forgiven for thinking them a bit crass. We believe their recovery is partly attributable to the fact that many had already encountered a similar experience in Columbine. Of course, the attack on New York was horrific beyond description, and the losses were nearly beyond teens' ability to comprehend.

Teen Perception of
Terror Threat

Most teens think another terrorist attack is "very" or "somewhat" likely.

(percent distribution of teens by their perception of the likelihood of another terrorist attack, by gender, age, race, and Hispanic origin)

	very likely	somewhat likely	not too likely	not at all likely
Total	17%	49%	30%	3%
Female	15	53	28	3
Male	19	44	32	4
Aged 12 to 15	16	47	33	3
Aged 16 to 17	19	47	30	3
Aged 18 to 19	17	53	25	4
Black	17	48	29	6
Hispanic	16	46	33	3
Non-Hispanic white	16	42	37	5

Source: The TRU Study, Teenage Research Unlimited, Inc.

Still, for many teens the terrorist attacks were far-removed from their daily life. They were more closely connected to the kids in Littleton. In fact, it could be argued that Columbine was this cohort's September 11.

Just a few months after the terrorist attacks, focus group panelists began telling us that the attacks had largely faded from their daily conversations, emerging only when a particularly big headline grabbed their attention. Many even said they had begun joking about "everything that's going on the news," a sure sign that the event had evolved from earth-shattering news into something more routine, perhaps even mundane.

Despite the seeming nonchalance about the national tragedy, teens repeatedly noted their appreciation for the national unity and resolve that followed in the months after the attacks. What's more, there was an upswing among teens in the popularity of time-tested American icons such as Chevy and Levi's. Other items popular among focus group panelists in the immediate aftermath of the terrorist attacks included comfort food such as Campbell's tomato soup and characters from old cartoons such as *Winnie the Pooh*'s Eeyore and Disney's Mickey Mouse.

When we asked teens in the summer of 2000 (about a year after Columbine but a year before September 11), how strongly they identified with the statement, "We're living in dangerous times," about 25 percent of respondents chose it as the one statement that most represents their generation. But teens interpret "living in dangerous times" differently than the general population does. In focus groups, teens imagine the statement refers to local or school-based violence, including threats posed by gangs and random school shootings. Remarkably (from our point of view), they rarely cite terrorist threats near the top of their list, and they frequently don't bring up terrorism at all. If we want to discuss the subject of terrorism, we have to ask about it specifically.

Still, the juxtaposition of "we're all about fun" (teens' most common description of the teen years) and "we're living in dangerous times" (the number-three response) caught our attention. When we asked about it in qualitative research, teens said both statements were accurate, explaining that fear of the unknown is no excuse for a "bunker mentality." Rather, they said, an unknown future is all the more reason to live life to the fullest. After all, one teen explained to us, "You never know what's around the corner. You'd better get some living done while you can."

Teen Attitudes Toward Patriotism

During the Persian Gulf War of 1991, teens and other Americans rallied behind the president, U.S. military forces, and the country at large. A sudden flurry of flags, bumper stickers, ribbons, and patriotic country-music songs attested to swelling national pride. However, once the conflict ended, the public returned to business as usual, and the senior President Bush's popularity plummeted so precipitously that he managed to lose an election most expected would be a slam-dunk. At that time, TRU recorded a similar trajectory in teens' own feelings of national pride. There was indeed an initial spike in patriotism, but six months later the sentiment was back at its normal level.

The War on Terror might be different. It's still too soon for most teens to see the attack on the World Trade Center as this generation's defining moment, but with the passage of time and with the help of hindsight, it's likely that the terrorist attacks will create more of a legacy than Columbine, which brought about relatively few long-term policy changes.

The Gulf War saw a sharp rise and an equally abrupt fall in patriotic attitudes, so we weren't surprised when terrorism dropped so dramatically on teens' list of top social concerns.

In fact, only a year after the terrorist attacks, significantly fewer teens reported an interest in actively participating in pro-USA behaviors. While 39 percent of teens say they would be willing to pay more for a product if part of the proceeds went to a pro-USA cause, only 29 percent report that it's important to them to purchase made-in-the-USA products.

Teens and Patriotism

While teens feel more patriotic than they once did, few are more likely to buy American-made products.

(percent of teens agreeing with statement, by gender)

	total	female	male
I feel more strongly about my country than I used to	67%	67%	68%
I feel really good about seeing an American flag in a TV commercial	46	44	47
I don't know which products are U.S.-made	40	43	38
I'd consider a government career	40	38	43
I'd pay more for products if some of the money went to a pro-U.S. cause	37	37	37
I like companies that let me know they contribute to pro-U.S. causes	33	31	35
I'd be proud to enlist in the U.S. military	30	22	37
It's important for me to buy U.S.-made products	27	22	31
Companies are wrong to say how patriotic they are	26	20	31
I'm wearing more red, white, and blue	25	28	23
I'd consider a military career	25	20	30
I want to buy red, white, and blue products	16	17	16
I look for labels that say U.S.-made	15	9	20

Source: The TRU Study, Teenage Research Unlimited, Inc.

White teens are more likely than African-American or Hispanic teens to say they feel more strongly about America than they used to and that it's important for them to buy USA-made products. Perhaps not surprisingly, perhaps thanks in part to NAFTA, more Hispanic than white or African-American teens disagree with the importance of buying products made in the USA.

Most teens appreciate the quality of life in the U.S., but few express much enthusiasm for the sort of blustering "We're number-one!" outbursts they have seen in TV advertising, programming, and news reports. They agree patriotism is a good thing, but don't expect to see them picketing in front of Pier One anytime soon. TRU believes a convergence of factors can explain this mindset.

About one-fourth of teens (26 percent) are distrustful of companies that boast about their patriotism. In the days following the attacks, some teens complained about ads that were garish and manipulative, seeming to capitalize on the tragedies.

Although most teens are not particularly cynical—not yet, anyway—they are pragmatic and impatient. When they undertake something, they expect to see the fruits of their labor almost immediately. For many, the expectation of immediate gratification discourages work on large or abstract social causes. Further, because most teens aren't old enough to vote, sign legal documents, or legally drink, they feel somewhat disenfranchised. They don't believe society values their contributions. As such, many don't go out of their way to contribute any more than they have to.

If you want to engage teens, let them know how their efforts can help not only down the road, but also right now.

Teen Heroes and Protectors

Although teens typically describe themselves as wild and carefree, the unsettling events of the last several years may have refocused their priorities a bit. When asked to name the biggest hero in their lives, teens increasingly look to spiritual and parental figures for strength and guidance.

Teens overwhelmingly name God as their biggest hero (particularly the youngest respondents and minority teens). Overall, 35 percent claim God as a hero—a greater percentage than listed mom and dad combined! This fact reveals an important difference between their parents' generation and their own. While Baby Boomers and Generation Xers were skeptical of religion, today's teens are more likely to embrace spirituality as one of their guiding principals. Spiritual life plays a particularly important role in African-American families. Further, teens gain a variety of benefits from their spiritual endeavors, including inspiration, perseverance, tolerance, and comfort.

Some teens—particularly those in the South—report active involvement in church youth groups and choirs. This involvement demonstrates that their commitment to faith goes beyond mere words and that their involvement is not simply meant to appease their families. (Still, it is probably safe to assume that parents have been influential in directing their teens toward religion.) Some religious-minded teens who show less interest in the highly structured environment of the church tell us they enjoy hanging out at places that play spiritual rock music and where others with similar values gather. Protestant Christians have made particularly strong inroads with these teens, and several rock bands that espouse a Christian message (whether overtly or covertly) have crossed over to mainstream success. These bands include P.O.D., Creed, and Lifehouse, among others.When we ask teens to create a collage showing what is important to them, it's not unusual to see religious icons in their work. When we have respondents from various regions perform this exercise, teens from the South—particularly the "old South"—are most likely to decorate their collages with religious symbols and phrases.

Interestingly, some teens—again, mainly in the South—talk about the important social role the church plays in many conservative communities.

To achieve a certain social status, they explain, one has to be an active member of the church, because the church is the focal point of social gatherings.

Mom is the second biggest hero to teens. Mom's long winning streak was broken this time around only because TRU expanded the question to include God. If anyone's going to end mom's streak, it might as well be an all-powerful deity.

Within the family unit, mom is God—especially according to daughters. Sixteen percent of teens claim mom (the de facto head-of-household) is their biggest hero. And as also found in other TRU work, African-American teens feel a particularly close, respectful bond with their mothers.

The genders diverge when it comes to dad. Teen boys rate dad slightly higher than mom, but it's no contest for girls: only 6 percent of girls name their father as a hero compared to 21 percent who choose their mother. And as much as African-American teens put mom on a pedestal, they display no such high regard for dad—he rates rather low in this measure.

Though celebrity and athlete heroes enjoy strong appeal with younger teens, they don't fare as well with middle to older teens—at least not compared to God or a parent. (Marketers beware: as much as teens look up to God, tapping into teen admiration for their parents would be more appropriate for brand marketing. But heavy-handed representations of the perfect, ever-adoring nuclear family could strike teens as being "fake"—a fatal flaw. Execution is of critical importance here.)

Teen Attitudes Toward Individuality and Open-mindedness

Teen attitudes toward open-mindedness, individuality, and diversity are in conflict with the realities of teen life. On the one hand, 24 percent of teens claim they are open to new ideas, and another 18 percent say individualism is an important component of their life. But only 13 percent say teens in general are accepting of differences.

Teen Heroes

The largest share of teens say God is the "biggest hero" in their life.

(percent of teens citing person as the "biggest hero in your life," by gender, age, race, and Hispanic origin)

	total	female	male	12 to 15	16 to 17	18 to 19	black	Hispanic	non-Hispanic white
God	35%	37%	33%	39%	31%	30%	47%	40%	31%
Your mom	16	21	10	13	16	22	21	19	13
Someone else	10	9	12	9	12	12	3	8	12
Your dad	10	6	14	9	10	11	6	12	11
Friend	6	7	4	5	8	5	1	4	7
Celebrity or athlete	4	3	6	6	3	1	3	2	5
Grandparent	4	3	5	3	5	6	5	2	4
Brother or sister	3	4	3	3	4	3	2	4	3
Teacher	2	2	3	2	3	2	0	2	3
Religious leader	1	1	2	1	1	2	1	2	2
Government leader	1	1	1	2	0	1	0	0	1
Coach	1	1	1	1	1	1	0	1	1
No answer	6	5	7	7	6	5	9	4	6

Source: The TRU Study, Teenage Research Unlimited, Inc.

Young people are well aware that the teen years are spent seeking the comfort of a close group of similar friends. Yet many boldly state that trying new things should be a life-long endeavor, although they acknowledge that experimentation is easier during youth than adulthood.

The most earnest proponents of experimentation during the teen years consider it a part of the growth process, as well as a good way to collect experiences. These respondents note that most adults seem reluctant to experiment, and they reason that this is because of the greater responsibilities of adulthood. In other words, the more you have, the more you have to lose. Many teens believe adulthood is the time to capitalize on experience. Having survived (and presumably learned from) youthful experimentation, teens believe that young adulthood is best suited for using that knowledge to one's advantage.

A surprisingly large segment of teens, however, argue that the teen years are not a particularly good time for experimentation because of limits and restrictions on their age group. Constrained by parental rules, not yet old enough to drink, and not financially able to have the experiences they would like (skydiving, for example), this school of thought argues that true experimentation must wait until college.

Chapter 4

Teen Types, Trends, and Music

In our more than 20 years of conducting teen research, we've examined almost every imaginable topic from the basics of new-product launches and advertising testing to innovative ethnographic projects on fashion, friendships, and fun. Yet, nothing else we do captures the public's imagination like our work on teen trends.

One reason for this relatively new-found preoccupation with the ebb and flow of teen trends is the increasingly crowded marketplace. Regardless of the product or category, brands that market to teens face unprecedented competition. When we founded TRU in 1982, we knew teens would become a formidable market segment, but the level of attention paid to the teen market over the last decade has surprised everyone who works in this business.

The practical upshot of marketers' headlong rush into the teen market is that consumers today have a much broader range of choices. The traditional means of selecting a brand—price vs. quality—is no longer sufficient because many points along the price–quality continuum offer more than one option. As such, imagery has become an increasingly important attribute in helping teens differentiate among brands.

Take American Eagle and Hot Topic, for example. Both are mall-based specialty-apparel retailers that cater to the teen market, and both offer good-quality clothing in a roughly equivalent price range. But the similarities end there. Whereas American Eagle sells a rather conservative mix of "preppy" styles with broad mainstream appeal, Hot Topic specializes in goth- and punk-inspired fashions for teens with a more adventurous sense of style. When visiting Hot Topic, the chain's core customer is drawn not only to the current selection of merchandise, but also to Hot Topic's brand

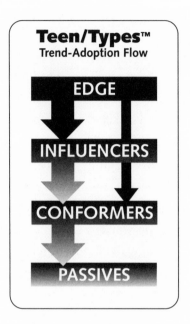

image as a purveyor of edgy, fashion-forward clothes. Such teens would likely consider American Eagle bland by comparison. On the other hand, a loyal American Eagle customer likely derives a great deal of satisfaction from the chain's image as a "safe bet" for popular styles. AE's products tend to mesh seamlessly with the fashions of the day, and they typically don't go out of style after a season or two. Many AE teens would reject most of Hot Topic's clothing as too "out there" for their taste.

Teen/Types

As the above example illustrates, different brand images appeal to different teens. Reaction to a given brand image is largely dependent upon a teen's personality. (Clearly, friends also are powerful influences, but the selection of friends is heavily reliant upon a teen's personality as well). The challenge, then, is to determine which personality types are most likely to embrace particular images, personalities, and other related attributes.

TRU's Teen/Types system is based on a statistical analysis of approximately 100 key behavioral and attitudinal variables that are included in The TRU Study's fairly lengthy questionnaire. The procedure, known as a cluster analysis, groups teens based upon a commonalty of response to these variables. The results segment teens based upon relevant characteristics—in this case, key behavioral and attitudinal attributes.

The graph on the following page shows the breakdown of these Teen/Types by size (i.e., the percentage of the teen population that is best characterized by each of the segments). When comparing the segments, it becomes immediately apparent that although they are of radically different sizes, their average age is approximately the same: about 15 years. Therefore, the variables that most strongly determine differences among Teen/Types are values, attitudes, and lifestyle, rather than age-dependent factors. This is key. If instead the segmentation yielded a group whose average age is 14 and another aged 16, we would imagine the differences to be age-driven. The objective of Teen/Types is to soundly segment the population in non-demographic terms, thereby reaching (through messages and media) teens based on lifestyle and personality.

Teens function in a hierarchical society, and the Teen/Types model reflects this dynamic. New products, fashions, and activities often start with Edge teens or with Influencers. They are then adopted by Conformers and finally by Passives. As telling as statistics are, it's also essential to confirm that "real life" supports the data. So, as a reality check, we routinely present Teen/Types (as well as other data) to high school audiences. Though each school may apply different names to our segments (for example, some will call Influencers "jocks" or "preps"), the students typically nod in unison upon hearing not only the description of each of the types but also how trends flow within the model.

What follows is an in-depth introduction to each of the four Teen/Types.

Teen/Types: Teen Segmentation System

Conformers make up the largest share of teens.

(percent distribution of teens by TRU's Teen/Types Segmentation System)

Edge	11%
Influencers	10
Conformers	44
Passives	35

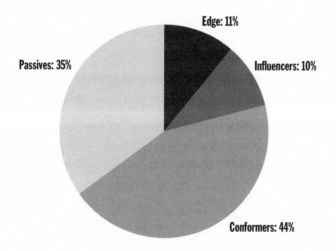

Passives: 35% Edge: 11% Influencers: 10% Conformers: 44%

Source: The TRU Study, Teenage Research Unlimited, Inc.

Edge Teens. If Edge teens are annoyed to hear that they are on the cutting edge of teen lifestyle and fashion trends, it's only because these fiercely independent youths often consider themselves removed entirely from the traditional teenage social strata. Edge teens are often rebellious, sometimes reckless, and always cool (though many won't acknowledge caring about such things). Many of the trends eventually adopted by the larger teen population start with Edge teens, including skateboarding, alternative music, body piercing, funky hair coloring, and tattoos. Still, this segment tends to bristle at being labeled "trendsetting." They are the least traditional and least family-oriented of the Teen/Types, yet Edge teens still frequently betray a fondness for "retro" activities like family dinners. Such contradictions define these teens, who sometimes mock the "constructs" of style and fashion, but swear by a wardrobe of Morbid Threads, Porn Star, and Menace.

Though some adults would automatically label them "antisocial," nothing could be further from the truth. They want out of the house as much as possible—to be with friends. They are most likely to be involved in "action" sports like motocross or skysurfing, and least likely to be interested in conventional sports like baseball or basketball. They like to push the envelope—whether at school, at home, or at play. They are experimental, experiential, and adventurous. In short, they've been known to break a few rules.

Edge teens are frequently quite bright—just as often, however, their grades don't reflect their abilities. As a result, they are not optimistic about future success, instead throwing themselves headlong into their current experiences and living for the moment. More than any other group, these teens have an abiding love for music, whether at an open-air concert or in a used CD bin at a local strip mall. They're the heaviest readers of *Rolling Stone* and *Spin*; they're also by far the biggest fans of dance and rave, hardcore, and punk music. They are less interested in rap, hip-hop, and

R&B. These musical preferences are a clear reflection that this group is disproportionately Caucasian; still, they are at the cutting edge of white music.

Edge teens are not a homogenous group, however. The population has many subcultures, and each smaller group has its own focus. While one faction may concentrate on politics and community involvement, others are just as likely to be anarchic in attitude. They revel in such differences and use fashion to accentuate them. From Day-Glo hair, tattoos, and body piercings to poetry, dancing, and the Internet, Edge teens choose their activities to fit their interests and their image. Still, they are accepting of differences in others.

These young people stand out from their peers in another important way. Their parents often let them "get away" with many of their behaviors and sometimes even facilitate them. Some Edge teens admit they successfully sneak riskier behaviors and more extreme styles past oblivious parents, while others say their parents know about their antics but let them slide. This is an important point. Groundbreaking teens need this kind of parental license, and the Edge seems to have more of it than other segments. In fact, other Teen/Types sometimes describe Edge teens as "those kids whose parents just don't care!"

Influencers. This is an exclusive group, and consequently it's smaller than other Teen/Types, comprising only 10 percent of the teen population. Membership in the Influencer segment is greatly sought after and highly prized. Despite its size—or more accurately, because of it—this segment remains the most influential among its peers. These are the teens that "wannabes" aspire to be and the ones that marketers are eager to reach. As far as teens are concerned, when Influencers speak, the world listens.

It is important to understand the differences between the two "influential" groups of teens. Influencers are popular with the "right" people. They are cool but not particularly edgy. These (generally attractive) teens care about how they look, what they wear, and with whom they associate. They love to spend time and money shopping, and they frequent a greater variety of stores than other teens do.

Although Edge teens believe others think they're cool, they're not as invested as Influencers in achieving or maintaining this status. Whereas the more independent-minded Edge teens revile the role of fashion in their lives (at least publicly), Influencers revel in it.

Influencers are a more ethnically diverse group than Edge teens—29 percent of Influencers are African American and 15 percent are Hispanic. The key personality traits that separate this group from the others include an outgoing nature, an active social life, and the self-confidence that such peer acceptance brings. These teens know they've "arrived"—they admit things are going "extremely well"—and that most people who know them think they're cool. Not surprisingly, Influencers enjoy being teen.

Influencers also enjoy being in the center of things. More so than other Teen/Types, they're involved in and enthused about the typical teenage social trappings, whether having boyfriends or girlfriends, owning cellular phones, cruising in cars, or just hanging out with friends. They also enjoy certain school activities more than other segments do, including sports, the hallway "scene," and joining and leading the desirable clubs.

Still, these young people feel a consistent need for self-affirmation; they need to stand out among their peers. They often accomplish this through careful attention to appearance and trends, taking their fashion cues from music videos and celebrities more than other Teen/Types do. Some, especially white Influencers, look to Edge teens for fashion and lifestyle ideas, but they wait until someone else initiates the style before risking their hard-earned reputation. (Conformers take this caution one step further: they wait to see fashions on Influencers before taking the leap.)

Noted examples of trends that originated with Influencers and have gone mainstream include rap music and hip-hop culture, low-rise jeans, a volume of youth vernacular, pro-sports clothes (including throwback jerseys, which are in vogue as of this writing), and many urban brands.

Conformers. Conformers are the teenage equivalent of Richard Nixon's "silent majority." Though they make up the bulk of the teen population, their main imprint on teen culture is that they popularize the fashions and lifestyles that their more trend-forward peers establish. Far from cutting edge, Conformers are "typical" teenagers, gravitating to the latest teen behaviors, styles, and trends. They tend to adhere to the social norms imposed by Influencers, although some Conformers directly emulate Edge teens.

Conformers require more peer acceptance than the Edge, and they lack the confidence and social status of Influencers. They have lower self-esteem: fewer Conformers than Influencers and Edge teens think they're "cool." This insecurity contributes to their reliance on external trappings and their compliance with already-developed fads. They aggressively seek out widely accepted lifestyle cues to help them feel more confident, both in how they see themselves and how they wish others to see them.

In fact, what most stands out about this group is the fact that nothing stands out! They often don't harbor extreme views or hold deep-seated concerns. They take part in the same kinds of activities (sports, parties, shopping) as members of the leading teen social groups, just not as often. They are content to let the trendsetters sort out what's hot and what's not, but after the treacherous trial-and-error period is over they happily purchase the prevailing look. In short, they are the consummate consumers.

Conformers' impact on teen culture makes the group hugely important to marketers. They represent an enormous portion of the teen population, and they have both the will and financial means to emulate the smaller, more trend-forward social groups. Advertising and promotions that show what the "cool" teens wear, do, or own tends to resonate with these teens, giving them much-sought-after cues about the trends they wish to follow. Additionally, marketing messages that offer solutions for typical teen problems—and, therefore, promote self-confidence—are especially compelling to Conformers. Marketers should take care, however, to present these messages in an engaging way: Conformers are becoming increasingly market-savvy, and they resent advertisements that blatantly play on their insecurities.

Passive Teens. Befitting their name, this group—though successful academically—struggles socially. To some extent, Passive teens exist on the outskirts of mainstream teen life. They yearn to be more popular and well liked, but they lack the confidence or the ambition to be proactive toward this end. Not only is this group the last to pick up on fashion trends, its members spend less time listening to music and they are generally less involved in all areas of teenage social life than the other Teen/Types are.

Although they do have friends, Passives tend to be more comfortable with others of the same Teen/Type. As a result, these teens spend less time participating in social activities like parties and large school gatherings—even talking on the phone and hanging out at the mall. Passives are not socially active enough to be dance fans nor experimental enough to favor emerging music. Little surprise, then, that these teens don't particularly like hip-hop, alternative, rave, techno, or punk.

Though Passives would not choose their particular rung on the teenage social ladder, they seem to accept it. Fewer Passives than other groups label themselves "cool." Instead, many of these teens say they are "pretty normal," noting that their friends are similar to them. More than half of these teens report that things are "really going well" for them. So, whether secure in their position and circle of friends or simply powerless to change, members of this Teen/Type do not actively strive to involve themselves in emerging trends.

Males dominate the Passive segment by a two-to-one ratio. This is not completely surprising: males tend to be less fashion-oriented than females, so more males find themselves at the end point of trend adoption.

Representing a sizable 35 percent of the teen population, Passives remain a worthwhile audience for many marketers. Most Passives don't actively resist trends, they simply require an unusually large degree of exposure before they feel comfortable with new fashions, styles, or activities. Most will (eventually) react favorably to the same kind of messages that appeal to Conformers. Marketing that offers optimism and relief from social stress should be especially effective with this segment.

Teens on Teen/Types

It's one thing to come up with a complex segmentation system to help explain how trends spread through teen society. It's quite another to get teens to sign off on its accuracy! We did both, and we were rewarded with some great teenage marketing perspectives.

For years, Teen/Types has been at the forefront of our quantitative research, breaking out our syndicated data by these four key lifestyle segments. More recently, we began offering the chance to stock qualitative research sessions with Edge and Influencer teens from our new Trendwatch panel.

Generally, when TRU invites a new recruit to join the Trendwatch panel, we tell the individual that he or she fits the criteria we're looking for. But we typically don't explain the methodology behind our decision— that we believe the recruit is either an Edge teen or an Influencer. Recently, however, curiosity and a desire to gain teen feedback prompted us to ask a group of Trendwatch panelists what they thought about our Teen/Type system. The results surprised us.

From the outset, we expected resistance. After all, teens have an uneasy relationship with labels and generalizations. On one hand, they tend to gravitate toward like-minded peers with whom they share common interests, be it fashion, music, sports, or some combination thereof. And when meeting new people, teens often look for external cues—most frequently in clothing—to help them recognize compatriots. Still, the teen tendency to celebrate individuality makes them wary of efforts by outsiders to pigeonhole or categorize them.

In order not to inadvertently prejudice respondents, TRU introduced Teen/Types simply as a marketing theory that we were investigating. We gave panelists free reign to comment in whatever way they saw fit, whether positively or negatively. And, as anticipated, one respondent expressed his misgivings right away. He insisted that to really know a person in all his or her complexity, a marketer would need to study the individual personally.

Remarkably, though, most of the other teens we asked seemed intrigued by the system. And, more important, after some debate, most agreed highly similar groupings exist at their school.

"I'd never really thought about it before, but I guess there is a kind of small group of kids that most of the people at school watch," one panelist said. "I mean, it's like Abercrombie. The cool people started wearing that quite a while ago, and for a long time it was tough to find anyone that didn't have 'A&F' stamped across their chest."

Surprisingly, even some of our Edge panelists, who tend to be most suspicious of efforts to categorize people, agreed that trend adoption follows a pattern similar to TRU's Teen/Types hierarchy. They suggested that the Edge segment might play a somewhat smaller role in the process because Edge teens intentionally seek out interests in which others aren't involved. Still, they acknowledged that ideas from the Edge do sometimes work their way into the mainstream—as seen with piercings and tattoos, which one panelist described as a "Blink-182 uniform."

Not surprisingly, as stated earlier, teens don't use the labels we do, but they have countless words of their own to describe Edge, Influencer, Conformer, and Passive teens. Panelists conceded that while the names of these groups may vary from school to school, their roles seem to remain fairly constant.

Teens and Fashion

Fashion plays a key role in distinguishing the Teen/Types; in fact, for the majority of teens, clothing choices have an oversized role in the entire teen experience. Fashion and style offer teens a way to display the many facets of their personalities. They can distinguish themselves from their peers through their clothing choices—or they can choose to assimilate completely.

Teens lead active lifestyles, and we've found that most—guys in particular—consider comfort every bit as important as appearance when choosing outfits. The teens we've talked to tell us their personal look combines both comfort and style; many argue that feeling comfortable establishes a sense of confidence they find indispensable. It's worth noting, however, that fashion varies rather significantly by region. Teens living in the Pacific Northwest are particularly adamant about comfort, while teen girls in some Southern states wouldn't dream of leaving the house without a full application of makeup and a pair of punishing high-heeled shoes.

The dominant teen clothing trend of the last several years—showing skin—seems custom-tailored for young people (although perhaps not for the youngest teens). The trend had roots in another teen-oriented fad: pop music. As the newest generation of pop fans became more familiar with (and perhaps a bit more resistant to) the slick, heavily produced sugar-bombs from Britney Spears to Christina Aguilera, the stars found it advantageous to up their sex appeal a bit. And as went the pop princesses, so went legions of teen girls across the country.

Indeed, teens like to wear clothes that get them noticed, and girls in particular are drawn to tight, low jeans, leather pants, and skimpy tops. Still, the "skin is in" trend peaked a couple of years ago, and many girls tell us they're increasingly interested in getting noticed without being overly provocative. To put it bluntly—as so many teens do—girls want to be "cute, not slutty."

In a testament to teen pop's decline and the ensuing rise of punk-infused rock music, more teens are now looking to punk- and goth-inspired fashions as a way to attract attention. Look for a steady rise in spikes, studs, and safety pins until the look is done in by its own popularity. Once mainstream kids adopt mohawks and bondage gear, the whole look will implode, leaving nothing but a strong whiff of irony in its place.

Punk styles are gaining popularity as of this writing, but fashion is not monolithic: teens embrace a wide variety of looks including "retro," "surfer," "urban," "preppy," and "skater." Still, it's misleading to suggest that any teen would restrict his or her wardrobe to one look. Most young people play different roles at different times and for different people, and they delight in experimenting with a variety of styles to reflect this diversity and to complement their various moods. Thus, some teens stock their wardrobes with mixtures of styles, while others accentuate their standard clothing style with interchangeable accessories, whether fun or formal. Guys and girls alike tell us that jewelry and watches, headbands, belts, sunglasses, bags, dog tags, tattoos, and body piercings are ways to further customize an outfit.

Fashion Influences

The style teens adopt depends heavily upon personal image and the look that prevails within the teen's social circle. Notably, best friends are not the primary source of peer pressure (on fashion matters or otherwise). Whether or not a best friend likes an outfit, they are less judgmental of the styles they see on their friends—or, at least, more judicious about their remarks. Fashion is one more example of how outer circles of friends can influence the type of person a teen wants to be and the image he or she wants to project to others.

Adults sometimes label teens as shallow for using fashion to portray their self-image, claiming that teens have so little substance that they must resort to wearing labels to differentiate themselves. But this argument

Where Teens Get Ideas for Fashion

**Most teens claim to get fashion ideas from themselves,
with friends coming in second.**

*(percent of teens responding when asked, "People often get ideas for fashion and
style from other people. Where do you get your ideas for what
to wear and how to wear it?" by gender)*

	total	females	males
Myself	61%	62%	60%
Friends	50	47	54
People at school	32	33	31
Advertising	24	21	27
Stores	22	15	30
Magazines	22	12	32
TV or movie stars	18	14	23
Music videos	16	14	17
Brother or sister	15	16	14
Catalogs	14	10	18
People on the street	11	10	11
Musical artists	10	9	11
Models	9	5	13
Pro athletes	8	13	3
Parents	8	8	7
Web sites	3	4	3
Other	13	15	10

Source: The TRU Study, Teenage Research Unlimited, Inc.

ignores the obvious fact that teens have a huge number of opinions and are unabashedly outspoken about most of them. Teens aren't simply using style as a substitute for substance. Rather, they use fashion as a quick-reference tool to help outsiders—especially like-minded peers—know about their attitudes, outlooks, and interests at a glance. Adults do the same thing—when's the last time you saw a loan officer decked out in leather pants and a tongue stud?

When we ask teens about their fashion influences, more than half tell us—in all seriousness—that they don't have any. They claim that they are their own inspiration and the looks they wear are simply an extension of their own personality. It sounds pretty good until you notice the huge Abercrombie & Fitch stenciled across their chest! In fact, most teens are much too concerned with their image and social standing to embrace an untested fashion statement that could be a hit, but stands an equal chance of being a complete disaster.

Most teens take fashion cues from friends, personalizing or accessorizing just enough to call the style their own. This helps explain the top two responses to this question: 60 percent of teens claim they come up with fashion ideas themselves, while 50 percent credit friends with sparking their inspiration. Another 32 percent say other people at school (not to be confused with friends) give them fashion ideas.

Notably, many teens admit that advertising plays a significant role in their clothing decisions—24 percent of teens said they get fashion ideas from advertising, showing how important, even at a conscious level, advertising is in shaping teen culture. This finding also answers the age-old marketer question: do we take cues from teens, or do they take cues from us? The answer: it works both ways. If you're reading this book, you obviously care about what teens think, and you want to reflect those insights in your teen offerings. Know, as well, that teens are closely watching you—not only your advertising, but also your new products and any changes in your brands.

The media (outside of advertising) are also a factor in influencing teen trends, but not a dominant one, according to teens. Our national sample rated magazines (22 percent) most influential, followed by TV or movie stars (18 percent) and music videos (16 percent). Musical artists (10 percent), models (9 percent), and pro athletes (8 percent) seem less influential on teens (although TRU believes these numbers are understated, as teens are reluctant to acknowledge that they take fashion cues from celebrities). Netting together the celebrity mentions raises the response, but still leaves it at a level that we believe understates the power of celebrity. Realizing this, Reebok—in addition to promoting its celebrity athletes—has also signed on popular rappers to promote new shoe lines.

Fashion Retailers

Teens give credit where credit is due. Nearly one-fourth of respondents, recognizing that they can buy only the merchandise a retailer stocks, say stores influence their sense of style. That acknowledgement is cold comfort for retailers. More retailers slipped than gained ground in the most recent wave of The TRU Study—thanks to the soft economy and recent, heavy expansion of the teen retail segment. Still, the big names (JC Penney, Sears, Wal-Mart, Target, Old Navy, Gap) remain big.

The best news for retailers comes from the beleaguered department store segment. In keeping with teen tradition, JC Penney continues to dominate here, with 57 percent of teens shopping the mainstream megalith in the past year. Sears trails at 43 percent. These two national giants are also teens' favorite department stores. Notably, two smaller department store chains enjoyed significant shopping increases. Macy's saw the percentage of teens shopping at its stores increase slightly from 18 to 21 percent, thanks to a renewed emphasis on in-store events and teen-appropriate brands such as XOXO. And Nordstrom climbed ever so slightly from 8 to 10 percent, thanks mainly to Brass Plum (also known as BP), a teen-targeted boutique that carries the kind of on-trend merchandise teen girls want at lower prices than the Nordstrom name might suggest.

Discounters Wal-Mart and Target remained flat. Some 75 percent of teens reported visiting Wal-Mart in the past 12 months, while 62 percent of teens shopped Target. Kmart, however, did not fare as well. The blue-light specialist saw its teen shoppers fall from 51 to 44 percent in six months. What's more, a paltry 5 percent of teens name the discounter as their favorite. This drop likely stems, at least in part, to the publicity surrounding Kmart's bankruptcy proceedings: nothing kills teen interest faster than the stench of death (real or perceived).

Specialty-apparel stores experienced a bit more flux. Old Navy attracts a healthy 56 percent of teen shoppers, but corporate cousin Gap's slow erosion continues: the retailer fell 3 percentage points in the latest TRU wave. Limited Brands, which controls the Limited, Express, and Express for Men lines, seems to be in a state of turmoil. Many of our male Trendwatch panelists admit being baffled by the company's decision to ditch the familiar and well-regarded Structure brand (one that was fairly popular with young men). The company dismantled Structure and replaced it with Express for Men, although guys think of Express as a "girl's brand."

When it comes to favorite specialty-apparel retailers, Hot Topic is on a roll. The punk purveyor is well positioned to take advantage of the pop backlash, which helps explain how the mall store vaulted from fourth to second place over a six-month period in The TRU Study measure on specialty apparel retailers.

Teen Trend Research

TRU employs several methods of keeping our clients up-to-date on teen trends. One of them is TRU View, a multimedia trend and news report delivered to our clients every other Friday. Happily, clients unabashedly tell us they look forward to receiving TRU View's coverage of teen marketing, fashion, and lifestyle news (and when people look forward to a marketing newsletter, you know you're doing something right!). TRU View, for the most part, is qualitative in nature. It provides coverage of notewor-

Teens' Favorite Stores

JC Penney is the favorite department store among teens, while Old Navy is their favorite specialty-apparel store.

(among teens who shopped at selected stores in the past 12 months, percent naming the store as their favorite, by gender)

DEPARTMENT STORES

	female		male
JC Penney	37%	JC Penney	33%
Kohl's	22	Sears	26
Macy's	14	Kohl's	12
Sears	10	Macy's	10
Nordstrom	8	Nordstrom	4

DISCOUNT STORES

Target	46	Wal-Mart	52
Wal-Mart	42	Target	30
Kmart	6	Kmart	9
Fred Meyer	0	Fred Meyer	1

SPECIALTY-APPAREL STORES

Old Navy	20	Old Navy	21
American Eagle	8	American Eagle	9
Abercrombie & Fitch	7	Abercrombie & Fitch	8
Hot Topic	7	Hot Topic	7
Gap	7	Gap	6
Express	7	PacSun	6
Wet Seal	6	Millers Outpost	4
Rave	5	Gadzooks	3
Aeropostale	5	Banana Republic	3
Gadzooks	4	Aeropostale	3

Source: The TRU Study, Teenage Research Unlimited, Inc.

thy and compelling fads and trends, as well as analysis of particularly good—and bad—teen-marketing strategies and tactics. Although we are able to support most of our recommendations and implications with either strong qualitative experience or actual quantitative data, much of TRU View is anecdotal. This is a key strength because when you're reporting short-lived trends, you can't wait around to see how they turn out!

How do we uncover the trends for TRU View? One way is through our Trendwatch panel. A major TRU initiative of the past two years has been to develop a large panel of Influencer and Edge teens who serve as our "eyes and ears" for teen culture. We named this panel Trendwatch to signal to both the teens and our clients their unique and empowered role. The teens on the panel, who live in the leading U.S. trend markets, are hand-selected (through a unique referral and auditioning process) as teens capable of ferreting out emerging trends before they show up in the larger population. One of the requirements for being on Trendwatch (aside from qualifying as an Edge or Influencer teen) is having home access to the 'Net, because much of our communication with these teens takes place online. In fact, we've set up a proprietary bulletin-board system to serve as a panel community and to facilitate a regular exchange of information with these trend-savvy teens.

Another way we find out about trends is through The TRU Study itself. Because it's the largest commercial study of teen behavior and attitudes, it's an extremely valuable tool for investigating and tracking macrotrends. Because it is nationally representative (unlike Trendwatch), The TRU Study is useful for gauging the rise and fall of mainstream fashions, activities, and attitudes. One of the primary tools for monitoring trends in the Study is our ongoing "What's In . . . What's Out" measure, which illustrates the often divergent passions and priorities of teen guys and girls.

Certainly, trend information (particularly related to fashion and style) can have an extremely limited shelf life. That's what makes writing about teen trends in book form challenging, knowing that at best we can offer only a snapshot in time. With that as a caveat, here's a quick look at some trends as of 2003.

What's In with Girls

With the incessant barrage of dance music in TV commercials, and the common (if sometimes inaccurate) depiction of rave and club scenes in movies, TV shows, and ads, it's clear that this once-underground lifestyle has hit the mainstream. Teen-savvy marketers know that once an "underground" trend reaches this point, it's only a matter of time before it's pushing up daisies.

It's no surprise, then, that one of the most notable changes in teen interests is the decline of dance/rave-related music and activities among girls. Significantly fewer girls in the past few months say that partying and raves are "in" (notably, rave-going is at its lowest point since TRU has measured this activity). In what appears to be a "cocooning" impulse among teens, other social events such as prom and homecoming—though still hugely popular—have trended downward in the past few months. Still, it's clear that girls aren't going to become solitary couch potatoes playing video games like their male counterparts: dating, cheerleading, and going to coffeehouses all increased in popularity among teen girls recently.

Girls seem to be rebelling against the hypergirly fashions of a few years back: hooded sweatshirts and NFL apparel, for example, are on the rise.

Girls still prefer their own hair long, but nearly all of them like guys' hair short. (It's worth noting, though, that shaggy and long styles on guys—while still edgy—are becoming slightly more visible in the mainstream.) And although dyed hair on guys lost some of its luster, it's still a widely accepted mainstream practice.

Pierced noses are still trending upward, as are high-top shoes, thanks partly to Nelly singing about those "Air Force Ones" and partly to garage

What's "In" with Girls

Most teen girls think silver jewelry, rap music, partying, healthy eating, and coloring your hair are "in."

(percent of teen girls saying item is "in")

FASHION

Silver jewelry	91%
Low-rise jeans	83
Hoop earrings	80
Hooded sweatshirts	78
T-shirts with graphics	77
Short skirts	76
Hats (nonathletic)	74
Studded belt	70
Necklaces with your name	55
Ripped clothing	41
Lace	37
Suede	26

MUSIC

Rap	79
Hip-hop	79
Alternative	63
Techno	31

ACTIVITIES

Taking photos	88
Partying	87
Having a boyfriend	86
Playing sports	85
Downloading music	85
Watching the news	47
Cigarettes	20
Ecstasy	17

ISSUES

Healthy eating	75%
Caring about environment	63

SPORTS

College football	62
Extreme sports	61
Snowboarding	56
Soccer	56
BMX biking	43
Yoga	37
Martial arts	30

HAIR STYLES

Coloring your hair	74
Spiky hair on guys	71
Shaggy hair on guys	40

OTHER STUFF

MP3 player	66
Digital video recorder (like Tivo)	60
Karaoke	49

Source: The TRU Study, Teenage Research Unlimited, Inc.

rockers and their stubborn infatuation with that longstanding (if cyclical) fashion icon, the Converse All-Star.

In music, rap, R&B, and hip-hop continue to dominate, while punk's popularity has markedly increased over the past few months. Both dance/rave and techno music have lost some momentum, and Top-40 is also down (by now, even the most boy-crazy young girls are finally growing tired of the boy bands).

Although the events of September 11, 2001, are still fresh in their minds, teen girls have moved on. Issues that fewer girls consider "in" in the past several months include the military, politics, and being patriotic. Although 73 percent of girls still say that displaying the American flag is "in," even that lofty score is down from the recent past. It may be that teen girls are experiencing "patriotism fatigue"—becoming desensitized to the ever-present news alerts dealing with terrorism and the Middle East. Or, perhaps, traditionally nurturing and peace-minded girls disagree with recent U.S. military actions.

What's In with Guys

Guys are fiercely competitive in some respects, but they tend to approach fashion and entertainment trends in an unhurried (perhaps even mildly suspicious) manner. Perhaps this explains why many guys continue to stand by such time-honored "in" staples as the NFL, playing sports and video games, going to the movies, listening to rap music, wearing hoodies, and enjoying a menagerie of electronic gadgets.

In fashion, casual mainstays such as hooded sweatshirts, athletic shoes, boxer shorts, and NFL apparel continue to dominate. However—and perhaps contributing to the woes of casual-apparel retailers such as Gap and Old Navy—cargo and khaki pants and shorts are losing status. Such "vanilla" fashions seem dull and character-free in a time when denim of every permutation rules the fashion runways and punkish pop idols have taken over the radio airwaves. Formerly edgy offerings, such as low-

What's "In" with Guys

Most teen guys think T-shirts with graphics, rap music, going to the movies, healthy eating, extreme sports, and spiky hair are "in."

(percent of teen guys saying item is "in")

FASHION

T-shirts with graphics	79%
Silver jewelry	75
Hooded sweatshirts	72
Hats (nonathletic)	71
White sneakers	59
Class rings	57
Sports headbands	46
Ripped clothing	28
Bowling shoes	15

MUSIC

Rap	70
Heavy metal	47
Punk	45
Hardcore	39

ACTIVITIES

Going to the movies	88
Having a girlfriend	85
Downloading music	83
Partying	80
Going to concerts	77
Shopping	76
Taking photos	63
Watching the news	41
Ecstasy	17
Cigars	16

ISSUES

Healthy eating	59%
Caring about environment	52
Sharing costs on a date	42

SPORTS

Extreme sports	68
College basketball	67
College football	66
Major League Baseball	59
Snowboarding	56
BMX biking	55

HAIR STYLES

Spiky hair on guys	58
Streaking color into your hair	55
Coloring your hair	52
Short hair on girls	52
Shaggy hair on guys	36

OTHER STUFF

MP3 player	70
Digital video recorder (like Tivo)	61
Comic books	30

Source: The TRU Study, Teenage Research Unlimited, Inc.

rise jeans and body piercings (which guys seem to appreciate more on their female counterparts than on themselves), have gained in the past wave of The TRU Study.

The urban flavors of rap and hip-hop continue to transcend ethnicity, making them guys' top two "in" music styles. Nevertheless, the styles making the biggest inroads with guys include reggae's Caribbean flair and punk's aggressive anti-establishment stance.

Perhaps in keeping with the last two music genres, substance abuse appears to be more popular with guys as well. The number of guys citing liquor, beer, or wine as being "in" rose in the past six months, while cigarettes and marijuana gained slightly. The popularity of video games continues to spearhead many guys "cocooning" impulses. Playing and renting home video games increased in popularity, as did playing computer games. On the other hand, extroverted pastimes suffered: going to raves declined slightly with guys, as did volunteering for community service.

Teens and Music

For spawning the most important and easily recognizable teen trends, music is fashion's only real competition. And there's a strong argument to be made that music has the edge—teens eagerly mimic the styles they see on their favorite musical performers and on MTV (whether they admit it or not!).

Traditionally, teens list "current hits" as their favorite type of radio format because it embodies characteristics that teens most prize: it's evolutionary but rarely revolutionary, and it's engaging without being challenging. Current hits provide a steady stream of new content from a broad cross-section of teen music genres, including hip-hop, alternative, pop, and R&B. The format draws from a broad spectrum of musical styles, giving it latitude to take the best and leave the rest. As such, many teens think of the format not just as "current hits" but as "radio's greatest hits." And if there's one thing teens appreciate, it's backing a winner.

True, the most music-involved teens tell us they thrill at discovering the "next big thing" before anyone else. But this is a relatively small subset of the population, especially in the conformist teen years. The majority of teen radio listeners have no problem allowing programmers to do the "grunt work," screening out the nonhits so they can listen to a continuous stream of hit material. And if music critics frequently dismiss top-40 fare as brainless, substance-free fluff, it's of no consequence to teens. After all, they tend to dismiss music critics as dreary, pompous blowhards.

Still, despite the format's traditionally high teen appeal, current hits recently fell by 6 percentage points in popularity, suggesting that many respondents are bored with the recently dethroned (and now widely shunned) pop genre that plays a large role in current hits programming.

The other teen radio powerhouse, the hip-hop and rap format, remains stable. But thanks to current hits' popularity decline, hip-hop is within a couple of points of the top spot, according to TRU research. This is an especially important genre to teens because it skews unusually heavily toward Influencers. In fact, when asked which music genre is most "in," teens almost always choose rap and hip-hop.

Rappers and hip-hoppers are permanent residents in the TRU*Score upper echelons, as well. Fully half of the performers in the most-recent TRU*Score top-10 are rap and hip-hop stars. Eminem retook the top spot, thanks to a successful album and a well-received starring role in the semi-biographical film *8 Mile*. Nelly, too, continues to fare well; his huge popularity with girls compensates for the relatively lukewarm reaction from guys.

What is it about this format that teens find so alluring? It goes way beyond the music. To teens, hip-hop is a lifestyle, an alluring symbol of freedom and rebellion for urban, suburban, and rural teens alike. It symbolizes everything to which teens aspire—independence to the point of arrogance, confidence to the point of cockiness, and success to the point

Favorite Radio Formats

Teen girls like the "current hits" radio format the best, while guys are most likely to favor "hip-hop/rap."

(percent of teens responding when asked, "Listed below are different types of radio stations. Which one or two types do you listen to most often?" by gender and age)

	total	female	male	12 to 15	16 to 17	18 to 19
Current hits	50%	61%	39%	50%	45%	54%
Hip-hop/rap	42	42	42	45	42	37
R&B	22	24	19	21	22	22
Alternative	19	18	21	15	24	24
Hard rock/ Heavy metal	19	11	26	20	21	14
Country	14	17	12	11	16	19
Classic rock	10	7	13	8	11	13
Christian	10	10	9	12	6	9
Oldies	8	8	8	9	7	9
Dance	6	8	4	6	5	7
Soft rock/ Easy listening	5	7	4	6	6	4
All sports	4	1	7	6	2	3
Spanish language	3	4	2	2	4	4
Jazz	2	2	3	3	2	2
All news	2	1	2	2	1	2

Source: The TRU Study, Teenage Research Unlimited, Inc.

of excess. It's the new rock 'n' roll—the ideological descendent of Elvis Presley—and none of the waifish pretty-boys that record companies have sent to defend rock are likely to change that fact anytime soon.

The third-place radio format is R&B. This genre is popular in urban centers, but unlike rap, it is not overtly political or antagonistic. Musiq, Floetry, R. Kelly, and Jaheim are prime examples of R&B. This format layers on liberal doses of love ballads and slick harmonies, so it's perhaps not surprising that girls are huge fans. Also not surprisingly, guys are less impressed—they like more angst and rebellion in their music.

Harder-edged rock music never went away, but for years it was relegated to the corners, typically the domain of a few teens who did not care that popular trends had left them behind. Today, however, the tables have turned. The natural result of a population burned out on pop is that punk, hard rock, and heavy metal are once again gaining ground on the competition.

Last year, the punk format tied alternative, and this year the genre is within 1 percentage point of R&B. A decade ago, bands such as Green Day and Offspring used catchy, up-tempo riffs and three-minute songs to lay the groundwork for the punk revival. Today, acts such as Good Charlotte, the Ataris, and AFI are carrying the torch, making punk music for the masses. Don't be fooled though—it may look markedly different from Britney Spears and Justin Timberlake, but today's punk is still pop. In fact, the progression into harder sounds and marginally more substantial lyrics is one way adults can watch today's teens growing up. Some of the same girls who were scrutinizing Britney's every move three years ago are now worshipping at the altar of self-described "anti-Britney," Avril Lavigne. Avril probably shouldn't get too comfortable at the top, either.

Punk (at least as many teens today know it) may be headed for a credibility crisis. When the genre was new, it was completely uncontrolled musical anarchy laced with strident political messages. Today, it's a different animal, a domesticated one. The politics are largely absent, replaced with standard pop-song themes. The clothing looks the same, but the meaning behind it is gone. The re-emergence of punk is a fashion trend in the truest sense of the word. Some fans may be spurred to investigate bands with more substance than Avril Lavigne and Blink-182 can muster, but the majority will likely adopt the costume only until it falls out of style.

What's Ahead for Music

We think it's back to the future for music as bands increasingly mine the 1980s for inspiration. According to TRU's Trendwatch panelists, anecdotal evidence, and our own observation, we believe the current trend toward revisiting '80s music is simply a continuation of the nostalgia that brought us the return of the '60s and '70s.

It makes sense: the youngest members of today's pop-culture audience aren't old enough to remember the 1980s in great detail, so it's new and exciting to them. And old '80s tracks allow younger teens to dance— something they grew accustomed to during pop's heyday, thanks to the likes of Christina Aguilera, Pink, and No Doubt. Still, because teens don't have a deep knowledge of '80s artists, look for them to focus on one-hit wonders and compilations rather than obsessively collecting albums and B-sides. They will be mostly interested in owning the catchy tunes they've heard on their local radio station's '80s at 8 programs.

On the other hand, older consumers (although still young enough to follow and/or drive trends) appreciate the retro kick on two levels. First, the excesses of the '80s generate an endless supply of irony—and irony is like oxygen to most Gen-X hipsters. Second, revisiting this period plays on aging Gen-Xer's rosy memories of youth, just as the '60s and '70s appealed to aging Boomers. Rather than devouring old '80s hits, this older crowd will likely drive demand for an updated musical style with heavy '80s influences. (After all, they have not only already experienced the old songs, but the music industry can't make nearly as much money from marginally successful reissues as it can releasing a parade of new hit singles.) There's

Trendwatch Slang: 2003

Clients regularly ask us not just what teens talk about, but what they say. Teens often speak in a language all their own, and marketers tend to regard this as a huge barrier to effective communication.

To a certain extent, they're right. After all, teen slang is purposefully designed to be obtuse. Adults don't understand it because that's the point—it's a highly guarded, ever-shifting collection of words and phrases that simultaneously imparts a sense of belonging to a select group while excluding everyone else. Generally, when the early adopters suspect adults (or even mainstream teens) are close to breaking the code, they'll change it.

Still, we believe that understanding the way teens communicate helps clients understand the way they think. So we recently asked our Trendwatch panelists to let us in on some of their current favorite phrases. You'll find their picks, definitions, and occasional usage guidelines below. For further reading, we recommend *Hip Hoptionary: the Dictionary of Hip-Hop Terminology*, by Alonzo Westbrook, which boasts an encyclopedic history of urban slang. Fair warning, however: TRU advises clients to exercise extreme caution when trying to communicate with teens (or anyone else) using slang.

- *Blow up spot* To embarrass or humiliate; to reveal something someone is trying to conceal. Example: "Wow, I can't believe you just blew up his spot like that!"
- *Boozin'* Drinking alcohol, getting drunk.
- *Bounce* Leave. Example: "Let's bounce!"
- *Getting served* Getting made fun of. (Also: Getting clowned on.)
- *Grimy* Stingy, selfish. (Also: Crusty).
- *Harsh* Bad luck or an unfortunate outcome. Example: "That's f***ing harsh!"
- *Harshing a buzz* Causing discomfort or paranoia for a person under the influence of drugs. Example: "Why'd you have to bring up my parole officer? You're totally harshing my buzz."
- *Put on blast* To be embarrassed or made to feel stupid. Example: "You been put on blast!"
- *Ribby* House, apartment. A derivation of "crib."
- *Shorty* A female, especially an attractive one. Also used to address someone who is physically shorter than the speaker or someone who is slightly inferior—a light-hearted put-down.
- *Sketchy* Sleazy; someone to be wary of. (Also: Dodgy).
- *Straight* Cool; fine; in the clear. Possibly derived from slang for sober. Example: "I thought I was going to get kicked off the team, but I guess I'm straight."
- *Tha business* Going on. Example: What's tha business?
- *That's the business on tha real fa sho* That's what's going on. Possible response to "What's tha business."
- *Tweakin'* Under the influence of stimulants, especially crystal methamphetamine. Example: "Are you tweakin' or something?"
- *What's (really) good* What's going on? Replaces "what's up?"

already a fledgling market for synthesizer-driven pop out there, and it will likely continue to grow (although the sound may have to change somewhat before it's adopted by the mainstream). More underground artists are also experimenting with the soaring vocals of '80s bands from Spandau Ballet to Howard Jones, although music's current focus on harder rock means that this, too, will likely simmer for a while before it cracks the mainstream.

Keep in mind that the modern "retro" kick will take cues from the '80s, but we won't see a *Groundhog Day*–style carbon copy. The youngest teens don't have the first-hand knowledge to recreate the decade, older consumers are still haunted by some of their own wardrobe choices, and technology's and society's collective experience dictates that we can't go back. Instead, look for a smattering of '80s influences to freshen and inform our current, more modern styles. Think of it as recycling useful bits rather than reissuing the whole decade.

Chapter 5

Teen Social Concerns

When adults contemplate teens' interest in social causes, they usually seize upon one of two contradictory stereotypes. They either envision teens as banner-toting, cause-driven agitators or they picture listless, self-absorbed brats who can't be bothered to lift a finger for anyone.

Although you're likely to find both kinds of individuals when combing through the teen ranks, we would (once again) like to discourage such snap judgments and generalizations. Involvement in social causes depends a great deal upon a teen's personality, environment, self-esteem, and upbringing.

For all their interest in independence and rebellion, most teens rely on their parents to help them build an ideological framework. To be sure, they will use their own experience to complete the structure (and if their experience contradicts their parents' beliefs, they may overhaul the framework at some point). Still, most teens reflect their parents' core beliefs. We've found, for example, that teens from conservative backgrounds are less likely to back more progressive social causes like environmentalism, but they are often drawn to subjects such as abortion.

Teens with naturally curious (and perhaps slightly rebellious) personalities are more likely to involve themselves in social concerns than their less rebellious peers. We've also found teens' involvement with social concerns is contagious: young people who associate with social-activist friends are more likely to participate in activism themselves.

In some circles, identifying with a cause can be the price of entry to a desired social group. Just as some teens use their love of music or cars as a bonding experience, others forge common ties through a desire to make the world a better place or by questioning the status quo. The tendency to gravitate toward likeminded peers serves dual functions for most teens, who use such groups for selfless reasons (advancing a political philosophy they support) and for more self-serving ones (seeking acceptance from a desired group). As sincere as some teens are in their cause-related concerns and activities, keep in mind that many teens use causes to help them carve out an identity.

In most clusters of teen activists (and probably in most group endeavors, whether teen or not), the amount and quality of work accomplished toward the "greater good" directly correlate to the ratio of selfless interest versus selfish desire. Many teens have a greater interest in the social aspects of their cause than in the avowed aims. As such, there is often a gap between teen attitudes and behavior. For instance, about two-thirds of teens maintain that eating healthy is "in." But only a tiny fraction of teens eschew drive-through windows and junk food.

Whether or not teens actively participate in finding solutions to social problems, many display a surprising level of issue awareness. Traditionally, young people have responded most vigorously to issues that either affect them directly or to which they can personally relate. Behaviors that involve both experimentation (an ingrained teen need) and serious, life-altering consequences frequently capture the teen imagination. Drinking and driving, drug abuse, AIDS, cigarette smoking, alcoholism, and unplanned pregnancy all fit into this category. But teens also are naturally concerned with issues that "hit home"(those that emotionally affect themselves as well as their friends, family, school, and community). These issues include child abuse, racism, and gang violence.

Teens believe adults can help solve many teen problems, according to TRU research. This perceived influence can help brands—or hurt them. Antismoking campaigns, for example, leverage teens' belief in the power of adults to solve problems to convince them not to smoke, showing them how cigarette marketers—or adults who should know better—prey on their insecurities.

Thanks in part to some particularly effective antitobacco advertising from the American Legacy Foundation (which developed the Truth national campaign), teens have become aware of the fact that tobacco marketers do not have their best interests at heart. The Truth campaign, as well as recent efforts from several leading states, is distinct from previous antismoking efforts because it refrains from attacking smoking (or smokers themselves) as stupid, ugly, or reckless. Rather than passing judgment on the user's decision to smoke, Truth reveals the marketing process that tries to convince young consumers that smoking will make them cooler, sexier, or more attractive. Truth details, in the plainest, least flattering way possible, how tobacco marketing executives have used brand-building to prey upon the image-conscious. In short, the campaign cuts through the smoke and mirrors to show how the industry uses lies and deception to fill its pockets. The increasing relevance of cigarette smoking as a teen concern (detailed later in this chapter) reflects the success of antitobacco campaigns.

On the flip side, marketers could do worse than to demonstrate that their company isn't interested in fostering addiction and illness. By showing consumers that a brand is interested in advancing the cause of the greater good, brand managers have the opportunity to set themselves apart from the competition.

Indeed, many brands have tied into social issues as a way to build goodwill with customers, from the support for the environment shown by quirky ice-cream brand Ben & Jerry's, to Benetton's long-standing attention to race relations. To successfully link a brand to an appropriate social issue, it's important to select the most compelling causes for the teen segment you're targeting. This is where some brands get caught up in a tug-of-war between two competing teen interests—being trendy and being authentic. Teens' fickle nature and their attraction to what's new leaves many marketers tempted to jump on issues as they're heating up, only to abandon them after the cool kids have moved on to something else. A word of warning: this kind of behavior will not build a brand image—it will simply confuse consumers. It's best to pick a subject that's likely to have long-term relevance, and stick with it.

When choosing a cause with which to align, the customary procedure is to avoid real controversy. The benefits of this strategy are obvious: no company wants to alienate a sizable percentage of its target audience. This is still the gospel for big, mainstream brands, but we've noticed an increasing number of smaller, niche brands embracing flatly confrontational causes that resonate well with their target. For instance, Phat Farm—an edgy urban clothing manufacturer—recently commissioned a series of ads calling for "Economic Justice Now." The Phat Farm campaign called for equal educational opportunities, stronger affirmative action, and—most controversially—slavery reparations. Such a campaign will not endear the brand to vast stretches of the American middle class. But for a brand targeting young, urban men who place authenticity and street credibility above all else, it sets the brand apart from competitors in a relevant, engaging way.

By now, you've probably read enough to anticipate a caveat, and here it is: teens inherently know when a connection doesn't work (such as "extreme laundry detergent"), and they will then question any other communications from the suspect brand. Imagine the confusion that would result if Abercrombie & Fitch, that bastion of middle-American preppiness, called for slavery reparations. The announcement would likely alienate people who couldn't make the connection between white-bred Abercrombie and a controversial race-relations issue. Likewise, although Chevrolet ranks highly as a cool brand among teens, the company would have some work to do before it could successfully link itself to environmental causes.

Ultimately, it's not enough to find a popular cause and support it. Marketers who stray beyond the boundaries of their brand risk, at best, muddling their image and, at worst, being labeled corporate "poseurs." Our recommendation: know your teen consumers. Only then can you understand your brand's boundaries and see the opportunities for shaping brand perceptions.

Having explored the possible benefits and drawbacks of adopting a pet cause, let's investigate the social issues teens are most concerned about. As you review the following list, however, note that some issues are more appropriate than others. As a rule of thumb, it's wise to tie into the consequence-based issues—drinking and driving, education, and AIDS—or teen-relevant topics such as child abuse or gang violence. Although terrorism is a much higher-profile concern, few in the private sector can say much about it without sounding like profiteers or racists.

It's also important to keep in mind that teens have a distinct bias toward local action. They prefer local news to national headlines, and they repeatedly tell us that they prefer companies that make a visible donation to their local community over those undertaking a massive nationwide effort.

Girls attach themselves to issues that push emotional triggers or challenge their instincts as a mother, caregiver, or potential victim (child abuse, abortion, prejudice or racism, sexual assault, eating disorders, and animal rights). Guys (particularly those nearing draft age) care more about global issues related to international tension, including terrorism, war, threat of nuclear war, and biological or chemical warfare. Guys are also concerned about issues surrounding their own potentially high-risk behavior (AIDS, drug abuse, and cigarette smoking).

Younger teens naturally feel strongly about child abuse, as well as drug abuse and cigarette smoking. Middle to older teens gravitate to issues such as drinking and driving, abortion, and suicide. African-American teens are more concerned about AIDS, education, and racism, while Hispanics are particularly concerned about child abuse and drug abuse.

Teen Social Concerns by Gender

Child abuse is the number-one teen social concern among girls, while terrorism ranks first among guys.

(percent of teens citing issue as one of the five they care most strongly about, by gender)

	total	female	male
Child abuse	43%	56%	32%
Drinking and driving	35	39	32
Prejudice or racism	32	34	29
Education	29	31	28
Abortion	29	38	20
Drug abuse	28	24	32
Terrorism	27	18	36
AIDS	24	23	26
Cigarette smoking	24	20	28
War	22	15	28
Sexual assault	20	27	14
Suicide	17	19	16
Animal rights	17	21	13
Violence/gangs	14	11	16
Environment	13	12	13
Women's rights	12	21	4
Alcoholism	12	11	13
Biological or chemical warfare	11	6	17
Divorce	11	11	12
Unplanned pregnancy	10	13	8
Threat of nuclear war	10	4	15
Unemployment/economy	10	7	13
Homelessness	9	12	7
Eating disorders	9	13	5
Health care	9	8	9
Gay rights	9	10	8

Source: The TRU Study, Teenage Research Unlimited, Inc.

Terrorism and War

September 11, 2001, added a chilling new topic to the national dialogue and created the need for The TRU Study to track two new social concerns. The new categories—terrorism and the threat of biological or chemical warfare—were threats most teens had never even considered until the attacks and ensuing anthrax scares.

Not surprisingly, terrorism debuted at the top of TRU's list in the immediate aftermath of September 11. Initially, the topic found itself in a two-way tie for the top spot, along with drinking and driving. Each issue strongly concerned 40 percent of teens. (The TRU Study allows each respondent to choose five concerns; therefore, percentages do not add up to 100.) Concern about terrorism has fallen in subsequent surveys, with terrorism placing seventh in the latest wave—well behind the causes toward which teens have traditionally gravitated.

Terrorism's addition to the list, beginning with the Spring 2002 study, siphoned mentions away from a handful of other topics. As one might expect during "wartime," most of the issues that saw significant downturns were nurturing causes, including AIDS, drug abuse, suicide, unplanned pregnancy, divorce, and eating disorders. Two topics dealing directly with victimization—sexual assault and violence/gangs—also dropped significantly.

The other new topic, biological or chemical warfare, is of significantly less interest to teens—only 11 percent cite it as one of their top-five concerns. Ongoing events could change how teens view this issue in future waves of the study.

Two other issues related to security—the threat of nuclear war and the topic of war in general—increased significantly from pre-attack levels. Twenty-two percent of teens claim war as one of their top-five issues. Another 10 percent name the threat of nuclear war. Predictably, significantly more guys than girls are concerned about these issues.

Although the events of September 11, 2001, still resonate with teens, corporate America must tread lightly when it comes to waving the red, white, and blue. Teens have told us that only the brands or companies that are true American icons (like Coke or Levi's) or those that had previously established a patriotic connection (such as Tommy and Polo) can get away with playing the America card without looking like cold, calculating marketers capitalizing on the country's fear.

Drinking and Driving

Drinking and driving is a classic bad news/good news topic. The bad news: many teens are enthusiastic about underage drinking—44 percent of total teens say that drinking is "in" and 58 percent of those of driving age (16 and older) say drinking is "in." The good news: dramatic and widely used educational programs warning of the dangers of drunk driving are paying off—35 percent of teens claim that drinking and driving is one of their top-five social concerns.

The fact that drinking and driving handily beats terrorism (undoubtedly a higher-profile concern) is another example of the power of community-based programs. Many of TRU's Trendwatch panelists (along with countless focus group respondents) have relayed their schools' and other local efforts in dramatizing the consequences of drunk driving. Although teens are quick to acknowledge that drinking is as a popular as ever (it's a staple at older teens' parties), they also explain that teens are increasingly careful about not driving when they drink.

Much of this relatively newfound caution likely stems from a concerted, organized effort by adults to present the issue to teens where they live. Some of the best examples of in-school confrontation happen during prom week (a time when teens are particularly at risk of drinking and driving). Teens have told us they take particular note when administrators place a car, utterly demolished in an alcohol-related accident, on campus grounds. But, for sheer shock value, nothing beats the "grim

Teen Social Concerns by Age

Child abuse is the number-one teen social concern, regardless of age.

(percent of teens citing issue as one of the five they care most strongly about, by age)

	total	12 to 15	16 to 17	18 to 19
Child abuse	43%	43%	43%	44%
Drinking and driving	35	34	37	35
Prejudice or racism	32	29	32	37
Education	29	31	28	28
Abortion	29	26	33	31
Drug abuse	28	32	22	25
Terrorism	27	27	26	29
AIDS	24	27	24	19
Cigarette smoking	24	27	23	19
War	22	22	19	23
Sexual assault	20	21	22	17
Suicide	17	18	20	13
Animal rights	17	20	13	14
Violence/gangs	14	17	11	10
Environment	13	14	11	13
Women's rights	12	14	9	11
Alcoholism	12	13	12	12
Biological or chemical warfare	11	10	12	13
Divorce	11	12	11	10
Unplanned pregnancy	10	9	12	11
Unemployment/economy	10	6	10	17
Nuclear warfare	10	9	10	10
Eating disorders	9	9	9	9
Homelessness	9	11	7	7
Gay rights	9	8	9	10
Health care	9	10	5	10

Source: The TRU Study, Teenage Research Unlimited, Inc.

reaper," an activity that allows students to experience the consequences of drinking and driving. Dressed in a black cloak and armed with a scythe, the reaper enters classrooms to "take" students. When the students return to class, their faces are pale with stage makeup and they're not allowed to speak for the rest of the day. Teens tell us that seeing their friends in "ghost" form is one of the most effective ways to discourage drunken driving.

The high level of teen interest in the topic, its moral weight, and the ability to reach teens locally, make drinking and driving an especially relevant topic for some brands.

Child Ause

Few things could be more personal or terrifying to teenagers than suffering violence at the hands of a family member or other adult. Child abuse is traditionally at or near the top of teens' list of social concerns—43 percent of teens list it as one of the five issues they care most strongly about. Teens often feel powerless in the face of adult authority, and most feel they've been wronged by well-meaning adults in the past. By their reasoning, if adults who love them and care for them could make their lives miserable, the power of a cruel and abusive parent or relative is almost unthinkable.

Abortion

Year after year, abortion is named as one of the issues teens care most strongly about, despite little focus on it in schools or public-service advertising.

Unlike other subjects teens list as highly important, abortion boasts fervent advocates on both sides. While most people agree that terrorism and drunk driving are inherently bad, abortion supporters and detractors both provide compelling arguments that resonate with teens, making it the most polarizing of teens' top concerns.

Teens often mirror their parents' leanings on political and moral issues such as abortion. But we've also noticed that this deeply personal issue inspires some teens to come to their own conclusions. In our experience, young teens—who in many ways still identify with the helplessness of children more than with the burdens of adulthood—are more likely to skew anti-abortion than their older peers.

Racism

Thirty-two percent of teens list prejudice or racism as a top social concern. Perhaps not surprisingly, the topic's importance varies greatly by ethnicity. Only 27 percent of Hispanic and 29 percent of white teens list prejudice or racism as an important problem, but 44 percent of African-American teens say this is one of their five most pressing issues.

Today's teens are not only more diverse than ever before, but they're also more comfortable with diversity than older generations. It's especially telling that the Influencer Teen/Type—the segment most teens look to for fashion and trend cues (and the segment that broadcasts those trends to the mainstream Conformers)—boasts a disproportionately large percentage of nonwhite teens.

Happily, more and more advertisers are recognizing that they ignore minorities at their own peril. Many leading teen brands are zealously pursuing diversity in their advertising and marketing, either through the use of entertainment celebrities and sports stars or simply by including a more diverse pool of talent in their commercials. TRU wholeheartedly encourages this trend, and not simply because of the weight of the moral argument. Teens' sensitivity to diversity means that any campaign that doesn't include a mix of races and ethnicities will look outdated or simply wrong. And because minority teens are integral to the spread of trends throughout teen culture, positioning your brand to be popular with these teens (particularly African Americans and Hispanics) can only boost your image. The opportunity to appear forward-thinking by courting these teens is well past. Now it's simply the right, smart thing to do. If your brand hasn't yet begun to pursue these segments, it's time to get on it.

Some companies deal with serious issues such as race through humor. And in fact, many of our Trendwatch panelists encourage a sense of humor

Teen Social Concerns by Race and Hispanic Origin

Social concerns vary by race and Hispanic origin.

(percent of teens citing issue as one of the five they care most strongly about, by race and Hispanic origin)

	total	black	Hispanic	non-Hispanic white
Child abuse	43%	42%	46%	43%
Drinking and driving	35	38	28	37
Prejudice or racism	32	44	27	29
Education	29	40	26	27
Abortion	29	21	30	31
Drug abuse	28	27	32	27
Terrorism	27	26	27	28
AIDS	24	52	29	16
Cigarette smoking	24	21	16	27
War	22	18	19	23
Sexual assault	20	23	19	20
Suicide	17	16	20	17
Animal rights	17	9	17	19
Violence/gangs	14	17	17	12
Environment	13	7	15	14
Women's rights	12	15	11	12
Alcoholism	12	10	11	13
Biological or chemical warfare	11	9	14	11
Divorce	11	7	11	12
Unplanned pregnancy	10	11	17	8
Threat of nuclear war	10	8	12	9
Unemployment/economy	10	12	12	9
Homelessness	9	10	12	8
Eating disorders	9	7	9	10
Health care	9	12	9	8
Gay rights	9	6	12	9

Source: The TRU Study, Teenage Research Unlimited, Inc.

in advertising. Being funny is a good idea—up to a point. History is rife with examples of humorous marketing campaigns that backfired utterly, alienating the very people they intended to attract. One example is Toyota, which had an ad campaign referencing the short-lived hip-hop phenomenon of tooth jewels, showing a golden sport-utility vehicle on a black man's tooth. Jesse Jackson criticized the image as offensive. To forestall a boycott, Toyota promised to spend hundreds of millions of dollars over the next ten years on diversity programs, including beefing up minority recruiting and boosting its spending with minority businesses by 35 percent.

Education

It may come as a surprise to many adults that education is important to teens—29 percent of teens list it as one of their top-five social issues. Teens have extensive experience with the subject, so it's only natural that their opinions are strong on this point.

Although many teens have told TRU they feel fortunate to be getting a quality education, many also express concern about what they consider unqualified, ineffective teachers, lack of adequate teaching materials, and overcrowded classrooms. Interestingly, this subject is almost as polarizing as racism: 40 percent of African-American teens say they care strongly about education, compared to 26 percent of Hispanics and 27 percent of whites.

One sign of declining confidence in the educational system is the way teens talk about their teachers. Teens' anecdotes about their teachers have become increasingly negative over the past several years, according to a few recent qualitative research projects we've conducted. (It's only fair to mention that teachers' views of today's teens are dimming as well.)

A great deal of the growing tension between teachers and students probably stems from cash shortfalls so common in schools today. When budgets run dry, everyone suffers, from the teachers who must tend to larger classes to the students who must share materials and work with outdated books. An appropriate marketing initiative in this area would not only help boost teen awareness but also satisfy an urgent need within the community. The matter should be approached carefully, however: parents are naturally suspicious of school-sponsored advertising messages.

Through qualitative research we've found the topic of education to be relevant to different teens for different reasons. Affluent teens, for example, focus on higher education sooner than the less affluent. Affluent teens can become obsessed with college before they enter high school, and their preoccupation nearly always involves getting into one of a handful of first-choice, brand-name colleges. Affluent teens are especially competitive, their high-school career guided by a long-term goal. Although many boast admirable self-discipline, some are under an inordinate amount of stress and can miss out on what makes high school fun.

Teens on the other end of the economic spectrum are no less fervent in their concern about education. But while this issue means costly weekend SAT prep courses to upper-middle-class teens, the financially disadvantaged seize upon education as their shot at a better future.

Drug Abuse

Drug abuse has declined as an important teen issue. Ten years ago, it was near the top of the list. Have we failed to convince teens of the seriousness of experimenting with drugs? As with all big questions, there's not one single answer. But, for this one, there is some good news. Drug use among teens is at a ten-year low. And the Office of National Drug Control Policy (ONDCP), which supports the national antidrug media campaign, is doing good work which should see a future payoff.

Some of the earlier public-service ads attempting to steer teens away from drugs have had a sort of *Reefer Madness* effect: they backfired and were parodied in many teen circles—beginning with Nancy Reagan's "Just Say No" campaign and continuing with some of the well-intended more recent attempts to link drugs with terrorism. Probably the biggest obstacle to making inroads in this area is that teens consider drugs—marijuana, in particular—to be normal. "Everybody smokes pot!" is a common teen refrain. Teens believe that far more of their peers use drugs than actually do, and this social norming has inflated teens' perception of the role drugs play in youth culture. To try to close the gap, some ads have tried to tell teens "it just ain't so," that the great majority of their peers do not do drugs. We're not convinced that this is a sound strategy. We've found teens quick to reject such messages as coming from clueless adults. After all, teens' own reality (or their perception of it) tells them something different.

We suggest testing new ads on their ability to positively shift social-norming attitudes by conveying either the negative consequences of drug use or the positive consequences of abstention. This effort may be more worthwhile than attacking teens' perception of drug use as normal.

From an advertising or marketing perspective, convincing teens not to smoke marijuana is an especially tall order—much tougher, I think, than convincing them not to smoke cigarettes or drink and drive. Why is it such a tough sell to get kids not to smoke pot? In addition to teens' perception that marijuana use is normal—as well as relatively harmless—teens also believe it has redeeming qualities (i.e., it's fun)! And, that's where it differs from tobacco. Except for the youngest of teens—for whom tobacco is a prop for feeling older or cooler—most teens see no redeeming qualities in cigarettes. We've worked with 16- and 17-year-old smokers who regret their decision at a younger age to smoke cigarettes, not understanding then what it meant to be addicted. These same individuals, so mature in their denunciation of tobacco, will in the next breath say they really like to smoke pot and find nothing wrong with it. They believe it's neither addictive nor particularly harmful. And, unlike alcohol, they think they're still in control when they're under the effects of marijuana.

Another difference between marijuana and tobacco is that a corporation is trying to sell them tobacco. The Truth antitobacco national campaign (as well as strong state campaigns in California, Florida, Iowa, Massachusetts, and Minnesota) has convincingly portrayed the tobacco companies as bad guys, leveraging teens' natural rebelliousness. This antitobacco messaging strategy has resonated with teens like none before. Unfortunately, there isn't an equally plausible bad guy when it comes to drugs. Some of the recent ONDCP ads have attempted to show that drugs lead to terrorism, betting that teens will rebel against smoking pot as many have with cigarettes. But while teens believe the tobacco industry is manipulative and deceptive, they haven't bought the argument linking tobacco and terrorism.

Swaying teens' thinking about marijuana is a societal and marketing dilemma. Teens can be convinced more easily about the dangers of harder drugs—ecstasy, inhalants, cocaine, heroin—than of marijuana. But I think there's hope. For one, the parent-directed "anti-drug" campaign is particularly smart, and I think parents are probably an easier target for an antidrug message. After all, teens not only respect their parents, but they also actively seek their approval and advice. Who better, then, to talk to teens about not smoking pot? Encouraging parents to closely monitor their teens' time (and giving parents ways to do that) and to maintain a dialog on the subject of marijuana may be more effective than any teen-directed effort. There's still reason to believe, however, that a long-term campaign hammering away at the myth that marijuana is harmless might ultimately prove convincing. In this regard, we like the current series of ONDCP ads that carry the adult-inclusive tagline: "It's more harmful than we all thought."

AIDS

Just a few years ago, AIDS was one of teens' top social concerns. It now ranks eighth, barely hanging on to a position in the top one-third of the list.

Even in the best of times, adults often find it difficult to convince teens to practice safe sex. Although young people know they are at risk of contracting AIDS, their behavior lags behind their awareness.

In our qualitative research, we find that teens understand the importance of using condoms and the consequences of not using them, but in actual practice teens engage in unsafe sex. They have a variety of rationalizations for their behavior, but it pretty much boils down to self-delusion. As much as teens understand the risk of AIDS, they simply don't believe it will happen to them. "We teens think we're invincible," explained a 16-year-old girl.

The second-most-common explanation for not using condoms is "heat of the moment." As one 17-year-old boy said, "When you're in the right situation, you're feeling things, not thinking things." Compounding this problem is alcohol and drug use. When teens (or adults) are under the influence of alcohol or drugs, they do not think. Many teens have told us that when they are drunk or stoned, they're more willing to have sex (especially girls) and less likely to use (or demand) a condom. "There's a lot of pressure to do drugs, drink, and have sex," said a 14-year-old girl. "If you don't do what the others do, you'll be left out. If you do this stuff, you might get AIDS."

Further, teen girls have told us they are embarrassed to buy condoms. Teens of both genders find going to the store, choosing (or asking for) condoms, and paying for them awkward, to say the least. Some retailers will not even sell condoms to teens, although the same clerks often will sell them cigarettes.

Teens struggled with these problems when AIDS ranked at the top of their list of concerns. Now, the sense of urgency is no longer there. To forestall another public health emergency, officials need to determine why the sense of urgency is gone and how to reverse the trend.

We've noticed an alarming fatigue among teens with the subject of AIDS in recent years. Clearly, HIV/AIDS is not a new phenomenon. First diagnosed in 1981, the disease is older than even the oldest of today's teens. With familiarity comes complacency. Young people have grown accustomed to (even weary of) the constant reminders to wear a condom. But, perhaps most important, they've paid just enough attention to the news to believe that medical science has a handle on the disease. They no longer see the virus as a death sentence; they think of it more as a chronic, treatable disease like diabetes. Many even believe, wrongly, that a cure is imminent. Unfortunately, this complacency is beginning to manifest itself in the rising number of AIDS cases, ending a period of stable infection rates.

Like so many other teen issues, AIDS becomes easily entangled in politics. Many social conservatives resist distributing condoms to teens, instead favoring abstinence education. But while TRU has indeed noticed an increase in the number of teens who are open to abstinence, we believe—and most teens agree—that condoms should be easily accessible. Even most socially conservative teens do not think teen abstinence is a realistic goal for all teenagers.

Cigarette Smoking

Cigarette smoking remains in teens' top ten list, with 24 percent mentioning the issue as personally important to them. The issue hasn't fallen in importance much in recent years, indicating that the ongoing Truth national campaign has been strong enough to compensate for cutbacks in state campaigns, which were finding great success. In many cases, state funding secured from the tobacco settlement for the purpose of advancing anti-tobacco campaigns has been diverted to fund other budgetary objectives.

Suicide

Seventeen percent of teens say suicide is one of their top-five issues. Suicide is an especially difficult subject for teens, and it's not one that comes up frequently in qualitative research. When the subject does arise, however, it can be both harrowing and heartbreaking. One teen girl, assigned to fill out a diary for a social-marketing client, submitted a final product so alarming it caused an internal debate within TRU over how to respond. On the one hand, we hold to the highest confidentiality standards—after all, it's hard to learn about teen life if respondents fear their parents will find out what they reveal. On the other hand, though, this young woman appeared to be under great emotional strain and was using her assignment as a call for help. The diary contained suicide threats, and we decided the situation warranted consulting with a psychologist with whom we've worked before. Following her guidance, we alerted the girl's school guidance counselor. We were relieved to hear that her teachers had already flagged her as a candidate for counseling, and our information fueled the urgency of getting this girl the help she needed.

As counselors often admonish, suicide is a permanent solution to a temporary problem. While this concept might resonate with adults, it often gets lost with teens, making suicide an especially confusing and painful issue.

Violence/Gangs

Although more teens named violence as a top-five issue after the Columbine shootings, only 14 percent claim this as one of their top concerns. Some teens seem to believe there's no point worrying about what you can't control, and others see gang life as a part of the teen experience.

This ho-hum attitude is well illustrated by a focus-group experience we had recently. We were meeting with a group of high school boys and talking about friendships. In the warm-up to the discussion, we asked the guys to introduce themselves and tell us about the "weirdest" way they had ever met a friend. One of the boys, after introducing himself, said he met a friend after the guy shot him. Although the backroom observers found the answer unexpected and provocative, to say the least, the other members of the focus group seemed to take it almost matter-of-factly. The respondent didn't give us many details about the incident, except to say that the experience had brought the two together and now they are close friends. His comments spoke to the reality of the world in which many teens grow up, one of pervasive violence that threatens them daily.

Chapter 6

Teens at Home and School

Each year we at TRU go before more than 100 companies and organizations with our "Key Findings Presentation," which combines cultural immersion with a teen-focused state-of-the-market address. For many clients—from Adidas, Fila, Nike, and Reebok to Coke, Dr Pepper/7 Up, and Pepsi, to ESPN, MTV, Seventeen, Teen People, and the WB—this is an annual foray, attended by many of the same people year after year. So, one of our most challenging tasks is not only to present new data but to explore completely new areas—in a sense, to assure clients that our faucet of teen findings is always turned on. TRU Vice President Michael Wood (who logs the great majority of these annual presentations) notes that without new material, he'd feel like a stand-up doing last year's routine. For a company that has been studying the same age group for more than 20 years, constantly coming up with new material is challenging, to say the least.

Not surprisingly, we take a systematic approach to developing new content. We follow a general outline, hitting almost all areas of teen life. As a matter of fact, TRU's Key Findings Presentation is similar in structure to this book. We cover teen trends, attitudes, shopping, marketing, and lifestyle. The lifestyle section is the most segmented because teens' lives are divided into three areas—home, school, and friends. Because of the breadth of information, the lifestyle portion of the presentation demands the most time.

This chapter focuses on two of the three segments of teen lifestyle: home and school. These may not be the parts of their lives that thrill teens the most, but they are the dual anchors of teen life—collectively shaping teens' core values and providing them with their formal education. When most adults think about teens, their first thought may not be of the classroom or the family room. Instead, most adults—just like the news media—gravitate to what teens do with their leisure time. It might be surprising for adults to learn, then, how teens prioritize family versus friends. In qualitative research for one of our packaged-goods clients, we asked teens to rate and discuss two seemingly conflicting value statements: "At this point in my life, my friends are extremely important to me; in many ways, my closest friends are like family," and "Even though we don't always get along, my family is a really important thing in my life."

Think you know which statement teens rated more highly? Maybe, maybe not! In fact, according to so much of our research, teens place their parents above all else. This doesn't mean that teen–parent relationships are not full of turmoil. Teens are only too happy to talk about the tough times they experience at home—some even trade parental horror stories like old war tales. But they're just as willing to identify family as the cornerstone of their lives. They explain that family provides them with identity and support—without question more so than their friends do. Although teens readily admit to considerable friction in their family relationships (particularly when it comes to their parents), they also say they appreciate family as a source of unconditional love.

For most teens, family is the bedrock of life—despite the frequent earthquakes they create beneath it. As much as teens' quest for fun often runs afoul of parental rules, teens nonetheless readily admit that without their families they would be sunk. In fact, two-thirds of teens (66 percent) even maintain they "really like to do things with family."

This sentiment is especially pronounced among Hispanic and African-American teens. In focus groups, many ethnic teens have told us about being raised in single-parent households (generally headed by mom). They describe how their mothers have made countless sacrifices on their behalf, giving them a heightened sense of respect and admiration for the value of family in general, and mom in particular.

Interestingly, when we have teens address the concept of "family" without reference to individual members, conversation almost exclusively gravitates to parents—few think of the role or impact siblings play in their

Teen Priorities: Friends, Family, or School?

Teens put family first, friends second, and school last.

(percent of teens responding when asked, "Which part of your own life right now is most important to you—family, friends, or school?")

	first	second	third
Family	60%	28%	12%
Friends	24	39	37
School	16	34	50

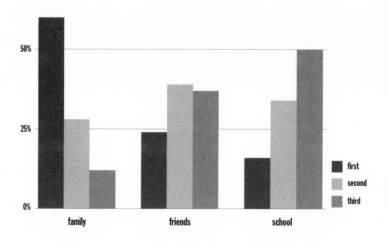

Source: The TRU Study, Teenage Research Unlimited, Inc.

lives. So, although many younger teens feel a nearly reverential respect for older siblings and older teens feel an obligation to be a role model for their younger brothers and sisters, teens recognize that their parents are the center of the family and the one constant in their lives.

Not surprisingly, teens acknowledge a dependence on parents (mostly for material goods, but also for emotional support). Most teens describe loving family situations, some saying they feel "sheltered" from the real world. And although nearly all teens speak of traditional teen–parent strife, most concurrently express some regret at the trouble they can cause their parents.

While many of the teens we interview describe having a healthy relationship with both parents, some admit favoring one parent over another—often depending on the situation. Generally, mom is the more trusted, nurturing parent, and she is widely regarded as the better counsel. Dad, on the other hand, can be more generous with cash and, therefore, is more often thought of as being "fun." Clearly, teens recognize the benefits of having strong relationships—albeit different ones—with both parents, but they're also realistic about their situation. It's not unusual to hear teens say they have "divorced" (or have been divorced from) a parent. Fortunately, in most of these cases, teens have a healthy relationship with the remaining parent and, at times, have also become close with another adult relative—a stepparent, aunt, uncle, or grandparent.

Most teens we speak to in research settings express complete loyalty to family; in fact, asked to compare the importance of friends and family in their lives, respondents explain that family love and trust is unconditional, while friends "come and go."

Respondents readily agree with the statement, "Family is the most important thing to me. I don't always let them know that, and we don't always get along, but I'd really be lost without the support my family gives me," freely admitting that family is what ultimately matters. In marked contrast, teens take issue with the statement, "There's nothing more important to me than my friends," not only because they contend that family is more important than friends, but—for many—faith or religion is also more important. (See Chapter 3 for more about the importance of religion in teen lives.)

Asked whether their parents are aware of how greatly they value their family, respondents frequently smile—or wince—at the mere suggestion of sharing such thoughts with their parents. Most teens acknowledge that they don't articulate these feelings and expect that their parents would be surprised by such sentiment. After all, who has time to engage in deep, meaningful discussions with family when there's fun to be had with friends? As TRU has quantified in its syndicated study, today's teens are closer to their families and place a greater value on family than teens did just a few years ago. Still, that doesn't mean they want to spend Saturday night in the den with a nice game of Jenga: when it comes to having fun, friends win hands-down!

Family, Friends, or School?

So far, this chapter has presented qualitative learnings. Sometimes, to see the big picture, numbers go a long way. So, we posed the following question to our national sample of teens in The TRU Study: "Which part of your own life right now is most important to you—family, friends, or school?" Forced to choose among the three, teens (in dramatic fashion) named family, validating our qualitative research. This choice is another indication of teens' underestimated maturity and larger perspective on life. They recognize the permanency of family in their lives, and they value it above all else.

More than twice as many teens (60 percent versus 24 percent) choose family over friends. Only 16 percent choose school. Half the sample name school as the least important part of their lives, compared to 37 percent who name friends. Only 12 percent say family is of negligible importance.

Distinguishing among friends, family, and school provides useful insights, to be sure. But don't rule out school as a viable media venue solely based upon this measure. Teens acknowledge that school is an essential and fundamental part of their lives. It's only when they are asked to choose among school, family, and friends that school's importance is diminished. If, instead, we asked teens to rate family, school, and friends independently, all three would get fairly high ratings (for different reasons, of course). Still, given the tough competition, we expect that school would still come in last.

Significantly more girls than guys (64 percent vs. 56 percent) choose family as the most important aspect of their lives. Girls' friendships tend to be much more fleeting than those of boys, partly because girls confide more in each other. On its face, this statement may seem contradictory. But, as countless teen girls have discovered, confiding in friends leaves one vulnerable to betrayal in a way that guys' typically more superficial friendships don't. And when friendships shift (as they are so apt to do), girls feel an almost gravitational pull toward mom (not dad!), who's often the one safe, stable person in their lives.

As found in other TRU quantitative measures on family and in our qualitative research, minority teens treasure family the most. Sixty-seven percent of Hispanic and African-American teens chose family over school or friends, compared to 57 percent of white teens—a significant margin that reveals key cultural differences.

The responses to this question also differ by age. It's the 16- and 17-year-olds who distance themselves the most from their families. Significantly fewer "middle-age" teens (who are new to driving and are doing the most experimenting) say family is more important than friends. Only 52 percent of 16- and 17-year-olds choose family, compared to 62 percent of 12- to 15-year-olds and 63 percent of 18- and 19-year-olds. To a certain extent, friends become even more important than family during this stage of their life, at least from a social perspective. As much as these teens recognize and value the importance of family, separating from the family is a natural, desirable, and ongoing process in this lifestage.

OK, we understand that the majority of teens enjoy being with their families. The next logical question is, "Compared to what?" To find the answer, we asked teens in our quantitative study, "If you could have a guaranteed great time, whom would you rather have it with, your family or your friends?"

The operative phrase here is "guaranteed great time." Either way, we are assuring teens of a more-than-satisfactory experience. Of course, what teens do with friends when they have a "great time" may be quite different from what they imagine doing with their family. It's not surprising, then, that teens—by a margin of almost two to one—choose friends (63 percent) over family (34 percent). Although teens enjoy spending time with their family, if they have a better offer from friends, they will almost always leave their parents at the doorstep. As much as teens love and appreciate parents, when it comes to socializing, parents take a backseat (unless they're dropping the younger teens off at the mall!).

As a parent of three teens who enjoys nothing more than family time, this has been an especially tough lesson to learn. But now that my youngest is in the midst of his teen experience, I'm finally getting it and not taking it personally. When we share these data with clients, the parents of teens nod their heads knowingly. They know they're lucky to get any quality time with their teenage children! Realistic parents also recognize that the time they spend with their teens will be more enjoyable for all if their kids haven't turned down another offer to accept (begrudgingly) a family invitation. As tempting as it is at times to mandate family time, it's important to show restraint.

For many parents raising their first teenager, the most difficult experience is having their children's friends supplant them as the people

With Whom Would You Rather Have a Guaranteed Great Time?

**Most teens would rather have a guaranteed great time
with friends, but many choose family.**

*(percent of teens responding when asked, "With whom would you rather have a
guaranteed great time—family or friends?" by age)*

	family	friends
Total teens	**34%**	**63%**
Aged 12 to 15	40	58
Aged 16 to 17	25	72
Aged 18 to 19	35	54

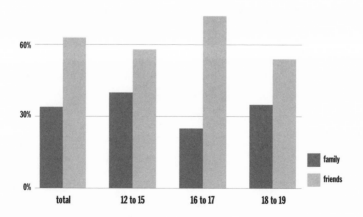

Source: The TRU Study, Teenage Research Unlimited, Inc.

with whom they most want to spend their time. Friends also are often the first people teens turn to when they have problems.

Many teens say they "survive" their day-to-day lives by looking ahead to the weekend or the next time they get together with their friends. In qualitative research, we have asked teens to diagram their social lives. At the center are the best friends—typically a handful of same-gender friends whom teens unconditionally trust and with whom they share almost everything. The next ring of the social circle comprises good friends with whom teens are happy to spend a lot of time. These individuals aren't confidants, really, but—in their vernacular—more their "posse," "crew," or even "entourage." The outermost ring is acquaintances teens are happy to see at parties or other venues. These are, more than anything, friends by proximity: teens see them frequently enough to have developed a rapport, but they're not people who teens would phone or invite to their home. In many cases, the outer ring wouldn't even make it onto their online "buddy lists."

We've already established that relationships between parents and children are most strained during the middle of the teen years. It's not surprising, then, that TRU's qualitative research suggests the middle-teen years are when ties between friends grow and strengthen. These are the most rebellious years, and teens in this stage are enjoying new freedoms: staying out later, partying, driving, dating, and generally pushing the boundaries. The late motivational-research expert Dr. Burleigh Gardner described the mid-teen state as "the cutting of the apron string," the time when teens feel compelled to separate from family in almost every part of their lives.

The youngest teen segment—in our study, predriving 12- to 15-year-olds—are still somewhat under their parents' wings (if not their thumbs). This explains why so many of these young respondents say they would prefer to have a good time with their family. In contrast, high school juniors and seniors frequently go out of their way to avoid spending leisure time with their parents. Recent graduates, however, regularly rediscover (and actually enjoy) their parents' company.

After asking respondents to choose whether they would want to spend a "guaranteed good time" with friends or family, we ask them why they made the choice they did. The overriding reason for those who choose friends is, "I can do things with my friends that there's no way I can do with my family!"

The other reasons teens give for choosing friends over family revolve around the theme of "I just want to be with my friends!" For example, 57 percent of teens say they prefer to be with friends because they already spend so much time with their family. We can only conclude that these teens must be counting the time they spend at home sleeping, talking on the phone or online, or simply hanging out behind the closed door of their room!

Those who choose to have a great time with their family say they appreciate the permanency of family in their lives. Parents of these teens should feel gratified by their response.

One of our all-time favorite responses to any of our syndicated questions came from someone who chose family over friends by explaining, "It's more unusual to have a great time with family!" This teen seemed to be saying, "Hey, having fun with my parents would be pretty weird. Why not give it a shot—it's only one night!"

Parents of younger children might find these data encouraging since they always hear people say, "Enjoy your children when they're young because when they're teenagers, it's all over!" These data suggest that they still might have something to look forward to.

To Whom Do Teens Turn for Advice?

For some products, depicting an advice-giver in advertising can be a viable tactic, especially for health and beauty aids. To shed light onto this

To Whom Do Teens Turn for Advice?

Teens are most likely to turn to a friend for advice, followed by mom.

(percent distribution of teens by the person they are most likely to turn to when in need of advice, by gender)

	total	female	male
Friend	55%	63%	48%
Mother	44	48	41
Boyfriend/girlfriend	23	26	19
Father	20	9	30
Sister	10	12	8
Other family member	7	8	6
Brother	7	3	10
Teacher	4	4	3
School counselor	3	3	3
Coach	3	1	4
Magazine/newspaper	2	3	2
Clergy (priest, rabbi)	2	2	2
Psychologist/social worker	1	1	1
Medical doctor	1	1	1
Crisis hotline	1	1	1

Source: The TRU Study, Teenage Research Unlimited, Inc.

dynamic, we asked teens the following question in our quantitative study: "Who is the first person you turn to when you need advice about a personal problem?" By a significant margin, the number-one answer is friend—mentioned by more than half the teens. Second is mother, followed by girlfriend or boyfriend, and (finally) father.

Of course, the nature of the problem will determine to whom a teen turns for advice. If the problem is, "I need help with algebra," a teen likely would turn to a competent parent. If the issue, on the other hand, is about sex or another topic some parents might consider off-limits, teens are more likely to turn to their friends. It's only the rare (and fortunate) parent whose teenaged children would come to them first when struggling with these issues. (Fortunately, a growing number of social service agencies are guiding parents on how to be effective in talking to their teenaged children about such topics. Schools are also becoming more proactive on such subjects, realizing that teens and parents avoid these issues at their own peril.)

There are a variety of reasons why teens are most likely to turn to their friends for advice. The problem they have may be too intimate or risky to broach with parents; a friend may have recently experienced a similar situation; or sometimes it's more comfortable talking with someone who is not an authority figure, who is less judgmental and more (from a teen's perspective) understanding.

More teen guys than girls go to their father or brother for advice, whereas more girls turn to friends, mom, or sisters. Dad ranks relatively low on this measure, for several reasons. First, many teens today come from single-parent homes headed by their mother; they may not have a dad close by to turn to for advice, or they may not respect him if they feel he has behaved irresponsibly. Second, even if a teen lives with both parents, dad is often less accessible than mom. Finally, in focus groups, teens tell us that their mother is more interested in their problems and more nurturing in her response than their father.

We often hear from teens that mom really listens and is empathetic; she might even offer potential solutions. Alternatively, when teens go to dad with a problem, they say he doesn't really "hear" what they're saying. Instead, teens say dad simply chooses from among his vast stockpile of prepared lectures. Clearly, this doesn't inspire repeat visits.

Nearly 25 percent of teens say they turn to their boyfriend or girlfriend for advice. If the data were limited only to respondents who have a boyfriend or girlfriend, the percentage would more than double. This reveals how important "significant others" are in sharing problems and giving advice. TRU data show that some 80 percent of teens want to have a boyfriend or girlfriend, yet only about a third do at any one time.

Our qualitative experience paints a somewhat troubling picture of the vaulted position a boyfriend or girlfriend can hold in a teen's life. Some teens use the expression "married" to indicate a serious romantic relationship. Although parents may wish it weren't true, many teens focus on a single member of the opposite sex throughout their high school career, developing extremely intense relationships where the individual supplants not only family members but also other friends as the most influential person in a teen's life. Some teens tell us that they, too, see unhealthy signs in friends' romantic relationships, explaining that the boyfriend or girlfriend takes up almost all of their friend's free time.

How Teens Describe Their Families

We wanted to quantify our qualitative findings about family by determining the words teens would use to describe their parents. Such questions give unrivaled insight into the kinds of relationships teens have with their parents.

Working with our Trendwatch panel of Edge and Influencer teens (who help us develop our questionnaire for each six-month wave of The TRU Study), we created a list of ten descriptors—five positive and five negative—that we put to our national sample to help them characterize

How Teens Describe Their Families

Most teens describe their families as happy, loving, and supportive.

(percent of teens responding when asked to describe their family)

Happy	68%
Loving	63
Supportive	63
Fun	54
Close	45
Tense	20
At each other's throats	18
Unhappy	12
Cold	6
Abusive	4

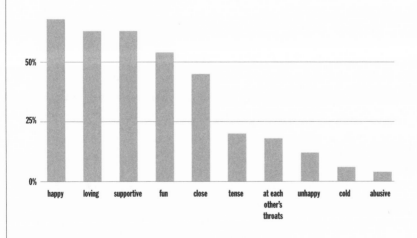

Source: The TRU Study, Teenage Research Unlimited, Inc.

their family. About 70 percent of respondents selected positive responses, while only 30 percent chose negative ones. Of the ten listed characteristics, the five most frequently selected were all positive.

Despite what many adults fear, most teens not only look up to their parents but actually feel good about them. Teens are more likely to characterize their families as happy than unhappy, as loving than abusive, as close than cold, as supportive than "at each other's throats," and as fun than tense. In addition to providing the list of potential descriptors, we allowed our sample to write in other responses. Most of those who wrote in an alternative response answered negatively, but fewer than 10 percent of the sample wrote in an answer. There were few differences in the selected family characteristics by gender, age, or race with one exception: the characteristic of "fun." More African-American than either Hispanic or white teens described their family as "fun." More younger teens, too, characterized their families as "fun." Younger teens are less involved in independent social activities—in a sense, they haven't begun to cut the ties to their family and, therefore, are more apt to think of families as fun.

What Teens Talk to Parents About

During the past several years, we've conducted a number of studies to determine how teens talk to one another and what they talk about. Clearly, technology has changed both how and where they converse: instant messaging is becoming a substitute for phone calls, while cell phones keep friends together even when miles apart. This type of tech talk will only increase as text messaging and an array of new digital and wireless services become more commonplace and affordable. Similarly, more teens are using technology to talk to their parents. In fact, many teens tell us that they convinced their parents to (at least partly) pay for their cell-phone service by saying, "You'll be able to reach me all the time!" While this sounds persuasive, in fact teens are adept at using technology to limit parental accessibility. I personally learned this a few years ago, when my oldest son

What Teens Talk About with Their Parents

The number-one topic of conversation between teens and parents is school and grades.

*(percent of teens responding when asked, "Which five things do
you most talk about with your parents?" by gender)*

	total	female	male
School/grades	55%	57%	53%
Other friends	40	48	33
Future	37	36	38
Life in general	36	36	35
College	34	33	35
Jobs	31	27	35
Current events	23	21	26
Brother/sister	18	22	14
Sports	17	10	23
Your attitude	17	18	16
Vacations	16	16	16
Your behavior	16	16	16
Boyfriend/girlfriend	15	20	11
Next weekend	13	12	14
Movies/TV shows	12	10	15
Deep feelings	11	13	9
Music	7	7	8
Last weekend	7	5	8
Fashion	7	9	5
Gossip	6	8	4
Someone you want to go out with	4	6	3
Sex	4	5	3
Video games/computers	4	2	7
Nothing	4	3	5
Eating habits	4	5	3
Secret stuff	3	5	1
Celebrities	3	4	3

Source: The TRU Study, Teenage Research Unlimited, Inc.

confessed that he had programmed two distinct ring tones on his cell phone to distinguish between his friends and his parents.

By getting a handle on how teens converse—and what they talk about—we help clients get a better idea of how to become part of that dialog. By doing this, communication with teens becomes more personal and relevant—and therefore more trusted and less intrusive. Based upon our qualitative findings, we decided to quantify what teens talk about not only with their friends but also with their parents. Comparing the two is especially enlightening—particularly for social marketers who dare not take a pedantic tone in their teen-communication efforts.

As expected, we found that teens talk about very different things with their parents than with their friends. When talking to friends, girls admit gossiping heavily, saying they spend a lot of talk-time on the subjects of boys and "secret stuff." Guys, in predictable contrast, say their conversations with friends focus either on sex or shared interests (such as sports, music, cars, and more sex).

Despite the gender differences in conversations with friends, both guys and girls have similar types of conversations with their parents. Adults and their teenage children frequently talk about school and grades, the future, college, family, current events, and (reluctantly) friends. Compare the two lists, and it's no wonder teens pull away from parents: they're boring! Conversations with friends are not only more enjoyable, but also more intimate and revealing.

School is the number-one parent–teen conversational topic. In fact, it's the only discussion that more than half of teens hold with their parents. Our Trendwatch panel contends this subject is pervasive because it's what parents constantly bring up. Although, most of our panelists say they value family dinners, they also say they dread the "What's going on with your grade in geometry?" line of questioning.

What Teens Talk About with Their Friends

Friends is a big topic of conversation among teens.

(percent of teens responding when asked, "Which five things do you most talk about with your friends?" by gender)

	total	female	male
Boyfriend/girlfriend	38%	44%	32%
Other friends	36	39	33
Life in general	35	39	32
Someone you want to go out with	35	38	32
Music	30	25	34
Sex	27	22	32
Gossip	26	39	14
Future	25	26	24
Next weekend	25	26	24
Last weekend	23	24	23
Movies/TV shows	21	16	26
Sports	21	8	33
Secret stuff	20	26	15
Current events	19	16	22
School/grades	18	20	16
Jobs	16	13	18
Deep feelings	15	23	9
College	12	13	11
Fashion	12	18	7
Video games/computers	11	1	20
Parents	9	13	5
Celebrities	7	9	5
Vacations	6	6	7
Brother/sister	4	6	3
Your attitude	4	5	3
Your behavior	3	4	2
Eating habits	2	3	1

Source: The TRU Study, Teenage Research Unlimited, Inc.

Close behind the subject of school, teens claim their parents can't resist bringing up the topic of their future. In fact, nearly two-thirds of the national sample say their conversations with parents include subjects such as the future, college, and jobs. Once that unpleasantness is out of the way, daughters say they talk to their parents about other people, while sons talk about events and activities.

These findings are relevant for marketers, because many brands have a dual teen–parent target (think food items—where teens are the users and mom is the shopper) and rely on traditional media for reaching both teens and parents together. The data show there are common, relatable, teen–parent conversations that can be depicted in advertising aimed at a dual target. Further, these findings present a new level of understanding about the critical teen–parent dynamic. Importantly, these insights are grounded in everyday reality, based on actual behavior rather than teens' typically optimistic (and less accurate) attitudes.

Talking to Parents About Tough Subjects

The undercurrent running through so much of this parent–teen data is of a mature teen perspective—of teens valuing parents' unconditional support and love above all else. So we wanted to push teen respondents further and find out whether they feel comfortable and secure enough about themselves and their family relationships to talk to their parents about any subject. Although many teens have trusting relationships with their parents, many teens also hesitate to talk with them about subjects such as sex, drugs, and drinking. Although two-thirds of teens say they can talk with at least one parent about these serious topics, an alarming one-third cannot talk about them with either parent.

Most teens contend that mom is the one parent they can talk to about intimate issues. Thirty-five percent say they can go to both parents with these topics, 26 percent say they can talk only to mom about them, and just 4 percent say they can talk only to dad. Mothers typically are more accessible

Can Teens Talk to Their Parents About Serious Issues?

Most teens can talk to at least one parent about serious issues.

(percent of teens responding when asked, "Can you talk to your mom or dad openly, honestly, and with detail about serious issues like drugs, sex, and drinking?")

Yes, both parents	36%
Yes, mom only	27
Yes, dad only	4
No, neither parent	33

Source: The TRU Study, Teenage Research Unlimited, Inc.

than fathers, and when teens have a need to spill it out, they're fairly impulsive about it. More important, teens explain that they're more comfortable discussing the intimate details of their lives with mom than with dad, because—as previously pointed out—they say mom is a better listener, more supportive, and at times even helpful.

On the surface these data indicate that teens talk with their parents about the private parts of their lives, but it's important to recognize that we asked respondents whether they "can talk" rather whether they "have talked" to their parents. Perception can be different from reality.

There are also important demographic differences in parent–teen communication. First, significantly fewer girls than boys say they are able to talk with their parents at all about these issues. Girls are especially reluctant to talk to their father about these parts of their lives. Only 27 percent of girls, compared to 43 percent of boys, say they can talk to both parents about these topics. Girls are also much more likely to go to (only) mom than boys are (35 percent vs. 17 percent). Finally, only 16 girls out of nearly 1,000 (fewer than 2 percent) in our sample say they can only go to dad!

As found in other TRU quantitative measures, fewer of the middle-age teens, 16- and 17-year-olds, maintain open lines of communication with parents. Interestingly, Hispanic teens—who often revere family—seem to have the most difficulty discussing highly personal topics with parents. Forty percent of Hispanic teens (compared to 31 percent of both African-American and white teens) say they're unable to talk to either parent about such subjects. It appears that Hispanic teens may demonstrate their respect toward their parents in different ways than teens of other ethnic backgrounds, which in turn may make it difficult for them to share personal information.

Social marketers—who, for example, attempt to educate and persuade a teenage audience about issues from cigarette smoking to drugs to sexual abstinence—need to incorporate a parental strategy as well as one geared toward teens. Because teens hold their parents in such high esteem, tapping into this respect and admiration (let alone the kind of access and attention parents can command and demand) can be highly effective. To be truly effective, however, parents need the skills and tools with which to talk to their teenagers about these issues.

For social marketers, learning that parents and teens can talk about intimate topics—although with some reluctance—provides a richer understanding of the parent–teen dynamic and how to accurately portray it. But be careful of whom you portray teens talking to. Even boys are unlikely to go only to their father to talk about sex, drugs, or drinking. So, showing girls talking to mom or boys talking to both parents would be the most accurate depiction of these interactions.

If teens and parents can talk about difficult subjects, they certainly can communicate about less serious subjects such as buying. Marketing efforts that encourage teens to talk to their parents about family purchases—or persuade them to take the initiative as influencers—are almost always viable. After all, in a world that discounts them as immature kids, teens love the opportunity to be "the expert."

Family as Friends

By now you're probably convinced that today's teens place tremendous value on family and enjoy spending time with their parents. But do they (or could they) consider their family members to be friends? We put forth this question to teens in The TRU Study, asking our national sample not only if they consider family members to be friends, but also which family members are accorded this status.

The findings are more good news for parents: on average, respondents consider a total of four family members or relatives to be friends, and 70 percent view at least one parent as a friend. Again, mom ranks number one, with nearly two-thirds of teens (among those who consider any family member a friend) naming her. Remarkably, a cousin is next, beating out dad. Dad follows, but (as is the case in much of our research) he trails significantly behind mom, with fewer than half of teens naming him. Brother and sister follow, each named by 41 percent of respondents. When brother and sister are netted together, nearly two-thirds say they consider a sibling to be a friend, suggesting that siblings can be powerfully depicted in advertising—especially ads that promote social causes and would benefit from including a slightly older, respected role model. In our antidrug and antitobacco work, the message to older teens that they're role models—that their younger brothers and sisters watch them closely and emulate them—resonates strongly.

Cousins are especially important to African-American teens. In fact, 22 percent of African-American children live in a household that includes extended family members, compared to 10 percent of whites. Cousins are attractive friends for teens. They can be the same age, but they don't carry

Family Members
As Friends

**Eighty-five percent of teens regard a family member as a real friend.
Among those who do, mom is most likely to be thought of as a friend.**

*(among teens who regard a family member as a real friend, percent
who name selected family members as friends)*

Mom	64%
Cousin	56
Dad	47
Brother	41
Sister	41
Aunt	35
Grandmother	32
Uncle	30
Grandfather	23
Another relative	17
Stepmom or stepdad	9

Source: The TRU Study, Teenage Research Unlimited, Inc.

the baggage of being a sibling (i.e., rivalries, etc.). Female extended family members are more important to African-American respondents than to Hispanics or whites. Significantly more African-American teens say they consider a grandmother or an aunt to be a "real friend."

Being of the same gender appears to facilitate close relationships. Significantly more girls are closer to mothers, sisters, and aunts; significantly more boys are closer to fathers, brothers, and uncles. Still, it's important to recognize that more boys name mom than dad as a close friend.

As discussed previously, 18- and 19-year-olds rediscover the enjoyment of spending time with their parents. For example, 62 percent of 16- and 17-year-olds consider mom to be a friend, but this number jumps to 71 percent for 18- and 19-year-olds. Dad experiences a less dramatic lift as teens age. And for middle-age teen boys, dad loses ground. Boys aged 16 and 17 (the most rebellious age segment) are struggling with the father–son relationship; while 58 percent of 12-to-15-year-olds consider dad to be a friend, the figure drops to only 45 percent among 16- and 17-year-olds.

Significantly fewer minority teens say they consider their father to be a friend, perhaps because fewer live with or maintain an ongoing relationship with their father. Census data show that 60 percent of African-American children are being raised in a single-parent family, compared to 21 percent of white children.

What Teens Like and Don't Like to Do with Parents

The generation gap today is smaller than a generation ago. Teens and their Boomer parents share many activities, interests, and even pop-culture preferences. We thought it would be interesting to quantify what teens like to do with their families, and—of course—what they don't. One thing's for certain: teens appreciate their parents' financial wherewithal. Activities requiring significant financial outlays—like vacations and dining at good restaurants—rank highly with teens as desirable family activities. Other activities—such as concerts and movies—teens view as off limits for parent–teen time.

What Teens Like and Don't Like To Do with Their Parents

Teens like to spend holidays with their parents, but they don't like to go to concerts or movies with them.

(percent of teens responding when asked, "What things do you like to do with your parents (or entire family) and which do you not like to do with your parents (or entire family)?")

Like to do with parents		Don't like to do with parents	
Spend holidays together	90%	Go to concerts	74%
Go out to a nice restaurant	86	Go to movies	67
Go on vacations	79	Play video games	63
Eat dinner at home	79	Play on a computer	63
Family parties	68	Play sports	56
Go to church, synagogue	66	Go shopping	54
Watch TV	66	Work on school projects	47
Go out for fast food	64	Having a talk/just talking	43
Watch videos at home	64	Go to sporting events	41
Play board games/cards	60	Go grocery shopping	38
Family outings (zoo, museum)	58	Go out in public	36
Go out in public	57	Family outing (zoo, museum)	35
Go grocery shopping	57	Play board games/cards	33
Having a talk/just talking	51	Watch videos at home	31
Go to sporting events	51	Go out for fast food	30
Work on school projects	45	Watch TV	30
Go shopping	42	Family parties	27
Play sports	35	Go to church, synagogue	25
Go to the movies	29	Go on vacations	19
Play on a computer	27	Eat dinner at home	18
Play video games	25	Go out to a nice restaurant	11
Go to concerts	16	Spend holidays together	7

Source: The TRU Study, Teenage Research Unlimited, Inc.

Teens like to do a variety of things with their parents. At least two-thirds of respondents mentioned spending holidays together, going to a "nice" restaurant, going on vacation, eating dinner at home, having family parties, and going to church or synagogue. These activities fall into two camps: those that offer teens a "free ride" (the aforementioned nice restaurants, vacations) and those that reflect teens' genuine desire to be with their family (spending holidays together, eating dinner at home, having family parties, attending religious functions).

As mentioned earlier in this chapter, teens value family dinners and the opportunity they offer for conversation—in part because family dinners are so rare, owing to everyone's busy schedule. Still, teens would much prefer talking about a movie with a friend than with a parent. Most teens don't even want to be seen at a movie or concert with parents. Their message to parents: back off! Pick your opportunities to socialize with your teens carefully, understanding their sensitivities.

Parental Punishments

Most teens are a rich mixture of creativity, boredom, and rebellion that can flare up with little or no warning. As anyone with teenaged children can attest, parents spend a good deal of time putting out these fires and trying to devise suitable disciplinary measures to discourage such problems in the future. According to a new measure from The TRU Study, the majority of parents use verbal punishment as a way to discourage unwanted behavior, and most also take away items or privileges important to teens as a way of making their point. For many, physical punishment is a last resort.

Fully 91 percent of teens report that their parents use verbal punishment to express their displeasure at problematic behavior. The most common form of verbal punishment is basic "yelling": two-thirds of teens say their parents are yellers (at least some of the time). Teens report that the next most-common disciplinary method is the often-lengthy and uncomfortable "talk," wherein parents calmly but sternly lay out their

How Parents Punish Teens

Yelling is the most common form of punishment experienced by teens.

(percent of teens responding when asked, "Which of the following have your parents done to punish or discipline you?" by gender)

	total	female	male
Yell	67%	70%	63%
Have a "talk"	59	58	60
Express disappointment	56	56	56
Ground	50	50	50
Guilt trip	45	51	39
Can't see certain friends	35	39	32
Take away TV	34	31	36
Take away phone	32	43	22
Early curfew	25	27	23
Take away Internet	25	27	23
Physical punishment	18	15	21
"Silent" treatment	16	20	12
Withhold allowance	16	14	17
Take away car	13	12	13

Source: The TRU Study, Teenage Research Unlimited, Inc.

position. Fifteen percent of teens mention the "silent treatment" as punishment. The teens who have experienced the silent treatment say they wish their parents would lay their displeasure on the table—whether by doing a little yelling or by having an open (but, hopefully, not overly lengthy) discussion.

Deprivation is often employed when verbal punishments don't work or when parents deem the trespass serious enough that a more punitive method is needed. Because teens can be both headstrong and mischievous, it's not particularly surprising that 77 percent report having had something taken away from them in punishment. Most often, it's their precious freedom: half of teens say they've been grounded for their misdeeds. Some 35 percent say their parents have forbidden them from hanging around with certain friends. More than one-third have lost TV privileges, and nearly as many have been barred from using the phone. Fewer parents seem to withhold money or allowances, and because few teens have their own car, only 13 percent say their parents have taken away their vehicle.

Physical punishment has played a role in the lives of 18 percent of teens. TRU's qualitative research shows that most parents use physical punishment as a last resort—the majority don't like it any more than their kids do. Unfortunately, there are exceptions to every rule: some parents dish out such punishments regularly and for relatively minor infractions. There are gender differences, too: significantly more girls than guys report experiencing verbal punishment, while more guys report physical punishment.

Most forms of punishment diminish as teens age for several reasons. First, older teens have taken some of the discipline to heart and have learned their lesson. No doubt, more experienced teens have also figured out how not to get caught. And, according to TRU interviews, some parents either have grown tired of punishing their teenager or feel that discipline is not effective and have, in effect, given up. Others simply say their teens have reached the age where both parties accept a certain amount of rule infractions.

Parental punishment is a fact of life, as much a given as death and taxes. In crafting a marketing message that appeals to real-life teens, it isn't necessary to shy away from such subjects so long as you use a sense of humor.

Family Trauma

So far, we've painted an optimistic portrait of teens and their families. Another recent measure from The TRU Study reveals that teens' optimism is at least part resilience. If you think growing up is hard to do, you're right. For American teens today, the passage to adulthood means more than surviving the typical teen trysts and fitting in while trying to keep your face from breaking out.

If the family is indeed teens' emotional anchor—as so much of TRU's data indicate—then teens remain optimistic in the face of realities that are all too frequently quite rough. Asked what sort of family trauma they have endured, respondents in our quantitative study revealed in startling detail the trials and hardships of the modern family. These statistics don't summon forth images of the TV families with which most of us grew up. But, as it turns out, those families never really looked much like us, anyway.

It's commonly known that nearly half of all marriages today eventually end in divorce. Nearly one-fourth of teens report that divorce has already affected their life. So, when we talk to teens about their "families," chances are their definition of family is different than the one their parents would have offered a generation ago. As latchkey kids, often growing up in one-parent families or shuttling between two households, many of today's teens have come to expect the family turmoil that parents traditionally have tried to guard against.

Divorce is hardly their only worry, though. Many teens report that they have witnessed mental illness—such as addictions and emotional

186

Teen Family Problems

Many teens have experienced a family crisis.

*(percent of teens responding when asked, "Which of the
following has your family experienced?")*

Divorce or separation	24%
Depression	24
Alcoholism	18
Unemployment	15
Death of a parent	11
Drug abuse	9
Someone kicked out	8
Someone went to prison	8
Violence between parents	7
Someone ran away	7
Mental illness	7
Teen pregnancy	6
Death of a brother or sister	6
Eating disorder	5
Discrimination	5
Child abuse	4
Sexual assault	3
Suicide	3
None of the above	31

Source: The TRU Study, Teenage Research Unlimited, Inc.

problems—in their household. In fact, 24 percent of teens report that someone in their family has battled depression. Another 18 percent say alcoholism has been a factor in family life, 9 percent list a struggle with drug abuse, and 7 percent report dealing with a family member's mental illness.

And it goes on.

A staggering 11 percent of teens report the death of a parent, and 6 percent say a sibling has passed away. Three percent report a suicide in the family.

The influence of ethnicity (and, more so, socioeconomics) is dramatic when comparing the responses of teen segments to this question. Significantly more African-American teens than those of other ethnic backgrounds report being affected by divorce, unemployment, death of a parent, prison time, violence between parents, and death of a sibling. On the other hand, significantly more white teens say a family member has suffered from an eating disorder. More white teens also list mental illness as a problem their family has experienced.

In analyzing this data, it's first important to again acknowledge just how important family is to teens and how vulnerable and fragile teens are when they lack reliable family support. As we know, nobody's opinion ultimately matters as much to teens as their parents', and they describe both mom and dad in generally glowing tones. Despite teens' positive feelings towards their family, they are surprisingly worldly in recognizing that families are less than perfect and that life comes with more than its share of setbacks. So, despite some teens' aversion to discussing family problems, such issues affect them deeply. Marketers should bear in mind that, although no one wants to be constantly reminded of the tougher aspects of modern life, teens recognize the difference between TV families (and families depicted in advertising) and their own. A more realistic portrayal—say, a blue-collar family facing real problems—can grab attention just because of its rarity (think *Roseanne* and *Malcolm in the Middle*).

The list of family problems encountered by teens gives enormous insight into their daily lives. TRU research has found that teens are deeply interested in their immediate community, and a company that shows concern—and possibly monetary support—for real people's problems is likely to make quite an impact on teens.

What Teens Would Change About Their Families

If this chapter has communicated anything so far, it's that the teen–parent relationship is a complex one, with many ambivalent feelings. On the one hand, teens readily acknowledge that they crave the attention, love, and security that only a family can give. Yet they also have a natural instinct to test family-imposed restraints (potentially jeopardizing those relationships). We thought it would be particularly insightful to learn how teens would change their family. So we posed the question in The TRU Study.

Perhaps because teens themselves are feeling the pinch of a tighter economy, financial status was the number-one thing teens would change about their family. Thirty-nine percent of respondents wished their family "had more money." With parents and teens working more hours to make ends meet, having "more fun" also ranked highly (mentioned by 25 percent) as did "less stressful household" (20 percent). Having more privacy (19 percent) and more respect and trust (18 percent) from their family also were popular choices among respondents.

Establishing a better parent–teen relationship (and having other family members get along with one another better) also found a prominent place on teens' wish list. Seventeen percent would like to "get along better with a brother or sister," while 16 percent would like their parents to "get along better with each other" or would like to "get along better with their parents." Interestingly, having "fewer rules" did not crack teens' top-five list of things they would change. This relatively low showing reflects either teen acceptance of a reasonable number of (well, reasonable) rules, or that teens are able to get around the rules in their household.

What Teens Would Change About Their Families

The largest share of teens wish their family had more money.

(percent of teens responding when asked, "If you could change three things about your family, what would you change?")

Your family has more money	39%
More fun	25
Less stressful household	20
More privacy	19
More respect or trust	18
You get along better with brother or sister	17
Fewer rules	16
Parents get along better with each other	16
You get along better with parents	16
Spend more time together	15
More understanding	14
More brothers or sisters	13
Fewer brothers or sisters	7
Livelier household	6
Quieter household	6

Source: The TRU Study, Teenage Research Unlimited, Inc.

The benefits of living in a harmonious, functioning family (security, acceptance, affection, encouragement) are timeless values that teens continue to appreciate despite their rather "independent" public personas. These data suggest that teens understand they have a role and a responsibility to help create an environment where family members get along. Yet there is also an implied quid pro quo (teens desire a larger role in defining themselves as individuals within the family nucleus). Teens are looking for more privacy, respect, and trust from family members in return.

In communicating their brands to teens, marketers should portray the themes of independence and family carefully. While teens will always be attracted to rebellious themes that sanction the exploration of their emerging independence, they still have a "sweet spot" for the nurturing values of family. Brands that accurately recognize and communicate this duality will likely gain teens' respect.

What Teens Like to Do at Home

Many teens think of their time at home as an opportunity to rest and re-cover from the nonstop action of their daily lives. Although adults often think of this time as a precious gift to be shared with the family, teens are rarely so enthusiastic. Most teens want quality family time, but they want it on their terms. And it's the rare teen who wants quantity family time. Teens prefer to use their down time at home and the resources of home (including free phone and 'Net access) to catch up with friends. Family interaction inevitably takes a back seat—even at home.

Teens, of course, are pop-culture junkies, and this pursuit requires a massive time commitment. Because of this preoccupation, entertainment activities such as listening to music, watching TV, going online, and playing video games account for a great deal of what teens do when they are at home. Young people are social beings, and although their own home is not the ideal setting for hanging out with friends (somebody else's is much preferred), it appears they would still rather connect with peers than parents

Favorite Things to Do at Home

When teens are at home, their favorite activity is listening to music.

(percent of teens responding when asked, "Of the following, which five are your most favorite things to do at home?" by gender)

	total	female	male
Listen to music	60%	62%	59%
Watch TV	50	42	58
Talk on the phone	41	53	29
Sleep	37	40	33
Go online	35	31	39
Have friends over	31	34	29
Spend time by yourself in your room	27	32	22
Play video or computer games	24	6	41
Eat	17	15	18
Spend time with your dog or cat	16	17	16
Read	16	19	13
Exercise or work out	16	14	18
Do your hobby	16	9	22
Draw, paint, write, be artistic, etc.	13	17	10
Talk with your sister or brother	11	12	10
Take a shower or bath	10	14	7
Hang out with your parents	10	11	9
Bother your brother or sister	9	7	11
Study or do homework	6	6	5
Spend time in your yard	5	4	6
Cook or bake	4	7	2
Have deep talks with your parents	3	3	3
Do something illegal	2	1	3

Source: The TRU Study, Teenage Research Unlimited, Inc.

192

when they are at home. Talking on the phone and having friends over rate highly in this measure.

Teens consistently complain about the hectic pace of their lives, so it's not surprising that they put a great deal of emphasis on relaxing at home. Respondents rate sleep a solid fourth in importance here. As will be discussed later in this chapter, teens require more hours of sleep than those older or younger; they also have trouble sleeping at what would seem logical times. Teens, for example, find sleep more natural at noon than at midnight.

A close look at how teens prioritize their at-home activities may be a little troubling, at least to parents. They are more likely to lock themselves in their rooms or spend time with pets than to sit down with their parents to hang out or talk. Parents need to be realistic and accept whatever time their busy teens give them. Even during family time, young people prefer to hang out with brothers and sisters more than with parents. In fact, teenagers rate their willingness to engage in "deep talks with parents" only slightly higher than their interest in doing "something illegal."

When teens are stuck at home (their words, not ours), they consider their room a safe haven. Whether listening to the radio, watching TV, or surfing the Web, young people are their own gatekeepers: they choose whom to let into their sanctuary, their bedroom. Beyond finding a message that won't turn a teenager off, it is a marketer's responsibility to give the teen a reason to keep advertising turned on.

The Teen Bedroom

To understand teens is to know not only who—but what—surrounds them. One of our favorite "homework assignments" in qualitative research is having teens complete a photo journal in advance of an in-person discussion. We design the journal so that it's both graphically engaging and particularly pointed—in order, obviously, to get the information and insight we need. We organize the assignment into key areas of teen life, which typically include friends, hobbies, hangouts, and families. One of the areas

Items Teens Want
In Their Bedroom

**TV is the number-one item teen boys want in their bedroom.
Among girls, a CD player/stereo is number one.**

*(percent of teens responding when asked, "Thinking of your own bedroom, which
three of the following are most important to you?" by gender)*

Female		Male	
CD player/stereo	35%	TV	40%
Photos	32	CD player/stereo	30
Phone	28	Video game system	26
TV	24	Computer/'Net	25
Door that locks	24	Alarm clock	24
Alarm clock	21	Door that locks	21
Music collection	21	Music collection	18
Stuffed animals	17	Hiding place for stuff	16
Hiding place for stuff	15	Phone	14
Computer/'Net	15	Trophies/awards	11

Source: The TRU Study, Teenage Research Unlimited, Inc.

we find fruitful for exploring the teen experience is their bedroom. For most, bedrooms serve as their inner sanctum, the one place they can escape to and call their own.

Based on this insight, we decided to quantify which items in their bedroom teens value most, believing that understanding the list would shed even greater light on teens' priorities.

The first revelation is that guys' and girls' lists are noticeably different. The six most valued items in boys' rooms are a TV, a stereo, a video game system, a computer, an alarm clock, and a door that locks. Guys' also highly rate their music collection, a hiding place "for stuff," and a phone. At the top of girls' list, on the other hand, are a stereo, photographs, a phone, a TV, and a door that locks, followed by an alarm clock, a music collection, stuffed animals/"blankies," a hiding place for secret stuff, and a computer.

As you can see, gender differences abound here. Girls' number-two item (photos) and guys' number-three (video game systems), don't even make the opposite sex's top-ten list! Further, more guys than girls name their TV, computer, and trophies as having high importance; more girls than guys name their telephone, stereo, and stuffed animals. On the surface these items seem to be nothing more than material possessions. But at a deeper level, they symbolize teens' underlying needs: entertainment, security, socialization, a sense of nostalgia (girls only), and sleep.

In-bedroom entertainment is, without a doubt, essential to teens' desire for continuous audio-visual stimulation, and the wide variety of devices they list is emblematic of their short attention span. Their televisions, stereos and music collections, video game systems, and computers promise nonstop entertainment and, as such, are either indispensable or coveted, depending upon a family's means. As parents see their teen growing more distant and mysterious, many are tempted to snoop in their bedroom. Today's teens value privacy—or, as they think of it, security—more than ever. It's no wonder that having a locking door and a place to stash "secret stuff" is so highly valued.

The walls of a teen's bedroom separate him or her both physically and symbolically from the rest of the home. Teens strive to make that space as comfortable and customized as possible (even if they share it with a sibling). Their careful attention to detail creates, in effect, a safe haven from which they can shut off the rest of the world (or, tune into it virtually, should they so choose).

What are the implications of this information, beyond simply getting closer to your target? For one, durable-goods makers might note that teens are drawn to their bedroom furniture and accessories for both functional and emotional reasons (it may be worthwhile to convey both in teen-targeted advertising). Marketers of any teen product should keep this list handy when depicting teen rooms in advertising. Keep in mind the things most important to teens (entertainment, security, socialization, a sense of nostalgia, and sleep) and then demonstrate how your brand understands, empathizes, and even addresses those needs.

Rethinking School

Teens view school as the ultimate social environment. It's the place where they get to strut their stuff, where Influencers can be Influencers and Conformers can pick up the social cues they need. School is where friends are. It is also the nexus for countless ritualistic behaviors, from meeting one another in the same spot each day, to hitting the vending machines en route to their locker, to hanging out in the cafeteria or another public space, to participating in locker-room humor.

We believe many marketers miss the point when it comes to the subject of school. Adults tend to think back to their (in some cases, not particularly pleasant) high school careers and can't imagine why school should be a marketing venue or even depicted in teen-targeted advertising. But to teens, school is their daily life. It's where they spend the majority of their weekday waking hours (although several of our Trendwatch panelists would argue that they spend significant sleeping time there as well).

Why should marketers think about school as an opportunity? For one, school delivers more teens per square foot than anyplace else! If you're looking for a targeted audience (and who isn't?), there's no more efficient place for reaching mass quantities of teens than school.

School also gives marketers the opportunity to support teens within their own community, where young people repeatedly tell us they are most eager to see companies devote their resources. Many of the nation's schools find themselves struggling financially—school-funding referenda are becoming more difficult to pass (especially in established, aging communities), and the federal government seems ever more interested in imposing rules than in increasing funding. If there's any bright side to this, it is that there are more ways to support schools—and become visible in them—than ever before. Opportunities to support schools financially can include donations of equipment as well as grants toward programs and curricula.

To be appropriately relevant in school, it's essential to know the "rules"—not only what each local school board permits, desires, and needs, but also what teens find appropriate and appealing in this special venue. What follows are some ideas about the teen relationship with school.

Favorite and Least-Favorite Things About School

To understand school from a teen perspective, we quantified what teens like and don't like about school. When presented with a list of items, including academic, extracurricular, and social factors, teens clearly (and perhaps predictably) show a preference for the latter. In fact, seeing their friends is by far teens' favorite thing about school. These results indicate that many teens view school as an ideal venue for socializing away from the prying eyes of their parents.

If you glance quickly at the list of teens' favorite things about school, you might miss any academic mentions: all but one are social or extra-curricular! Friends, boyfriend/girlfriend, extracurricular activities, free

What Teens Like and Don't Like About School

Friends are what teens like most about school, and getting up early is what they like least.

(percent of teens responding when asked, "What are your three most favorite and least favorite things about school?")

Most favorite		Least favorite	
Friends	79%	Getting up early	52%
Assemblies/special days/		Tests	52
field trips	43	Homework	51
Sports	34	How long the days are	27
Seeing boyfriend/girlfriend	32	Peer pressure	25
Extracurricular activities	25	Classes	24
Free periods/recess	23	Gossip	21
Learning	22	School administration	19
Lunch	20	Teachers	18
Being away from home	18	Just being there	14
Other students	14	Grades	14
Gossip	12	Being away from home	8
Teachers	12	Other students	7
Clubs	11	Learning	6
Grades	11	Clubs	5
Classes	10	Assemblies/special days/	
Just being there	9	field trips	4
School administration	3	Lunch	4
Tests	3	Sports	3
How long the days are	2	Extracurricular activities	3
Homework	2	Seeing boyfriend/girlfriend	3
Peer pressure	2	Free periods/recess	2
Getting up early	1	Friends	1

Source: The TRU Study, Teenage Research Unlimited, Inc.

periods, and lunch are all more favored than anything academic. The only consolation for teachers and parents is that learning actually cracks the top ten. But the means by which teens learn—teachers, classes, grades, and tests—all rank low, mentioned as something they like by 12 percent or fewer teens.

Despite what some marketers believe, school scenes need not be taboo in advertising to teens; after all, school is a huge part of their social life. Marketers should concentrate on the aspects of school that teens appreciate the most, however—namely, the social interaction. When teens are vegging out in front of the TV, with one hand on the remote and the other in a bowl of chips, a commercial that brings them back to the daily irritations of classes, teachers, tests, homework, and grades runs the risk of alienating them. Still, there are no real "rules" when it comes to advertising; even classroom scenes—if handled humorously—can work. After all, you would be hard-pressed to come up with a more relatable setting for the country's more than 30 million teens.

A look through TRU's data shows that what teens don't like about school could fill a standard-size yellow school bus. Young people's complaints range from classwork to social pressures to simply having to drag themselves there! But three things stand out: getting up early, taking tests, and doing homework.

Teens' need for (and love of) sleep shouldn't be underestimated. This age group, after all, is increasingly sleep-deprived. This may be hard for some parents to believe: many live in wonder that anyone can sleep as much as a teen. But appearances can be deceiving. Based on their accelerated rate of development, teenagers need more sleep than younger children. But they invariably stay up later than younger kids—and even most adults. In fact, a growing body of scientific evidence is proving the obvious: teens are naturally predisposed to different hours than the rest of us. Researchers are increasingly convinced that the hours teens keep—late to bed, late to rise—are biologically hard-wired into them. They claim the biological clock shifts to a late-night cycle with the onset of puberty, although no one seems to know why. Interestingly, some progressive school districts around the country—including those in Dallas and Minneapolis—are pushing high-school start times back to help ensure that teens will be awake during first period. What's keeping the rest of the country from following this lead? Stubbornness may play a small part, but more important is the logistical problems such an endeavor entails. Typically, the same bus that drops students off at high school then goes back to pick up elementary-aged students. Allowing teens to start the day later generally means increased transportation costs. Additionally, pushing back the high school schedule often disrupts athletic and other extracurricular activities.

An organization no less hard-nosed than the U.S. Navy is taking note. The Navy's only boot camp recently made the bold decision to delay reveille, coming to terms with the fact that—no matter how hard officers push them—young recruits are going to be more trainable when they're awake. Drill sergeants at the Great Lakes Naval Training Center in North Chicago, Illinois, recently changed the time at which they rouse the newly uniformed. Although the Army and Marine Corps still rise at 4 a.m., naval recruits get to sleep until 6 a.m. Boot camp still tries to impart discipline and mental toughness to recruits, but officials at Great Lakes believe the Navy doesn't gain anything from forcing teens to function during hours unnatural to them. According to officers, the experience is the most intense of their lives, and they "want them awake for it."

Here's a fun experiment: ask a teenager how he or she spends a weekend day, and the typical response is "Well . . . I get up . . . ," and then the teen stops. Teens long for sleep and devote weekend mornings (and oftentimes afternoons) to this passion. In the data on what teens dislike about school, more than twice as many cite getting up early as peer pressure, grades, teachers, classes or even the (dreaded) school administration.

Another TRU measure shows that grades are teens' biggest everyday worry. For a variety of reasons, teens do care about getting good grades.

The reasons range from improving their chances to get into a college of their choice, to placating their parents, to maintaining athletic eligibility, to simply making their life easier. Tests are a variation of grades. Having to study for tests is as distasteful to teens as tests themselves. When netted together, 74 percent of teens cite tests or homework as what they don't like about school.

Although being with friends is teens' favorite thing about school, the pressures surrounding peer relationships can make school unpleasant and even stressful for some. When netted together, 40 percent of teens cite peer pressure, gossip, other students, a boyfriend/girlfriend, or one or more friends as things they dislike about school.

What's Big at School

If you think schools today are an unrecognizable mix of educational fads and new-fangled computer clubs, think again. We recently posed the question, "What's big at your school?" to our national sample of teens. Despite the 1950s-era images athletics and school dances evoke, these are still some of the most popular school activities.

More teens name sports as dominant at their school than any other activity. Sixty-one percent of teens mention sports, making it the only answer agreed upon by the majority of respondents. (Note: these figures may seem a little low; here's why: in an attempt to determine only the most relevant activities, we restricted teens to two choices. Had they been allowed to choose all that apply, no doubt all scores would be higher).

The appeal of sports is hardly surprising. In addition to the physical benefits, joining an athletic team encourages camaraderie, effectively expanding a teen's social network. Then there's the irresistible possibility of honor and glory in the eyes of one's peers. And who doesn't want that?

Two other sports-related responses score highly, as well. Forty-five percent of respondents say school spirit is really "big." Although spirit exists independently of sports, it is often most evident when students are

What's Big at School

School sports is big for most teens, followed by prom and school spirit.

(percent of teens responding when asked, "Which of the following are really big at your school?" by gender)

	total	female	male
School sports	61%	59%	62%
Prom	45	50	41
School spirit	45	49	42
Homecoming	39	43	36
Competition	38	37	39
Joining school clubs and organizations	35	40	30
Drugs	33	32	33
Cheating	30	30	30
Skipping school	29	29	28
Smoking cigarettes	28	29	26
Senior ditch day	27	30	25
College prep	24	23	24
Performing arts	20	23	16
Great assemblies	14	14	13
Charity drives	13	14	12
Getting involved in causes	13	15	11
Safety precautions	12	13	12
Gangs or violence	12	10	14
Racism	11	10	12
Sadie Hawkins or turnabout	6	6	6
Apathy	5	4	5

Source: The TRU Study, Teenage Research Unlimited, Inc.

cheering for their team (or against an opponent). Another 38 percent say competition is a big factor at school. This figure likely includes students thinking of their athletic accomplishments as well as college-bound teens feverishly engaged in competition for the best grades

In selecting a single event that outshines all others, prom is it (although homecoming is also big—for many schools it has become the fall version of prom). These events provide the opportunity to fulfill two important teen desires. Aspirationally, teens love the feeling of maturity that a formal occasion confers upon them. And, from a purely youthful standpoint, they enjoy parading around with their friends in front of the entire school "society." The actual dance itself isn't the draw. It's the events surrounding prom (and, for many, homecoming as well) that get most teens excited.

One look through the prom issues of teen-girl magazines will tell you the importance of getting the right dress. And, in marked contrast to the rest of their school experience, this is one kind of homework that teen girls can't get enough of: TRU research indicates that prom shopping with their friends is one of the most anticipated elements of the entire process. For guys, on the other hand, prom is about the postparty, where teens celebrate with friends—typically without adult supervision.

Perhaps surprisingly, teens also say that joining school clubs and organizations is a popular activity at school. Gone are the days when joining a club meant plotting chess moves with other socially stunted bookworms (just kidding, save your angry letters!). The proliferation of different after-school clubs now lets teens gather to discuss a variety of topics, including academic achievement, acting, automobiles, card games, cooking, ethnic heritage, hackey sack, religion, and issues of sexuality.

One-third of teens say that drugs play a sizable role in their school, a percentage that beats out other vices including cheating (30 percent), skipping school (29 percent), smoking cigarettes (28 percent), gangs and violence (12 percent), and racism (11 percent). Fittingly, teens responded with complete disinterest to the subject of apathy (5 percent), which they relegated to the bottom of the list.

As discussed in this and other chapters, 16- and 17-year-olds are the "most teen" of all teenagers. When listing what's "big" at their school, those in this age range respond more enthusiastically than their younger or older peers. Their higher involvement stems from this age group's greater social connection—they are the teens most invested in high-school life. Most have recently obtained their driver's license and are exploring their newfound freedom. Most also are now upper classmen in high school, and they're about as popular as they're likely to get. For many students of this age, it's good to be a teen! As a marketer, it's wise to target your message a few years older to leverage teens' aspirations (see Chapter 2 for more on age aspiration), but you'll likely find some of your most enthusiastic customers in the 16- and 17-year-old age bracket. Remember, for age-specific messages, you likely won't find a more appealing image around which to base your message than that of sports or prom.

"Labeling" at School

There's a strict social hierarchy that exists in teen communities—most notably in school. Though the specific groups that exist in each school vary, there's a commonality of structure. It's this structure that's replicated to a strong degree in TRU's Teen/Types segmentation model (see Chapter 4).

When we ask teens to talk about cliques and labels, they sometimes do so reluctantly and almost always emotionally. Those who are on the higher rungs of the teen social ladder are, predictably, more forthcoming in discussing this dynamic. Those who are struggling socially, on the other hand, prefer to focus on other parts of their lives. We decided to quantify this issue in our syndicated study so as to understand the degree to which labeling exists and how it affects teens. Although respondents strongly maintain that these labeled groups are "stupid" and unimportant, they admit that they exist in their school and can cause a lot of stress. There are

How Teens Feel About Labeling

Although teens don't like labeling, few say there is no labeling at their school.

(percent of teens responding when asked, "At most schools, people are 'labeled' into different groups—like jocks, nerds, and preps. Which of the following statements do you agree with about these groups?")

Once you're labeled as part of a group, it's hard to lose the label	64%
Being labeled in a group that you don't want to be in can cause a lot of stress	61
These groups just happen, they're a part of a school	60
These groups are stupid	58
Not being in a group that you want to be in can cause a lot of stress	45
These groups make being at school hard	38
These groups are important	13
People in my school aren't labeled	13

Source: The TRU Study, Teenage Research Unlimited, Inc.

two ways in which labeling can be stressful: 1) being unable to gain membership in a desired group because you're pegged as being "unworthy", and 2) being labeled as a member of an undesirable group. It is the latter experience that is more stressful to teens.

Teens grudgingly accept that these groups are part of school life—that they just happen and can't be avoided. Only 13 percent say these groups don't exist in their school. More than one-third of teens say the groups make going to school more difficult. Still, in qualitative research, teens say they have developed strategies for dealing with it. Further, some teens say they've learned to turn a deaf ear to this part of their life. As long as they have outside interests and a friend or two, high school social life doesn't have to be as painful or all consuming as it is sometimes made out to be.

Nonetheless, our data confirm that school can be harsh, populated by a variety of socially distinct groups, some of which are thought of highly and others not so. For better or for worse, teens tend to be at least as materialistic and brand-conscious as the general population: Teens are just as likely to abandon a brand if they believe it is connected with an unpopular group as they are to embrace a brand favored by their school's elite.

Marketers must walk a fine line here. Although it may be possible to prey on teen insecurities by pitching your product as a badge item that will give socially awkward teens entry into the clique of their choice, doing so is unwise. Totally apart from the dubious social message involved in such an undertaking, these ploys for the most part work only on the very young—and often only once. After eager teens have made their purchase, it doesn't take long before they realize that the new shirt didn't magically vault them into the next social caste. In the wake of this letdown, they're likely to feel worse about themselves and dramatically worse about your brand. After all, you made a deal with them and they held up their end. The long and the short of it is that your brand lied, and they're unlikely to trust it again.

This isn't to say that teen concerns about image and social standing don't sell products. In truth (and much to the chagrin of parents and social scientists alike) vast quantities of goods are sold precisely because of these factors. Trying to fit in is a natural reaction to the turmoil and insecurity of the teen years. Wise brand managers should be thankful for any boost in sales they receive from the whims of teen fashion. At the same time, however, they should not chase trends that don't logically fit their brand or try to convince the target that the brand is something it's not.

Study Time

Of all the annoyances that pervade teen life, homework is the most irksome. Still, except for a small percentage who report never doing homework, teens manage to fit it in somehow. An understanding of how and when teens study can help marketers determine when best to reach them—when they're free of school work—and give them a richer sense of one of the basics of teen life.

The word "homework" is something of a misnomer because the most common venue for completing homework is school—either during a free period (38 percent) or in class (34 percent). The big benefit to teens of getting their homework done at school is that they have more free time *after* school. Two other benefits are being able to collaborate with classmates and not having to lug heavy textbooks home.

Other common times for completing homework are right after school (35 percent), after dinner (36 percent), or late at night (29 percent). In fact, it's not unusual for high-achieving teens to finish homework in the wee hours of the morning when most other students are asleep. Some teens tell us they like to do homework at home where they can relax, raid the fridge, and tune into the background media of their choice.

Not surprisingly, teens are happiest when their homework doesn't spill into weekend time. Almost one-quarter of them report "never" doing homework on weekends.

When Teens Do Their Homework

Many teens do their homework at school.

*(percent of teens responding when asked, "When do you
mostly do your homework?" by gender)*

	females	males
Weekday homework		
Free period at school	41%	34%
After dinner	39	32
Right after school	42	28
During class	34	34
Really late at night	30	27
In the morning before school	13	13
Never	2	7
Weekend homework		
During the day	41	29
During the night	45	39
Never	19	29

Source: The TRU Study, Teenage Research Unlimited, Inc.

What Else Is Going On When Teens Do Their Homework

Most teens listen to music or have the TV on while they do their homework.

(percent of teens responding when asked, "What's going on while you do homework?")

Music is playing	67%
TV is on	50
You're with family	44
You're on the phone	27
You're online	25
You're with friends	21

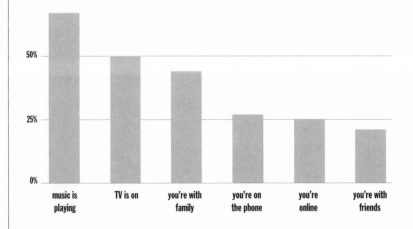

Source: The TRU Study, Teenage Research Unlimited, Inc.

Girls are more conscientious about doing their homework—significantly fewer girls than guys say they never complete their at-home assignments. In fact, a review of many of TRU's school measures shows the same pattern: girls are more serious about school, spend more time studying, and exert more pressure on themselves to do well.

As much as teens protest, homework is an inevitable part of academic life. And because teens would rather spend their time writing e-mails to friends than writing essays, they've developed homework-tackling strategies. Not only do many teens crack the books during school time (so they can avoid finishing it at home), they explain that the noise of school around them makes the drudgery more tolerable. Although teens may not mind a few distractions while doing their homework, they cannot focus on marketing messages (nor should they!) during their studies. Instead of devising ways to reach studying teens, consider a different tactic. Create messages that empathize with teens and acknowledge that homework can be annoying. Offer them products and services that help them manage their workload and reward them for completing it. If you're not in the business of manufacturing loose-leaf binders, don't worry: a growing number of marketers are offering discounts and incentives to students who perform well in school. This tactic will not only boost sales, it should earn high marks from parents, teachers, and school administrators as well.

Classroom Behavior

An understanding of what school means to teens (and what it could mean to you) would be incomplete without knowing what teens do in class. Some of our Trendwatch panelists amaze us with their stories of what really goes on (their tales make *Fast Times at Ridgemont High* pale in comparison). Naturally, we decided to quantify what teens do when they're sitting in class. We presented our national sample of teens with a list of in-class behaviors (developed collaboratively with our Trendwatch panelists) and asked them to choose the three activities in which they participate the most.

Teen Classroom Behavior

Most teens claim to pay attention in class, but many also talk to friends and daydream.

(percent of teens responding when asked, "During a typical class at school, which three of the following do you do most often?")

Pay attention	63%
Talk to/write notes to friends	41
Fantasize/dream	38
Look at the clock	37
Do homework/study for another class	33
Doodle	23
Sleep	18
Goof off	14
Nervous habit (bite nails, tap pen on desk)	14
Eat/drink	9
Read a book or magazine	7
Make hand gestures to friends	3
Play calculator games	3

Source: The TRU Study, Teenage Research Unlimited, Inc.

A quick look at the accompanying table is both gratifying and misleading: the number-one in-class activity (by a whopping 20-point margin) is "paying attention to what's being taught." Closer examination, though, reveals that more than one-third of respondents do not name "paying attention" as even one of their three most frequent classroom activities. In fact, when combined, far more respondents report participating in a noncurricular activity (from passing notes and looking at the clock to sleeping and goofing off) than paying attention.

A look at what's high on teens' list of frequent classroom behaviors shows that teachers are faced with stiff competition. Being social creatures, teens can't resist communicating with friends—whether by passing notes or talking. And, these days—with more schools allowing cell phones in class—teens are also text-messaging one another. Teens are adept at shutting out classroom instruction. When a teacher is lecturing, chances are most students aren't fully listening—instead, they're thinking about next period, the game after school, the weekend's festivities, or sex (you heard it here first!). So, as a marketer, if you feel challenged in your quest to "break through the clutter" in gaining teens' attention, consider how tough it would be if your "communications" budget bought you only a lesson plan, a few dry-erase markers, and a textbook from the 1970s!

As we've stressed throughout this chapter, the inclusion of school scenes in teen-directed advertising can work. Remember, school is an easily relatable backdrop for teen life and is the center of their social world. Remembering teens' ambivalence toward school, however, it's wise to focus on the funny and the familiar.

Rating Their School

Over the past few years, we've found teen opinions about their schools and teachers becoming increasingly negative. One of the original TRU measures from 1983 asked teens to identify their heroes. Back then, parents and teachers topped the list. Parents rate as highly today as ever before.

But, teens' opinions of their teachers and the quality of their education have dropped. For example, over the past few years, education has declined as one of the issues about which teens care most strongly. To better understand this trend, we developed a measure in which teens rate their schools across a host of attributes. The results show that teens give a less than ringing endorsement of their teachers and schools. Teens grade schools more highly for having high-tech equipment and offering a variety of clubs than for employing caring teachers and having strong security measures.

More than half (57 percent) of teens agree that their school offers a high-quality education, but only about one fourth (27 percent) agree strongly with this statement. More than four in ten (43 percent) don't feel they are getting a quality education. Teens rate their fellow students the lowest of any measured item: only 12 percent strongly believe other students care about grades.

On which measures do teens rate their schools the highest? More than one-third (34 percent) strongly believe their school offers a variety of clubs and extracurricular activities, and 30 percent say their school has become high-tech, offering Internet access and computer labs.

The findings are similar regardless of demographic segment: teens of both genders and all age and ethnic groups rate their schools about the same.

There are more opportunities than ever before for businesses to sponsor educational programs. Our data show that teens feel the quality of their education is lacking. By developing sponsored educational curricula, advertisers can demonstrate their willingness to fulfill a highly relevant, valued need—not only to the school and community, but also to students themselves.

Implications of Reaching Teens at Home and School

Every now and then, we ask teens to chart their lives, breaking the whole into parts. More often than not, they break their life into three parts: 1)

How Teens Rate Their School

Barely half of students think their school has teachers and counselors who really care.

(percent of teens who "strongly" or "somewhat" agree with each statement)

Offers a variety of clubs and after-school activities	58%
Provides an overall high-quality education	57
Offers students good preparation for the future	55
Is high-tech (Internet access, computers, etc.)	54
Has teachers and counselors that really care	51
Has good security against violent acts	43
Is a place where most students really care about their grades	32

Source: The TRU Study, Teenage Research Unlimited, Inc.

their own time (for most, comprised of friends and fun), 2) family time, and 3) school.

The smart marketer looks for creative ways—via media, promotions, and distribution channels—to reach teens at play, at home, and at school. Because teens are barraged by marketing messages, it becomes increasingly important for marketers to find new ways and new places to reach them. (See Chapter 8 for reaching teens at play—on their own turf.)

Home is the primary (but not the only!) place to reach teens with traditional media, especially TV, magazines, newspapers, and the Internet. Teens also listen to radio at home, but probably spend more time tuned into radio when they're on the go. And, of course, home is where most direct-marketing programs reach teens. In fact, TRU's through-the-mail methodological design gets our syndicated study a strong response rate, in part because teens rarely get mail—and when they do, they pay attention to it.

Whereas the best media for reaching teens at home are mostly the traditional ones, the best media for reaching them at school are a combination of traditional media and sponsorship opportunities. The traditional media include in-school advertising through both national vehicles, such as Channel One, Scholastic, and GymBoards, and local ones such as school newspapers, radio stations, and even Web sites at some schools. There are a number of additional ways to give your brand prominence at school, including vending machines, cafeteria lines, scoreboard signage, and sponsorship of curricular programs and extracurricular activities.

One successful place-based teen marketer is Richard Ellis, president of 12 to 20, a firm specializing in events and promotions that reach teens where they work, learn, and play. His programs have been adept at offering partnership opportunities at various levels, thereby allowing smaller brands a chance to get in on the action (as well as to benefit from the halo of "cool" associated with larger brands whose budgets allow them primary-sponsorship opportunities). Because Ellis grew up in the record business, his programs typically have a strong music component—from giveaways of new CD singles or downloadable MP3s to mall tours featuring up-and-coming acts. And, when music is front and center, teens listen. One of Ellis's recent mall tours included a seeming hodge-podge of sponsors—headed by Pepsi and Ford, but also including Arista (who supplied the music talent that drew the teens), Do Something (a Web-based teen volunteer advocate) and even the current "Anti-Drug" campaign from the Office of National Drug Control Policy (handled particularly well to get across its message in a creative, inclusive manner—no preaching there!). The presence of Do Something and the ONDCP not only helped decommercialize the program, their participation allowed it to expand into schools. The variety offered by the range of sponsors—all of whom 12 to 20 guided in creating an engaging presence—makes these tours real "events."

The power of school-based marketing is especially clear in a recent soft-drink case study. Although more and more schools are banning soft-drink vending machines (mostly because of all the attention being given the alarming rate of obesity in kids and teens), schools remain a fertile ground for cultivating a grassroots campaign. Assuming you've done your research and are confident of your product's teen appeal, placing it with a hand- picked group of Influencer teens within the school environment gives it an unparalleled opportunity for visibility. The viral nature of peer broadcasting can be invaluable. Being able to place your product within a segment of society known for being the first to try something new is so much the better

When Mountain Dew Code Red first came out, the school buzz was incredible. Pepsi leveraged its strong in-school distribution, and Code Red's awareness and trial grew rapidly. But Pepsi didn't stop there. Understanding the value of being where teens are, free samples of Code Red showed up at beaches, amusement parks, and almost every variety of summer festivals populated by teens.

By following teens during their day, you are employing a pervasiveness strategy. And that's the key. Find ways to appropriately pervade your target's life. One of the most successful examples of a pervasiveness media strategy is fostered, unfortunately, by tobacco companies, which have a vested interest in recruiting teens before their current customers die off. From adorning t-shirts, jackets, and other teen gear with logos to placing their products in movies, the tobacco companies have successfully pervaded teens' lives. The same sort of pervasiveness strategy can work against tobacco companies, as well. In the media strategy for California's antitobacco campaign, Bruce Silverman, now president of the Los Angeles office of ad agency Wongdoody, followed a pervasiveness model. As a principal architect of California's antitobacco campaign while president of Asher Gould, Bruce mimicked the tobacco industry's own strategy by seeding antitobacco messages and icons where teens commonly see those from tobacco companies. With an antitobacco pervasiveness strategy, the California campaign successfully countered the tobacco companies' efforts.

Marketers of all types of consumer products can learn from such a strategy and creatively (and appropriately) pervade teens' lives, reaching teens at home and at school. Chapter 8 discusses how brands can connect with teens when they are away from home and school, supporting their hobbies and interests and becoming a part of teen life.

Chapter 7

Teens and Friends

Some adults believe the most important part of the teen experience is the painful, awkward, or generally unpleasant "life lessons" that are supposed to lay the foundation for adulthood. Most teens, however, find this idea far-fetched, to say the least. Ask just about any teenager what best characterizes his or her lifestage, and the answer will be the opportunity to kick back, hang out with friends, and actually enjoy youth.

Having fun is also about having a wide variety of activities to choose from and, for many teens, a wide web of friends with eclectic character traits. Teens seem to revel in collecting friends who bring something new to the party (figuratively, and perhaps literally).

To teens, friends serve as colleagues, conspirators, and confidants. Most teens feel that great times aren't really all that great without someone with whom to share the experience.

Teens also depend on their friends during difficult or uncertain times. To explore this facet of teen friendship, we have conducted several projects in which we've asked our Trendwatch panelists to describe their friendships in writing: we've found that for certain topics, a diary format elicits more introspection among teens. Many panelists write passionately about friends with whom they can safely trade secrets in exchange for empathy and advice.

In fact, few things have a greater impact on how individuals feel about their teen years (both at the time and looking back) than the friendships they form. It's no surprise, then, that the Influencers—the Teen/Type blessed with confidence, a natural gift for socialization, and lots of friends—are among the happiest and most optimistic of teens. (Influencers and Edge teens each make up approximately half of our Trendwatch panel.)

Even teens who don't boast a circle of friends quite as large or as varied as Influencers still find a handful of close friends with whom they share common interests. By definition, Passive teens have less patience than their peers for the fickle and complex world of teen friends. In fact, these teens find the all-consuming teen quest for popularity confusing, somewhat vacant, and not really worth the effort. Still, to label them anti-social would be to make a grievous mistake; they like nothing better than to hang out with likeminded peers, whether studying, sharing in a hobby, or making plans for the future—when they plan to employ the very same Influencers that so vex them today!

In fact, regardless of their demographic, social, and economic differences, teens tell us there's nothing they would rather do than hang out with friends: 87 percent of teens get together with friends at least one night per week, according to The TRU Study. That number is meaningful on its own, but a deeper look reveals important wrinkles.

Rebellious, experiential Edge teens are able to see their friends more frequently than any other Teen/Type—possibly owing to more permissive parents or a knack for getting away with things. Whatever the reason, 93 percent of Edge teens say they get together with friends at least once each week. However, the popular, socially oriented Influencers are the undisputed champions of quality time: they see their friends an average of four nights per week, and 18 percent report getting together with friends every night. Conformers, the mainstream masses that make up the bulk of teen society, are quite sociable, as well—90 percent visit with friends at least once a week, and they average three nights a week with friends. Passive teens, in general, would like to be more sociable than they are. Unfortunately, they often find their circle of friends limited. But if these teens find it difficult to carve out a place for themselves in the larger teen society, they typically still have friends they can count on to pass the time. On average, 80 percent of Passive teens get together with friends at least once a week.

There's a distinction to make about the importance of friends, however. Although teens tell us that—all things being equal—they would rather spend time with friends than with family, they usually note that friends are the second most important aspect of their lives. Friends are a great way to pass the idle hours, teens say. But their families have displayed a level of support and dedication that most friends—even the closest ones—can't hope to match. Friends are undoubtedly more fun to joke around and spend lots of time with, but most teens recognize that their families have an obligation to them and they feel similarly obligated to their families. In certain cases, teens report that their best friends are almost "like family," but this description tends to apply only to the closest, most loyal members of a teen's circle of friends. Any individual vying for such stature should be prepared to work for it over a matter of years.

Where Friendships Form

A teen's ability to make friends depends on a complex variety of factors, including—but not limited to—natural confidence and sociability, personality and sense of humor, interests and hobbies, position within the greater community, and, to some extent, physical appearance. (Parental influence, of course, plays a huge role in all of these factors, so it should come as no surprise that parental rules and attitudes may also play a part in the kinds of friends with whom teens associate.)

Few teens excel at all of the above factors, but far fewer excel at none. In general, young people learn to use their strengths to their advantage when trying to convert strangers into friends—for instance, masking a lack of confidence with a sense of humor.

So, assuming that the vast majority of teens are able to meet an acceptable cadre of friends, the question remains: where do they meet them?

Proximity, more than fate, brings them together. Because teens spend more time at school than in any other social situation, it comes as little surprise that school is where most teens meet their closest friends. According

Where Teens Meet Their Friends

Most teens met their closest friends in class.

*(percent of teens responding when asked, "Where did you
first meet your closest friends?" by gender)*

	total	female	male
In class	64%	69%	59%
In the neighborhood	26	24	28
In school sports	16	13	18
At a school activity	14	15	14
Through family friends	10	12	9
At a church	9	9	9
On a nonschool sports team	6	5	7
At a job	5	4	5
At a youth group	5	5	5
At summer camp	4	4	4
On the Internet	2	2	2

Source: The TRU Study, Teenage Research Unlimited, Inc.

to The TRU Study, 64 percent of teens meet friends in classes they share, 16 percent claim school sports as the main impetus for new friendships, and 14 percent say the connection happens at another school activity. On the other hand, 26 percent meet friends in their neighborhoods, 10 percent through family friends, and 9 percent at religious services or functions. Smaller percentages list meeting people at a job, a youth group, a summer camp, or the Internet. And although teens frequently go online to chat with existing friends, most tell us they avoid talking to strangers online. If they do, they tend not to develop a close relationship with those whom they might casually "meet" in a chat room or by posting to an electronic bulletin board. In many cases, this predilection is based on safety-conscious parents who have warned their teenaged children that the Internet is rife with dangerous people. However, other teens have told us that it's just too easy for others to lie—about age, gender, interests, appearance, whatever—on the Internet. These teens note that meeting new people through actual human interaction is much more reliable and desirable.

Not surprisingly, demographics play a role in determining where teens first establish friendships. More girls than boys say they meet their best friends in class, while more guys cite their neighborhood and sports teams as sources of friends. Significantly more young teens meet their friends at summer camp, while older teens more often befriend coworkers.

Although we would never discount the importance of a first impression, we find it interesting that teens don't always tenaciously stick to their snap judgments. Some tell us they hated their best friend when they first met him or her!

Why Friendships Form

For a teen friendship to take root, a common bond must form—otherwise, teens tell us, there's just no reason to go through the trouble of getting to know someone new. And, for teens, attempting to form a new friendship implies risk. Theoretically, anyone has the opportunity to befriend anyone else. But teens frequently find themselves surrounded with a clique, the members of which often have similar opinions, interests, or backgrounds. These similarities may not always be glaringly obvious (race or gender), or even easily distinguishable (socioeconomic status, religion). But they are there—even if it's something as simple as music preference or style of dress. After all, teens point out that jocks hang out with other jocks because they consider it preferable to "slumming" with the chess club kids!

One of the most interesting findings we've come upon is that all teens seem to admire and look up to their closest friends in some way. Be careful in how you interpret this, however. It doesn't mean that teens believe their friends are better than they are. It's simply a recognition of the other person's strengths and an affirmation that teens feel everyone benefits when they surround themselves with a group of people with varied talents.

Far and away teens' most widely regarded attribute for close friends is simply "having a good personality," and this characteristic seems to be the quickest way for teens to judge compatibility with their peers. Note that teens have wildly divergent ideas of what constitutes an engaging personality—some look for a sense of humor, others demand intelligence. Many teens enthusiastically describe friends as wild, crazy, goofy, or flirtatious. But others look for more subdued companions, describing friends as laid back, respectful, loyal, and sweet. One of the most important litmus tests of a successful teen friendship seems to be having things in common. Although teens love having a broad variety of friends, many seem most comfortable with a best friend whose outlook and background are similar to their own. As one girl from Denver recently explained of her best friend, "We relate to each other, meaning we think alike and have the same style in clothes."

The teen years are a tumultuous time, and teens may be forgiven for trying to reduce some of the drama in their lives. Teens often say they seek out people they believe will be trustworthy. After all, they reason, what hurts more than being betrayed by someone close to you? Teens frequently describe their close friends as individuals in whom they can confide anything—including the kinds of problems they would never discuss with parents. Similarly, they tell us friends who have survived tough times and those who have proven themselves willing to look out for one another are much more valuable than those who simply provide occasional entertainment.

The rarest form of praise from teens—and perhaps the most heartfelt—is the description of a friend as being "like a member of the family." This kind of closeness demonstrates that the friendship has been tested, and that it has passed that test. In many cases, the analogy is rather literal, with other family members—most notably parents—giving the individual their seal of approval as well. In these cases, it's not uncommon for friends to use each other's homes (and their contents) interchangeably with their own.

TRU has spent a great deal of time conducting qualitative research, including a number of ethnographic studies, to understand the intricate relationships between teens and their friends. In addition to continually including new quantitative questions focusing on friends in each wave of our syndicated study, we've been commissioned on numerous occasions to delve into this area for the benefit of our custom-research clients. Typically, these studies have shed light into how friendships form and evolve, including how teens communicate with each other within and outside of established friend groups. These learnings have provided the strategic insight for a number of advertising campaigns as well as new-product launches. Overall, we've been struck by the similarity of responses on the subject of friendship, regardless of whom we interview or where they live. With remarkable consistency, teens imagine their friendships as akin to the concentric circles on a dartboard.

Best Friends

The center circle, or bullseye, represents a teen's best friend. Obviously, a best friend serves as a teen's companion of choice for all types of leisure-time pursuits. But he or she also fills an important role when life isn't quite as easy or carefree, serving as a confidant when teens face difficult decisions, stressful situations, and an uncertain future.

Teens regularly tell us that best friends are indispensable for a variety of reasons. First and foremost, close friends understand what it's like to be a teen, whereas teens tend to believe their parents rely on outdated—and sometimes faulty—recollections about their own teen years. And unlike parents, best friends don't spend much time teaching lessons or determining effective punishments. Rather, young people tell us their best friends work with them to try to solve the problem at hand—no judgment, no guilt. Of course, it's a matter of perspective: many parents would argue that such a situation is nothing more than the blind leading the blind.

Many teens explain that they typically have one best friend (in some cases, two or three) in whom they can truly confide. Although a guy and a girl sometimes acknowledge each other as best friends, the realities of teen life conspire against such arrangements. It generally takes a great deal of shared history for teens to reach the position of best friends, and younger guys and girls typically don't have this shared history because they mature at dramatically different paces. To put it plainly, younger teen boys and girls generally don't get along well enough to make a deep friendship viable. Older teens, on the other hand, often find their increasingly nonplatonic interest in the opposite sex can spell doom for a deep and significant male-female friendship.

The biggest exception to this rule: older teens frequently explain that a romantic interest may become a best friend. (This seems more common among girls than guys.) Although many teens claim the friendship that develops out of a romantic relationship seems stronger than that of a platonic best friend, these new friendships rarely take the place of a teen's original best friend.

Secondary Friends

The next circle out from the bullseye represents teens' secondary friends, usually the group (or clique) they run with. Still very close to the center, these friends haven't earned the same trust as the best friend, but they do boast a high level of access.

Although friends in this group usually share many things in common, including interest in specific sports, music, or activities, teens often note that each group member contributes something unique to the dynamic. Sometimes teens even admit that group members—and even outsiders— can identify the part each member plays in the clique (e.g., "the smart girl," "the funny guy," or "the partier").

Almost by definition, teens see the individuals in this circle on a regular basis. In fact, it can be proximity that places some friends at this level. It's worth noting that not everyone in this circle enjoys the same level of regard, because teens don't necessarily always like everyone in their clique. Typically, they get along well as a group, but teens have told us that some individuals (usually friends of friends) interact like oil and water. Although teens might consider hanging out alone with preferred members of this inner circle, they likely also have at least one or two individuals with whom they would prefer not to deal on an up-close and personal basis.

Other Friends and Acquaintances

The outer circle (or circles, depending upon how many strata a particular teen can distinguish) represents lesser friends, friends outside their imme- diate group, and acquaintances. Members of this group may include class- mates, kids from the neighborhood, or coworkers at a part-time job. These individuals aren't typically a teen's first choice for companionship, but they can be useful as a spur-of-the-moment distraction or as a "Plan B" if an- other option falls through.

In certain cases, teens describe having a friend or two who do not fit neatly into their various groups of friends. Although a teen might genuinely like such a friend, this individual's position outside their defined friend-group means that most of the time the two spend together takes place separately from their other friends. Fair or not, this perceived need for distance or discretion is often enough to place such individuals in an outer circle. As some teens have told us, there's just not enough time to go around. Spending time with friends from outside the core group takes time away from their best friends. It seems that part of being a teenager is lacking either the wisdom or the savvy to maintain and manage different types of friendships.

Interestingly (and perhaps counter-intuitively), peer pressure seems to emanate mainly from the outer circles. TRU research has found that peer pressure is based on internal fears and insecurities more than direct pressure from outside parties, but teens still look to the larger teen population when deciding how best to fit in. Although the opinions of closer friends are arguably more important to teenagers, these close friends are also likely to be more forgiving and less judgmental of quirks than passing acquaintances. Individuals from the outer circle also tend to be more prone to spreading potentially hurtful or embarrassing gossip. (As an aside, TRU's qualitative research has repeatedly documented teens' ingrained mistrust of unfamiliar peers. Prior to our warm-ups in qualitative sessions, it's not atypical for our moderators to find a room full of teen guys in the midst of self-conscious posturing. Girls simply tend to cross their arms and make guarded small talk.)

Comparing differences among demographic groups, younger teens associate with larger groups of friends. Younger teens' feelings of self-worth are tied more closely to external barometers (such as hanging out with or being one of the "cool" people). Consequently, the social circles of younger teens often emphasize quantity over quality. A change occurs as teens mature, however; older teens often describe smaller friendship circles. As teens graduate from high school and enter college or start full-time work, the transformation becomes even more striking. The oldest teens and young adults may still have an extended network of friends, but they prefer to concentrate on closer, more meaningful relationships.

Duration of Friendships

Friendships during the teen years are particularly emotional. Several factors unique to this lifestage make teen friendships more intense—and often more volatile—than relationships among adults. First, the entire teen experience is something akin to sensory overload. The highs seem higher, the lows lower, and every emotion—from boredom to ecstasy—takes on an added urgency that would quickly exhaust most adults. What's more, teens' limited experience with friendship exaggerates the highs and lows. The result, to paraphrase an old nursery rhyme, is that when friendships are good, they're very, very good. But when they go bad, they're horrid.

When we ask teens to sum up their closest friendships, most suggest that their relationship with their best friend is the kind of true friendship that withstands all challenges and lasts forever. Their close friends offer a sense of permanence, stability, and loyalty that they can't imagine being without, they say. Some even tell us that their closest friends offer a level of love and support that even some family members can't give.

Unfortunately, not all of these bonds survive the test of time. Some teens describe friendships that have withered away, or worse, crashed and burned. Apart from the obvious culprits (arguments, changing interests), quintessential teen issues such as a nasty breakup or a family-mandated move may also doom a friendship.

The most striking demographic difference in regard to this subject is age-based. Younger teens place greater stock in new friendships than do their older counterparts, who have accumulated more relationships and describe some friendships as transient or cyclical—a view most younger teens reject. One interesting finding is that fast friends sometimes meet fast ends. Stories abound of teens developing an instant rapport with a peer who would eventually become a lifelong friend. But teens also repeatedly tell us that's the exception rather than the rule. They say their closest friendships need time to mature because relationships that grow over time normally give each party the opportunity to test limits and gauge loyalty.

In fact, some of the most disastrous friendships seem to follow a pattern, beginning when an individual from a teen's outer circle of friends rises quickly from relative obscurity. The reason for this sudden "promotion" is less important than the result. In relatively short order, the two become nearly inseparable—they may even refer to one another as best friends. But in their rush to build the friendship, they often find they didn't spend enough time on the foundation. When cracks develop, they require quick and careful attention or the whole thing is liable to collapse, often in rather spectacular fashion.

The fact that teens frequently point to failed friendships as a valuable learning experience while simultaneously pronouncing their current crop of friends "the real deal" is another example of this age group's boundless optimism. That positive attitude is one of the things we appreciate most about teens!

Friends as Influences

Teens have, seemingly without intent or realization, developed one of the most effective trend-distribution networks on Earth. The beauty of their system is in its simplicity. No one has to purchase a subscription to anything, there are no complicated telephone trees, and an individual's opportunity for involvement is limited only by his or her personal interest. It's also the most democratic model yet devised; the masses decide for themselves which styles thrive and which linger on the clearance racks.

This ingenious system, when distilled to its essence, is nothing more than teens spreading trends by word of mouth and co-opting the looks they see on others. Still, the impact is huge.

Nearly two-thirds of teens claim they are responsible for their fashion sense. And, given that they are likely choosing their own clothes, such a response is not surprising. Still, watching groups of teens in their natural element belies this statement: cliques share remarkably similar senses of style.

In fact, more than half of teens report that they get ideas about what to wear from their friends. There's a sizable discrepancy between the percentage of girls (61 percent) and guys (50 percent) who admit taking cues from their friends. This difference is easily explained. Girls are generally more fashion-conscious than their male counterparts (although guys have made significant gains in recent years). Both girls and guys carefully monitor their friends' clothing choices, but girls often feel freer to experiment: they frequently engage in a bit of friendly competition over who has the newest look or best accessories. Guys, on the other hand, are historically more conservative with their clothing choices. While girls may subconsciously push each other to update their wardrobes, many guys actually seem to hold each other back—they don't want their peers making fun of them, so they stick to the tried and true.

Fashion is one of the easiest ways to observe teens' influence on one another, but it's far from the only one. In fact, respondents to our syndicated study suggest it isn't even the most important.

The TRU Study reveals that teens believe they influence their friends in a variety of ways. Forty percent say they have a role in shaping their group's personality and attitude, nearly double the response for any other variable. This influence is a two-way street—especially among younger, insecure teens who frequently allow themselves to be defined by their associations with different groups. Sometimes they even actively seek out such characterizations. After all, they reason, there's safety in numbers.

The next most prominent area in which teens say they influence their friends is activities, where 23 percent say they play a defining role. Music

How Teens Influence Their Friends

Teens believe they have the most influence over the personality and attitude of their friends.

(percent of teens responding when asked in which area they influence their friends the most, by gender)

	total	female	male
Personality/attitude	40%	44%	36%
Activities	23	18	28
Music	19	15	23
Fashion	16	22	10
Language	12	12	13
School	10	8	12
Shopping	7	9	5
Food	5	5	5
Art	3	3	3

Source: The TRU Study, Teenage Research Unlimited, Inc.

and fashion follow at 19 percent and 16 percent, respectively. This finding is interesting because, as we saw above, more than half of teens admit that their friends influence their fashion sense, but only a small fraction seem to believe they have the same power over their friends!

Where Teens Hang Out

Teens love places they can call their own. After all, they're constantly reminding adults that they aren't kids anymore, and adults are constantly reminding them that they aren't yet grown up.

Most of the popular places people go to socialize are intended for either children or adults. Adults have the best entertainment options, obviously. But most teens, lacking a valid form of ID that can get them into the bars and clubs they find so endlessly fascinating, can only wait impatiently for their state-mandated coming-of-age.

At the same time, teens aren't obsessed with nightspots. Most acknowledge they would really like to gain entry, but they claim what matters most is being in an environment where they feel they can be themselves—unguarded, uninterrupted, and most importantly, understood. That said, there are three main requirements that teens look for in a hangout destination: the company of other teens, limited adult interruptions and supervision, and access to food—in that order.

Not surprisingly then, places that offer teens all of the above (such as homes, malls, cinemas, restaurants, schools, and parks) remain perennial teen favorites. In explaining what makes their chosen hangout special, teens tend to give a variation on a single answer: "It's just where everybody goes." To the outside observer, this answer doesn't seem like much of an answer at all, simply opening up more questions. What they mean, however, is that the ideal hangout would have individuals that a) the teen already knows and likes, or b) are similar enough in personality and preferences that the teen would like to know them, or c) are attractive to look at.

Where Teens Spend
Their Free Time

**Teens hang out at different places on weekends than
they do after school or on a date.**

*(percent of teens responding when asked to name the three places where they are
most likely to spend time after school, on weekends, and on a date)*

	after school	weekends	on a date
Home	63%	30%	6%
Friend's house	55	52	6
School/around school	30	7	2
Sporting facility	28	25	4
Boyfriend's/girlfriend's house	26	34	36
School dances	18	20	17
Mall	17	44	11
Downtown/uptown/city	17	32	14
Video arcade	16	23	4
Restaurant	16	32	36
Park	15	28	17
Party	8	48	26
Bowling alley	8	22	9
Movie theater	8	43	55
Church/place of worship	8	36	2
Roller rink	7	24	9
Teen/dance clubs	7	23	15
Beach	7	39	13
Concerts	4	26	18

*Note: "On a date" was asked only of those who said they date at least once a week.
Source: The TRU Study, Teenage Research Unlimited, Inc.*

Geography often plays a key role in choosing an appropriate hangout. For younger teens (or those without cars), a hangout will likely emerge as close as possible to the midpoint of a group of friends. Older teens may choose such a centrally located meeting spot in deference to their transportation-challenged peers, but most teens of driving age will choose a location solidly in the middle of the action.

Girls often name malls and outside places as their favorite hangouts, while guys seem to prefer homes—typically a friend's but sometimes their own. These guys explain that homes offer access to everything they want—including free food, home-entertainment equipment (stereos, DVD players, gaming systems, etc.), or even a makeshift sound studio to play guitar. When it comes to choosing between one's own home and that of a friend, most teens choose the location where they're given the widest latitude to do their own thing without parental interference. In cases where a teen's older friend has a place of his or her own, this apartment often becomes Party Central.

Here's a quick equation to help determine a suitable venue: hangout = central location + teens – adults. Though teens don't always explicitly state that their favorite hangouts are places where adults aren't, other TRU lifestyle research shows that it's no coincidence that the homes in which teens typically congregate are those that feature a basement or other room offering privacy from parents' prying eyes.

Weekends are clearly teens' time to unwind. With no school and fewer obligations, they stand a much better chance of staying out late, socializing with friends, and doing the sorts of things that an earlier bedtime and a geometry test the next day would preclude during the week. But as much as the weekend differs from school nights, other TRU research has uncovered further subtle but important differences between Fridays and Saturdays.

Guys, Girls, and Fun

When it's just girls, going to the mall is a popular activity. When's it's just guys, playing video games is a frequent choice.

(percent of teens responding when asked, "Which five of the following do you do most often when you're out with just the girls/guys? Now, which five of the following do you do most often when you're out with guys and girls together?")

Just the girls		Just the guys	
Hang out at someone's house	69%	Hang out at someone's house	66%
Go to the mall	59	Play sports	53
Eat	53	Eat	48
Go to a movie	49	Play video game	45
Try to meet boys	36	Try to meet girls	37
Rent a movie	32	Watch TV	33
Go to a party	30	Go to a movie	32
Drive around	30	Drive around	30
Watch TV	29	Go to a party	25
Go to the beach or pool	26	Go to the mall	19

Guys and girls together

Hang out at someone's house	59%
Go to a movie	52
Eat	40
Go to a party	37
Rent a movie	29
Go to the mall	27
Watch TV	26
Go out to dinner	26
Drive around	25
Go to the beach or pool	20

Source: The TRU Study, Teenage Research Unlimited, Inc.

Fridays tend to be party-intensive. From the moment they wake up, many teens are gearing up to blow off steam on Friday night. In many cases, they go directly from worrying about the rigors of the school week to trying to forget them. As such, teens' Friday-night destinations tend to be places where they can "cut loose."

Saturdays, on the other hand, give teens an entire day to lounge around, talk on the phone, plan events, get ready, and head out early to meet with friends. As such, Saturdays tend to be less rushed and frenzied: whether teens are going out to eat, to a party, or just hanging out at the beach all day, the pace is a bit slower.

Still, not every teenager lives like Tara Reid and Carson Daly, even on Friday nights. For every teen firmly entrenched in a rock 'n' roll lifestyle, there are probably at least two who are perfectly content (or at least willing) to hang out at home and watch movies on Showtime.

Some teens make the best of their homebound Friday nights, inviting friends over and sequestering themselves in the basement, garage, or den. Their activities depend on several factors, including personal interests, available options, and, of course, parental oversight. Many watch cable, videos, or DVDs. Others simply talk and eat. Video games are particularly popular among guys. It's worth noting that snacks and soft drinks play a large role in most of these evenings.

Friendships by Gender

Regardless of whether it's a girls' night out or an evening with the guys, teens aren't far apart in how they choose to spend time with friends. Eight of the top-10 things teens do with friends of the same gender are identical for males and females. The most popular pursuits include hanging out at someone's house, eating, trying to meet members of the opposite sex, watching TV, driving around, and going to parties. Girls are more interested than guys in going to the movies, renting films, and going to the beach. Guys are more eager to play sports and video games.

But part of the point of socializing is to go out with members of the opposite sex. So, what changes in "mixed company"? Not much. In fact, "going out to dinner" was the only top-10 mixed-gender activity that wasn't also an option for a guys' or girls' night out. (Nevertheless, despite all that guys and girls have in common, it's still a problem to determine who pays.)

Aside from hanging out at someone's house (the overall favorite activity regardless of the company), teens also favor going to the movies (52 percent), going out to eat (40 percent), and going to parties (37 percent).

Teens have told us they're reluctant to go out with friends of the opposite sex if there's a chance this will prevent them from hooking up with someone they meet during the course of the evening. Or, in an even worse scenario, if the friends hook up before they do! This reluctance would explain the unenthusiastic responses teens gave to such mixed-gender options as going to clubs (9 percent), trying to meet members of the opposite sex (9 percent), and going to concerts (6 percent). TRU's Trendwatch panelists have explained that guys and girls often prefer different sporting events, which explains why only 8 percent think this is an appropriate gender-neutral activity.

Teen Parties

Parties can be the best of times for eager teens, but they can be the worst of times for worried parents. Socialization is among the highest of priorities for the average teen, and parties are the top rung of the sociability ladder—81 percent of young people say that partying is "in." After all, if music, refreshments, lots of friends, absent parents, and a little insanity are good by themselves, imagine the possibilities when you combine them!

What's the big draw? Not only are parties social events where teens can interact and meet new people, they also serve as a way to let off steam. It is at such "escapes" that some teens experiment with drugs and alcohol.

Adults often have only vague ideas about what goes on at teens' parties. Those ideas usually are built around memories of their own teen years, are informed by the media, or arise from late-night thoughts and fears. Too few adults base their assumptions on candid conversations with their own teenaged children. In an attempt to correct this knowledge deficit, TRU gave teens a non-judgmental forum to discuss what partying means in their social circle. The results of this qualitative measure indicate that friends are, far and away, the most important party ingredient. Sure, other things are needed as well (it's not really a party if you're hanging out at the mall). But even so, most teens indicated that without their friends, the best party in the world wouldn't be any fun: there would be no one to share it with (and this includes not just the party itself, but also recounting the evening's events in great detail afterwards).

Still, a party consisting solely of five friends isn't much of a party. Teens tell us the affair should also include each clique member's outer circles of friends—people who may not already know each other. A variety of new people (particularly members of the opposite sex) is key because teens are always looking to expand their social connections, and a party is the ideal forum in which to do so. Guys, particularly, are always looking for potential hook-ups, so they like to have the "talent pool" refreshed regularly.

Even if many of the party goers have never met before, it's critical that everyone get along. Some teens explain that if they don't feel comfortable with the group "vibe" at a party, they simply leave.

Listening to music (which was listed by 91 percent of teens) and dancing (81 percent) are the two most common party elements. Three-fourths of teens also reported "hooking up" with someone—though that phrase can mean different things to different teens. For younger teens or those of a more conservative mindset, hooking up simply means meeting or talking to someone. Slightly more adventurous teens claim the phrase signifies making plans or exchanging phone numbers. For the oldest teens, however, hooking up is more often than not a euphemism for having sex.

What Teens Usually Do at a Party

Teens say most parties for people their age include alcohol and many include marijuana and other drugs.

(percent of teens responding when asked, "Which of the following goes on at most parties for people your age?")

Listening to music	91%
Dancing	81
Hooking up with girl/guy	75
Drinking alcohol	56
Watching TV or videos	51
Playing games	48
Smoking cigarettes	44
Smoking marijuana	36
Having the cops show up	28
Doing other drugs	20

Source: The TRU Study, Teenage Research Unlimited, Inc.

Of course, no party is complete without food and drink. The scope of available beverages typically extends beyond innocent soft drinks and fruit juices (although some teens volunteer that these make perfectly useful mixers). Beer is a popular choice because teens say it's relatively easy to obtain and alcohol intake is easier to regulate than with liquor. On the other hand, liquor fans argue that bottles are easier and less conspicuous to transport, that the alcohol itself is visibly masked by the mixer, and light-drinking parents may be less likely to notice a lower level in their liquor bottles than missing bottles of beer. Further, unlike many adults who have more access to—and experience with—alcohol, many teens drink with the intention of getting drunk. These teens tell us that beer can be an acquired taste, but they appreciate the fact that they can dump alcohol—especially vodka—into a sweet mixer to help mask the flavor. Wine is relatively rare at teen parties because it can be expensive, it doesn't last long, and it's not particularly easy to get. Cheap wines are an exception to this rule, but even teens say they can tell the difference!

More than half of teens acknowledge a typical party involves drinking alcohol. Although only 35 percent of teens aged 12 to 15 report that drinking takes place at parties, 75 percent of equally underaged 16- and 17-year-olds say their parties include friends knocking back a few.

Drugs are also fairly widespread in teen culture. Nearly half of 16- and 17-year-olds say they either smoke pot at parties or know people who do. In fact, some minority teens (especially African-Americans) report their parties feature people smoking pot more often than tobacco. Overall, 44 percent of teens say the typical party involves smoking cigarettes, while 36 percent claim the same about marijuana.

Teens have an interesting take on substance abuse. Many young people genuinely and steadfastly believe that marijuana is a lesser threat than tobacco or alcohol. After all, they contend, both cigarettes and alcohol have been proven addictive time and again, but the scientific community has yet to come to a consensus about the addictive properties of marijuana.

The relatively widespread prevalence of marijuana brings us to another component of a good party: munchies. Teens always seem hungry to begin with, so there's no great surprise that they're keenly interested in having food around when they get together with friends!

Music overwhelmingly arises as another key ingredient of a great party. Our panelists, in discussing parties, emphasize that good, loud music (perhaps even with the help of a DJ) sets the mood and atmosphere for fun. Music also encourages dancing, which many panelists recommend as both fun and a great way to "get to know" other teens. These teens recommend a mix of music genres and a combination of slow and fast songs to energize the crowd, bring it back down, and set the tone.

Perhaps nothing dictates mood and atmosphere as much as a well-chosen location. Though the classic house party is the most common, some teens noted a preference for hotels or large, open spaces such as the beach or the woods. Raves are widely acknowledged to be "so '90s."

Of course, teens are nearly unanimous in the assertion that the lack of parents is generally a necessity if the party's going to "go anywhere." Without that kind of unsupervised license, it can be difficult for teens to guarantee the privacy needed to do just about any of the above activities.

The youngest teens—those aged 12 to 15—typically find it difficult to secure such an arrangement with their parents. As a result, more of them report playing games and watching TV or videos at their parties.

At this point, we suspect, concerned readers who are also parents of teens are frantically trying to figure out how to confine teens to their rooms without interfering with their education. But all is not lost. Although many of our panelists express great interest in huge parties (complete with entertainment, food, alcohol, and drugs), many others hesitate. Remember that although a majority of teens report the presence of alcohol at the typical party, most other high-risk behaviors are safely in the minority. Don't get us wrong: it's easy to see why parents might be alarmed that 28 percent of teens say a good party involves having the cops show up. But the majority of young people know there are certain lines that shouldn't be crossed—even if they place those lines a bit closer to the edge than their parents would like.

Teens who say they would prefer a laid-back get-together over an all-out house party generally have their parents to thank. These teens cite the fear of getting caught by parents, neighbors, and other authority figures, the fear of things being broken, and the fear of never leaving the house again if their parents were to find out! Some recalled the consequences from previous infractions, while others explain they just don't want to violate their parents' trust (chalk one up for mom and dad!).

Keeping in Touch with Friends

Between school, homework, errands, sports, and after-school activities, teens tell us it can be tough to find the time to make social plans with friends. For that matter, it can be tough even to find their friends! Yet, for all this frenetic activity, when teens want to get in touch with friends a surprisingly large number still use the traditional landline phone. Slightly more than half of teens (54 percent) say the regular telephone tops cell phones, e-mail, and even instant messaging for staying in touch on a daily basis.

At first, this finding seems counterintuitive. No matter where they go, teens always seem to be talking into their cell phones. Further, the proliferation of home computers (and the relatively slow pace of broadband adoption) means that getting a dial tone at home is never guaranteed, and sending bite-sized snippets of information via instant messaging is easier than ever. So what's responsible for the landline's popularity? The same thing that works in Wal-Mart's favor: ubiquity. It may not be glamorous, but it's still handy, and it gets the job done for the greatest number of teens. Plus, mom and dad foot the bill.

Instant messaging is a distant second behind the telephone—18 percent of teens say it's their primary method for getting in touch with

How Teens Keep in Touch With Friends

When teens communicate with friends, the old-fashioned telephone still rules. But instant messaging is in second place.

(percent of teens responding when asked, "When you are not with your friends, which one way do you most often use to keep in touch with them?" by gender)

	females	males
Regular phone	53%	55%
Instant messages or online chatting	17	19
Cell phone	11	11
E-mail	9	7
Letters or notes	3	1
Pager	1	1

Source: The TRU Study, Teenage Research Unlimited, Inc.

friends—though we suspect this number has grown since we quantified it in 2001. This form of communication is distinctly teen; even non-tech-savvy users can carry on a conversation with several friends independently of one another, and if the discussion gets dull, they can check out Web sites, listen to music, or watch videos. Instant messaging is a much more appropriate teen online forum of conversation than e-mail, which teens say is more appropriate for communicating with an out-of-town aunt. Teens love the impulsiveness, informality, and immediate gratification of trading instant messages. They simply log on and they can instantly send and receive messages to anyone and everyone on their buddy lists. Clearly, AOL's instant-messenger service has been the single feature that's resonated the most with teens, who don't particularly need (nor care about) AOL's proprietary content. Potentially bad news for AOL: the advent of broadband and the increasing availability of instant messaging by other means has resulted in declining teen use of America Online.

Somewhat surprisingly, only 11 percent of teens say cell phones are their preferred way of keeping in contact with friends. However, given the complexities of many calling plans and the punitive fees they can rack up when they go over their limit, teens tell us mobile phones are best for getting and giving brief updates or for possible emergencies. Typically, examples of "worthy" calls include checking voice messages or conveying location, destination, or direction information to parents or friends. Cell phones are not as attractive an option for long, rambling conversations that may or may not have a point. Still, for many teens, cell phones are the primary means of communication among their closest friends. After all, teens are always on the go, and mobile phones are the communication technology that best suits this active lifestyle. Besides, cell phones offer more than one communication option: teens love to send text messages to friends via their mobile phones as well. We've seen the average age of initiation into the cell-phone category fall from 16 (when teens get their driver's license) to 14 (when they enter high school). Currently, 45 percent of all teens own a cell phone—33 percent of 12- to 15-year-olds, 52 percent of 16- and 17-year-olds, and 62 percent of 18- and 19-year-olds. As with many forms of communication, girls are more involved in this category than guys are. In fact, the majority of teen girls own a cell phone.

Teens are skilled at choosing the optimal means of communicating with friends based on their objectives and the situation. For example, if a teen wants to tell a friend something after 10 p.m., she'll often go online (if she doesn't own a cell phone) rather than use the telephone and risk disturbing her friend's family. Once logged-on, she will scan her instant messaging "buddy list" to see if her friend is also online. In this case, instant chatting is preferred to e-mail because it enables immediate response and ongoing commentary. If the friend can't be found, then a quick e-mail will have to do.

Still, if her friend has her own phone line, our teen would likely prefer to use that. In addition to the call being free for the teen, it's also much easier to interpret conversational nuances when you can hear the sound of someone's voice. We don't know if kingdoms have been won or lost because of misunderstandings spawned from online communication, but if they haven't yet, they will!

Look for teens to quickly adopt text messaging via cell phones. Already one of the preferred forms of communication among teens abroad, text messaging has been slower to catch on here. But cell phone manufacturers and wireless providers are teaming up to increase the technology's use stateside, and teens' reactions have, so far, been quite enthusiastic.

Demographically, age seems to correlate with communication preferences. Significantly more younger than older teens prefer the traditional telephone. Obviously, this choice has much to do with the lower incidence of cell-phone ownership among the youngest age group. Still, younger teens also report chatting and instant messaging online more than older teens. It's a technology they've grown up with, and one with which they're comfortable. Not surprisingly, significantly more females than males write letters or notes to friends.

Love and Dating

What's love got to do with it? According to teens, a lot! Love is an essential rite of passage—and, for some, one of the most alluring and elusive. Nearly 90 percent of teens tell us this is what they want, teen-targeted lifestyle magazines are filled with articles about boys and boyfriends, and teen TV shows are similarly obsessed with the subject. And we won't even waste time rehashing how important female companionship (and the ensuing prospect of sex) is for teen guys.

When teens talk about their social lives (or, alas, lack thereof), the understood subtext is usually dating. Sure, they love socializing with a group of friends. But as they're prowling the mall or lounging at the local fast-food joint, they are probably scanning the crowd for someone—anyone—with dating potential. For many, dating is the holy grail of teen life: maddeningly elusive, but worth the effort. On the other hand, the process can be stressful and frustrating: over the past few years, during discussions, many teens have told us that dating at their age seems absurd, rarely leading to anything serious. What's apparent, though, is that teens use the term "dating" fairly broadly. To today's older teens (and certainly those who are in college), the traditional definition can apply. But to most teens of high school age, "dating" simply means getting together less formally with a boyfriend/girlfriend or with someone who sparks a romantic interest. This new definition of dating can often include whole groups of friends.

Finding Love

Love means different things to different teens. Most believe that love tends to blindside a person: it happens unexpectedly and uncontrollably. They warn against underestimating love's power, and complain that people throw the term around too loosely.

The self-proclaimed hopeless romantics declare that love is life's ultimate goal. These teens describe love as a beautiful, euphoric, intoxicating, once-in-a-lifetime occurrence that endures all the challenges it may face.

Many teens start out wide-eyed idealists, but it usually doesn't take more than one or two unpleasant incidents to make them more cautious. A surprising number of teens have told us that love at first sight simply doesn't happen. Rather, they say (rather maturely) that budding relationships must pass through certain stages before being considered "real." Being friends, hanging out, and even "kicking it" together may all be ingredients of love, but these teens claim they aren't the real deal.

A number of teens—the ones for whom a nasty experience is still fresh in their minds—sound skeptical and even bitter about the subject. We've heard love described as "blind," "misleading," "hurtful"—even "deadly." Other teens, speaking hypothetically, claim that love isn't a right and it isn't guaranteed. Sadly, they say, true love may never happen at all.

All this teen speculation led us to quantify how many teens believe they've personally been in love. We found that more than half claim they have indeed been in love—and a few seem downright preoccupied with love. Nearly one-third (32 percent) of teens have been in love only once. Another 16 percent have fallen twice, and 5 percent have been stung by the love bug three times. And for the 1 percent of teens who claim that they've been in love more than 50 times, the question remains—quantity or quality?

Dreams of a fairy-tale romance are firmly rooted in many girls' minds, whereas young guys seem more likely to fall in love multiple times (or at least are quicker to use the "L" word in describing their experiences). Our qualitative research into this topic shows that guys are also less willing to openly express their feelings of love, often waiting for the girl to say it first. Some guys find it difficult to differentiate between "love," "like," and "lust." Older teens can more clearly identify when it's love and when it's not. Approximately 65 percent of 18-to-19-year-olds affirm they've been in love (compared with 53 percent of 16-to-17-year-olds and 45 percent of 12- to-15-year-olds). Conversely, younger teens are more hesitant to call what they're feeling love. Twenty percent of 12-to-15-year-olds and nearly 22 percent of 16-to-17-year-olds are not sure they've been in love, compared to only 12 percent of 18-to-19-year-olds.

Ever wonder why affluent, middle-aged, divorced guys often marry "trophy wives?" TRU data suggest they may be trying to relive their youth, when they were looking for the same qualities in a mate. Teen guys—especially younger ones—are highly motivated by physical attraction. In fact, one blunt, young Casanova actually explained to us that competing with friends for girls can be an ego trip. Other guys tell us they simply enjoy meeting and experimenting with lots of girls. Although boys reinforce one common stereotype, they broke several others down, revealing that they place high emphasis on intelligence, personality, and an emotional connection. Girls report being interested in solid, long-term relationships.

Teens' romantic priorities can be placed into three clusters: Love and Security, Personality and Mind, and the Trophy Date. More than half of girls (52 percent) say they look for a mate who cares for them, while about one-third of boys (35 percent) answered similarly. In explaining what girls perceive to be appropriate "caring" by teenage guys, one of our Trendwatch panelists (with unbridled romantic pride) told us, "My boyfriend really cares about me. He knows exactly what to order for me from Wendy's."

Conversely, the majority of boys (52 percent) are looking to snag a "hottie." Only 30 percent of girls listed physical attraction as an important attribute. In a revelation that speaks volumes about attitude differences between the sexes, TRU qualitative research indicates most boys think their female peers are not exactly being truthful when they say looks aren't as important to them! At least at this time in their life, guys are comfortable with their teenaged shallowness: they're quick to admit that the first thing that attracts them to a girl is how she looks. Refreshingly, a couple female Trendwatch members (who, by definition, are more confident than their peers) matched guys' unabashed candor by explaining that they have plenty of time to find a smart guy; for now, they want somebody who's hot.

More than one-third of both genders say they want their crush to be "fun," and a similar number mentioned a good sense of humor as important. More than one-third of boys—36 percent—say their girlfriend should be "smart." Before you parents of boys flush with pride, however, you should

What Teens Look for in The Opposite Sex

To teen girls, the most important quality in a boyfriend is someone who cares for them. Most important to teen guys is a girlfriend who is good looking.

(percent of teens responding when asked, "What three things do you most look for in a boyfriend/girlfriend?" by gender)

Female		Male	
Cares for me	52%	Is good looking	52%
Has a good sense of humor	37	Is fun	37
Is fun	34	Is smart	36
Is good looking	30	Cares for me	35
Won't cheat on me	28	Has a good sense of humor	32
Is a good listener	28	Has similar interests	28
Is smart	26	Won't cheat on me	26
Has similar interests	23	Is a good listener	15
Is outgoing	17	Is affectionate	15
Is affectionate	16	Is outgoing	13
Is spiritual	9	Is spiritual	8
Challenges me	5	My friends will like her	7
Is older than me	5	Challenges me	5
My friends will like him	4	Is popular	5
Has money	4	Has money	3
Is popular	3	Is "experienced"	3
Dresses "cool"	3	Dresses "cool"	2
Doesn't follow "the rules"	3	Has a car	2
Has a car	2	Doesn't follow "the rules"	2
Is "experienced"	1	Is older than me	1

Source: The TRU Study, Teenage Research Unlimited, Inc.

know that teen boys define "smart" as a girl who can talk about things that interest guys, such as sports, cars, music, and video games!

Younger teens are more motivated by popularity and peer pressure, so it's not surprising that 12-to-15-year-olds list desirable attributes in a love interest that older people consider shallow. Some 46 percent say good looks is most important to them, and another 7 percent admit to looking for someone who's popular. Such answers drop considerably among older teens. Significantly more girls than boys want someone who's outgoing and a good listener. Significantly more guys than girls place greater importance on looks, being popular, and finding someone friends will like.

Relationships

Once teens have found that special someone, they work their significant other into their day-to-day life. And, as many teens have told TRU, this can be a tricky, complicated task: after all, teens have established social behaviors and circles that they don't want to compromise by adding a romantic interest to their lives. Teen guys, in particular, say one sure way to "get grief from your buds" is to desert your friends in favor of a girl; for understandable reasons, teens call such a state being "married." For many, it's something they want to delay as long as possible.

Although 22 percent of teens report that they have never had a boyfriend or girlfriend, most try to establish a dating history in middle school. Precocious kids may start even earlier.

Only 37 percent of teens say they are currently in a relationship, but that number increases rather dramatically in the upper age bracket: 58 percent of 18- and 19-year-old females say they are in a relationship. This number is significantly higher than for similarly aged males. But rest assured, there's nothing scandalous going on here: older teen girls often ignore their male contemporaries, preferring to be with slightly older and (to their mind) more mature guys.

Do Teens Have a Boyfriend/Girlfriend?

Most teens do not have a boyfriend or girlfriend.

(percent of teens responding when asked, "Do you currently have a boyfriend or girlfriend?" by gender)

	total	female	male
Yes	37%	40%	34%
No	55	53	56

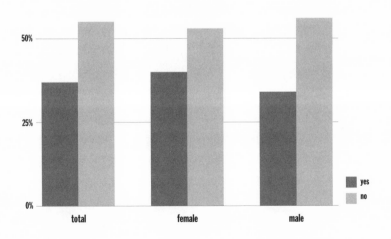

Source: The TRU Study, Teenage Research Unlimited, Inc.

253

A typical teenage relationship lasts only a few months: 44 percent say their last relationship lasted between one and six months. It's important to view these durations within the context of a teen's age. A six-month relationship for a 14-year-old high school freshman, for example, amounts to one-fourth of his or her teen years to date. Still, for one-fifth of teens, romance is particularly short-lived: these teens claim their fling lasted less than three weeks! Another 20 percent report being involved in a relationship that lasted more than a year. Girls are more likely than guys to define their present dating status as "a relationship," while guys are more likely to claim they are just "going out."

What comes up must come down, and breakups are as big a part of teen life as are relationships. Teens employ many ways to notify the other party of their new status as an "ex." The 41 percent plurality courageously breaks the news in person. These teens need to be commended for not taking the easy way out! Another 24 percent place a phone call—hardly flawless etiquette, but especially understandable for teens who don't go to school with their new ex and better than the 14 percent who "just stop talking" to the former boyfriend or girlfriend, the 12 percent who send a friend to do the dirty work, the 7 percent who send a note, and the 2 percent who dump via e-mail. Ann Landers would be appalled. In fact, teens tell us that the "dumpee" is often the last to know. "Her friends tell your friends, so you're just waiting around for it to happen," explained one of TRU's Trendwatch guy panelists. "Then, we all go out and forget about it!"

Chapter 8

Teen Lifestyle

"Lifestyle" is one of an increasing number of words whose meaning has been muddied by overuse. In the marketplace, "lifestyle" may be linked to anything from a section of the newspaper to a contraceptive device. The word's meaning from a marketing perspective, however, is simple: it's what consumers do with their time. We've devoted two chapters to the origins of teen behavior—Chapter 2 on Teen Psyche and Chapter 3 on Teen Attitudes—which help explain teen motivations. Whereas those chapters are devoted to the psychology of teens—seeking to shed light onto why teens do what they do—this chapter intentionally doesn't dig as deep. Instead, it focuses on what teens do.

The prevailing thought among psychologists and researchers alike is that attitudes drive behavior—that is, somebody must first feel or think something before she or he acts upon it. But, we don't think teens always follow such a linear path. They're not that predictable—so many of their actions are anything but premeditated. In fact, we think teens' behavior at times can drive their attitudes. Because teens can be impulsive, they sometimes act before knowing how they feel—whether trying a new activity or hanging out with a new group of peers. In such cases, teen behavior drives the resulting attitudes.

Teen behavior probably tells a more realistic story than do teen attitudes about who teens are and what they like. As the previous chapter on psyche explained, teens' aspirations are so strong, so motivating that they can cloud a clear depiction of teen behaviors. As stated earlier, teens are living a few steps ahead of where their feet are planted. And while understanding teens' aspirations offers critical implications to marketers, it's equally important to know what teens actually do. That's what this chapter is all about. For example, when teens are asked to select the activities they would most *like* to do, most choose something different from what they *actually* do. Understanding the distinction between what they do and what they would like to do is key to reaching teenagers.

What teenagers do with their leisure time segments them, profiles them, and offers opportunities to marketers. In many ways, teenagers *are* what they do. They choose their friends based on shared interests. That's why teens who are into basketball hang together, as do those who volunteer, work on cars, create music, go to the mall, or do drugs.

Weekly Activities

To understand teens, it's best to start with the basics. In each wave of The TRU Study (more than 40 to date), we include a grid in the questionnaire that asks teens how many hours they spent in the past week on a variety of activities, from sports and shopping to working at a job and working out. A quick glance at these data shows just how much teens fit into a single week! As avid multitaskers, they combine their favorite activities with the more mundane. For example, listening to music—whether on the radio, TV, stereo, or computer—accompanies many of their other activities, from doing homework and playing video games to talking on the phone and driving in their cars.

Although youth fashions, music, and lifestyles change quickly, there are also many constants in teen life. The teen years are a time of testing limits, learning to make decisions, and becoming responsible for one's time. By getting a handle on how teens divide their hours, marketers benefit from a deeper understanding of why teens make the choices they do.

In analyzing our data on teens' weekly activities, we look at both the incidence of participation (i.e., the percentage of teens who engage in an activity during a given week) and involvement (the number of hours teens spend on each activity). Not surprisingly, the activities with the greatest participation are also those that teens spend the most time doing. For example, during an average week more teens (97 percent) watch TV than

What Teens Do, By Gender

Eighty percent of girls went to the mall in the past week compared with 64 percent of guys.

(percent of teens who participated in selected activities in the past seven days, by gender)

	total	female	male
Watching TV	97%	97%	98%
Listening to CDs, tapes, records, MP3s	96	97	94
Listening to the radio	92	94	90
Hanging out with friends	86	87	86
Talking on a regular phone	85	91	80
Going online/using the Internet	81	81	82
Doing chores or running errands	81	86	77
Going to the mall	72	80	64
Using a computer (not online)	71	71	72
Reading magazines for pleasure	67	73	61
Watching rented videos	66	68	64
Working out	66	62	70
Reading newspapers	65	63	66
Playing video games at home	61	42	80
Going to the movies	61	64	58
Playing sports	59	49	68
Cruising in a car	58	60	56
Preparing meals	58	67	49
Reading books for pleasure	57	64	51
Instant messaging	55	59	51

	total	female	male
Talking on a cell phone	54%	63%	46%
Playing computer games (not online)	53	49	57
Attending religious services	52	53	51
Going to parties	49	50	49
Going shopping for family	46	53	39
Doing homework	44	46	43
Downloading music	42	38	46
Dating/being with boyfriend or girlfriend	39	44	34
Babysitting	31	42	20
Going to sports events	30	29	32
Playing a musical instrument	30	28	32
Working a a regular paid job	28	28	27
Volunteer work (community, charity)	22	25	19
Going to a library, museum, or gallery	21	23	20
Going dancing	21	27	16
Downloading movies or videos	18	14	21
Playing video games at an arcade	14	9	18
Reading magzines for school	13	12	14
Going to concerts	12	13	12
Going to amusement or theme parks	12	13	12

Source: The TRU Study, Teenage Research Unlimited, Inc.

What Teens Do,
By Age

Playing video games is more popular among younger than older teens.

(percent of teens who participated in selected activities in the past seven days, by age)

	12 to 15	16 to 17	18 to 19
Watching TV	98%	98%	97%
Listening to CDs, tapes, records, MP3s	95	97	97
Listening to the radio	91	93	93
Hanging out with friends	83	91	87
Talking on a regular phone	86	89	82
Going online/using the Internet	79	84	84
Doing chores or running errands	79	83	85
Going to the mall	70	74	74
Using a computer (not online)	73	72	67
Reading magazines for pleasure	66	68	68
Watching rented videos	65	67	68
Working out	68	68	62
Reading newspapers	56	70	77
Playing video games at home	68	57	51
Going to the movies	60	65	59
Playing sports	65	55	49
Cruising in a car	44	72	74
Preparing meals	53	60	65
Reading books for pleasure	60	55	55
Instant messaging	53	62	51

	12 to 15	16 to 17	18 to 19
Talking on a cell phone	41%	63%	72%
Playing computer games (not online)	59	48	45
Attending religious services	53	50	52
Going to parties	43	54	57
Going shopping for family	45	43	51
Doing homework	51	52	23
Downloading music	39	50	40
Dating/being with boyfriend or girlfriend	26	50	53
Babysitting	36	31	20
Going to sports events	32	30	26
Playing a musical instrument	34	33	20
Working at a regular paid job	11	35	53
Volunteer work (community, charity)	19	28	25
Going to a library, museum, or gallery	23	18	22
Going dancing	18	23	26
Downloading movies or videos	16	21	17
Playing video games at an arcade	17	12	9
Reading magzines for school	14	13	11
Going to concerts	10	15	14
Going to amusement or theme parks	15	11	9

Source: The TRU Study, Teenage Research Unlimited, Inc.

take part in any other leisure-time activity. They also spend more time each week watching TV (10.24 hours) than they spend doing any other activity. Some activities with high participation, however, have low involvement levels. For example, nearly two-thirds of teens read a newspaper during an average week, but they spent only 1.93 hours doing so. Recognizing the difference between teen participation and involvement is important for marketers who want to promotionally tie into or depict an activity in advertising. Don't be misled by the size of the audience; as with most things teen, it's the quality as much as the quantity that counts.

There are significant gender differences in teens' weekly activities. Girls, for example, prefer activities that involve entertainment. Their top-three activities (listening to recorded music, listening to the radio, and watching TV) consume nearly 29 hours of their time each week! And where entertainment leaves off, the social life picks up. Girls' interactions with friends consume just as much time, whether it's going out, talking on the phone or computer, or simply hanging out. Guys also enjoy being entertained. They, too, devote plenty of time each week to the "big three" of TV, radio, and recorded music. Where guys differ is in other electronic entertainment, specifically console and computer gaming. Girls are more social in their online time while guys are more competitive and adventurous. This gender distinction appears offline as well, with guys spending more time than girls playing sports and working out.

All is not fun and games for teens, however: the money to pay for their entertainment has to come from somewhere. Work plays a prominent role in the lives of both genders: 53 percent of teens aged 18 or older have a job, as do 35 percent of 16- and 17-year olds. These numbers explain why marketers are courting teens like never before.

Based on our qualitative research with teens and parents, we believe teen employment is a double-edged sword. Certainly, it teaches a work ethic and helps teens understand the value of money. Many teens take the work ethic to an extreme, however, allowing their jobs to consume a disproportionate amount of time and energy. If a teen works more than 15 hours a week (and we've met some who work 30-plus hours a week), something has to give. What gives, typically, is studying, extracurricular activities, and unscheduled "chill-out" time (in other words, time to enjoy being teen). Finding the right balance is key.

Not only are teens working for money, many also work to help others. Doing chores, running errands, preparing meals, grocery shopping for the family, and doing volunteer work take up nearly nine hours of the typical teenagers' week.

Girls spend almost six-and-a-half hours a week reading books and magazines for pleasure. Boys spend about four-and-a-half hours reading books and magazines. Clearly, there are more magazines written specifically for teen girls than for guys. In just the past couple of years, some leading publishers have entered the teen-girl arena, trotting out new titles such as *Teen People*, *CosmoGirl*, *Elle Girl*, and *Teen Vogue*. It may appear that guys aren't getting equal treatment, but a boy's version of *Seventeen* has never proven to be commercially viable. (Much more on this in Chapter 10, Teens and Media.)

Boys spend at least some of the extra time that girls devote to reading to playing electronic games. Whether on a PC, a game console, or at an arcade, guys spend almost ten-and-a-half hours per week in furious battle with pixels and program code. (Girls also like games, by the way. They spend close to five hours each week playing them). In fact, in TRU's Web site development research, teens always tell us to include fun and new games, and this request comes almost as often from girls as guys.

The world of electronic gaming is an exciting one, with continual technological advances making the experience more visceral, more engaging than ever before. It seems that almost every year "next-generation" systems

How Much Time Teens Spend Doing Activities, by Gender

Teens spend almost as much time online each week as they do listening to the radio.

(among teens who participated in an activity, number of hours spent doing the activity in the past seven days, by gender)

	total	female	male
Watching TV	10.24	9.89	10.57
Listening to CDs, tapes, records, MP3s	9.19	9.97	8.46
Hanging out with friends	8.27	8.74	7.82
Listening to the radio	7.55	9.02	6.16
Going online/using the Internet	6.83	7.02	6.66
Talking on a regular phone	5.03	6.38	3.76
Instant messaging	4.68	5.34	4.05
Playing video games at home	4.37	2.09	6.53
Dating/being with boyfriend or girlfriend	4.14	5.14	3.19
Playing sports	3.95	2.97	4.87
Going to the mall	3.83	4.77	2.96
Cruising in a car	3.81	4.20	3.44
Using a computer (not online)	3.75	3.52	3.98
Doing chores or running errands	3.75	4.42	3.12
Working at a regular paid job	3.71	3.67	3.74
Working out	3.62	3.29	3.94
Watching rented videos	3.60	4.01	3.21
Reading books for pleasure	3.29	3.95	2.66
Downloading music	2.87	2.67	3.06
Talking on a cell phone	2.83	3.69	2.03

	total	female	male
Going to parties	2.73	2.84	2.63
Playing computer games (not online)	2.70	2.24	3.14
Going to the movies	2.63	2.81	2.47
Doing homework	2.34	2.59	2.10
Reading magazines for pleasure	2.23	2.52	1.96
Attending religious services	2.14	2.39	1.90
Preparing meals	2.07	2.62	1.55
Babysitting	1.98	2.83	1.18
Reading newspapers	1.93	1.83	2.02
Playing a musical instrument	1.80	1.49	2.10
Going to sports events	1.53	1.49	1.57
Going shopping for family	1.45	1.82	1.10
Downloading movies or videos	1.19	0.85	1.51
Going dancing	1.01	1.40	0.64
Volunteer work (community, charity)	0.88	1.00	0.76
Going to a library, museum, or gallery	0.80	0.77	0.83
Going to amusement or theme parks	0.71	0.85	0.58
Playing video games at an arcade	0.59	0.40	0.78
Going to concerts	0.58	0.62	0.54
Reading magzines for school	0.42	0.39	0.44

Source: The TRU Study, Teenage Research Unlimited, Inc.

How Much Time Teens Spend Doing Activities, by Age

Older teens work an average of more than eight hours a week, while the youngest teens work less than an hour.

(among teens who participated in an activity, number of hours spent doing the activity in the past seven days, by age)

	12 to 15	16 to 17	18 to 19
Watching TV	10.77	9.65	9.75
Listening to CDs, tapes, records, MP3s	8.47	10.71	9.16
Hanging out with friends	7.55	8.89	9.10
Listening to the radio	7.35	7.92	7.57
Going online/using the Internet	6.63	7.68	6.39
Talking on a regular phone	5.45	5.53	3.71
Instant messaging	4.80	5.40	3.73
Playing video games at home	5.24	3.95	3.04
Dating/being with boyfriend or girlfriend	2.22	5.48	6.64
Playing sports	4.49	4.00	2.82
Going to the mall	3.88	4.18	3.40
Cruising in a car	2.65	4.97	4.99
Using a computer (not online)	3.83	3.77	3.57
Doing chores or running errands	3.62	3.85	3.91
Working at a regular paid job	0.73	4.92	8.37
Working out	3.44	4.12	3.48
Watching rented videos	3.55	3.60	3.71
Reading books for pleasure	3.32	3.01	3.48
Downloading music	2.54	3.60	2.82
Talking on a cell phone	1.95	3.56	3.89

	12 to 15	16 to 17	18 to 19
Going to parties	2.32	2.96	3.32
Playing computer games (not online)	3.16	2.36	2.12
Going to the movies	2.69	2.76	2.39
Doing homework	2.58	2.78	1.43
Reading magazines for pleasure	2.17	2.34	2.25
Attending religious services	2.17	2.19	2.01
Preparing meals	1.93	2.02	2.41
Babysitting	2.34	1.92	1.32
Reading newspapers	1.60	2.06	2.47
Playing a musical instrument	1.90	2.51	0.93
Going to sports events	1.54	1.81	1.23
Going shopping for family	1.40	1.41	1.56
Downloading movies or videos	1.05	1.31	1.34
Going dancing	0.98	0.99	1.10
Volunteer work (community, charity)	0.74	1.22	0.81
Going to a library, museum, or gallery	0.74	0.74	0.99
Going to amusement or theme parks	0.93	0.62	0.56
Playing video games at an arcade	0.80	0.47	0.31
Going to concerts	0.40	0.86	0.66
Reading magzines for school	0.44	0.47	0.31

Source: The TRU Study, Teenage Research Unlimited, Inc.

arrive in the stores, and teens (guys especially) go out and buy them. Several years ago, when Nintendo was preparing to launch its first next-gen system, Super Nintendo (which since has been surpassed not only by Nintendo 64, but more recently by the company's current console, Game Cube), the company was concerned about the degree to which teens and their parents would resist investing in a new system to remain current. The outcome is instructive. When given the opportunity to own a superior system—better graphics, faster play, newer games, and an overall better gaming experience—teens jumped at the chance (and pulled their parents along with them). We've interviewed parents who tell us they're almost grateful that video game systems become obsolete after a few years, explaining that they typically feel hard-pressed to come up with a birthday or holiday present for their teenaged son. (Advice from TRU: cash always works—as do gift certificates!) These days, teens are particularly intrigued by the capabilities of hooking their console up to a fast 'Net connection and competing with friends and new virtual acquaintances. Regardless of technological advances that make the entire gaming experience more realistic, if the game isn't fun, they're going to run! Or, in Clintonese, it's the games, stupid. (Incidentally, we've heard from some of our Trendwatch panelists lately that they're digging their old systems out of basement storage just to relive some of their favorite "old-school" games.)

How can marketers use the information about teens' top activities to reach this on-the-go audience? Consider these facts: in a given week, teens spend more than one full day (almost 29 hours!) using traditional media (Internet, radio, TV, magazines, and newspapers). They spend another 32 hours per week participating in activities that expose them to other marketing messages—whether at concerts, sports events, fast-food restaurants, or simply driving around. So, the opportunities to (appropriately) pervade teens' lives with your messages are abundant, and the payoff is rich—the chance to become a part of their lifestyle.

Where Teens Spend Their Free Time

A few years ago we were conducting focus groups to expose teens to preliminary advertising ideas for a top youth-targeted brand. The storyboards depicted teens heading to a movie theater after school, which proved to be an instant "disconnect" for several respondents. They explained that none of their friends (and, they suspected, few teens anywhere) ever went to the movies after school. This might not sound like a big deal, but we've found time and again that once teens disconnect from an ad (even for the most minute of details), it's almost impossible to get them back. You immediately lose your credibility—you might as well shout, "We just don't get you!" Though we caution companies never to "become teen" in their ads (nothing kills credibility like faking someone's lifestyle), teens appreciate it when advertisers understand them. So, something as seemingly innocuous as an afternoon movie can spell trouble for an otherwise strong message. Execution is key in advertising to teens; even if the strategy is sound and well communicated, you can still lose big time if an execution doesn't feel or look "real."

The above is an obvious example of an activity that does not match the occasion. But it led us to develop a measure to determine which teen venues are appropriate for specific occasions. Do teens do the same things after school as they do on weekends? Do they go to different places with their boyfriend or girlfriend than they do with friends?

We presented our national teen sample with a list of activities and asked them to identify those in which they participate after school, on weekends, or with a girlfriend or boyfriend. As expected, the findings show that teens frequent different places at different times and for different reasons (reflecting the media challenge of reaching a moving target). For example, nearly two-thirds spend their free time after school at home, while only about one-third spend their leisure time on weekends at home. Only one in 20 chose their own home as the place to go with a date!

The top two places teens go after school are their own home or a friend's house. The next-most common after-school place is school itself— frequented by those who take part in sports or other after-school activities.

On weekends, teens can be found most often at a friend's house, a party, or the mall. On a date, they tend to go to a movie, a restaurant, or their date's home (especially those in established relationships).

Dating has evolved from the guy-calls-girl-and-asks-her-out routine familiar to the parents of teens. These days, teens are far more casual. They spend less one-on-one time with their significant other, preferring instead to be with a group of friends as well as their boyfriend or girlfriend. Don't be fooled, however—they still remove themselves from the larger group now and then for a bit of one-on-one time. As teens tell us, a certain amount of exclusive "date" time is mandated whether they're in a serious relationship or are interested in pursuing one. So, despite the changing face of teenage dating, the types of places teens go remain largely unchanged.

Except for leisure time after school, teens prefer to spend their free time at someone else's home. On weekends, teens prefer to get together with friends just about anywhere but their own home. Similarly, when teens date, they say they prefer to go to their boyfriend's or girlfriend's home rather than their own. This is another life-stage truth. Think back to your own teen years and, chances are, you'll remember who had the most popular house. Most teens have at least one friend who has what they often refer to as "the party house." It's usually a friend whose parents aren't home, or— as teens tell us—whose parents "don't care." Although parents admonish their children not to behave differently in someone else's home than they are expected to behave in their own home, teens look for friends' homes where they can do just that.

Girls frequent a broader range of venues than boys do. With the exception of sporting facilities and video arcades, significantly more girls than boys spend time at each of the listed venues, regardless of occasion.

Where Teens Prefer to Spend Their Leisure Time

Teens prefer to spend their after-school leisure time at home and their weekend leisure time at a friend's house.

(percent of teens citing location as one where they prefer to spend their leisure time after school, on weekends, and on a date; respondents could pick up to three places)

	prefer to spend leisure time		
	after school	weekend	on a date
Home	63%	30%	6%
Friend's house	55	52	6
School/around school	30	7	2
Sporting facility	28	25	4
Boyfriend's/girlfriend's house	26	34	36
School dances	18	20	17
Mall	17	44	11
Downtown/uptown/city	17	32	14
Video arcade	16	23	4
Restaurant	16	32	36
Park	15	28	17
Party	8	48	26
Bowling alley	8	22	9
Movie theater	8	43	55
Church/place of worship	8	36	2
Roller rink	7	24	9
Teen/dance clubs	7	23	15
Beach	7	39	13
Concerts	4	26	18

Note: "On a date" was asked only of those who date/get together with their boyfriend or girlfriend at least once a week.
Source: The TRU Study, Teenage Research Unlimited, Inc.

In general, younger teens (aged 12 to 15) prefer to spend their free time at places requiring little planning or travel, such as the mall, movies, skate parks, video arcades, or school (for school-sponsored activities). Older teens, particularly 16- and 17-year-olds, enjoy the widest variety of venues, including restaurants, friends' homes, the city, concerts, parties, and clubs. These are the teens for whom a car (their own or a friend's) means newfound independence and empowerment.

Favorite and Least-Favorite Weekend Evening Activities

Weekend nights hold a special allure for teens. It's the time for them to do what they want—to be with friends, the opposite sex, and sometimes push the limits of age restrictions. On weekends, teens get a reprieve—albeit a temporary one—from the rigors of school, work, and, often, family. For many, it's what keeps them going during the school week. But what are teens doing on weekend nights, and what do they really want to do? Knowing the answers to these questions gives marketers useful information for creating advertising that excites teens and for developing promotions that both motivate them and reach them where they play.

Most older teens spend weekend nights with friends; younger teens, on the other hand, are often saddled with family time (though, in fairness, some actually enjoy it—even on the weekend). Half as many teens say they spend time with a boyfriend or girlfriend on the weekend as spend time with family or friends, and 17 percent go out on dates. Further, one-third of teens go to someone else's home (probably the "party house" discussed above), and one-fourth spend time talking on the phone (even if they're restricted to their home, they can escape behind a closed door to talk with similarly restricted friends). And, these days, homebound teens communicate with each other online—mostly through a continuous stream of instant messages. Finally, both big and small screens play an important weekend role. More than one-third say they usually watch TV on a weekend night, with as many teens renting a movie as going to see one in a theater.

Favorite and Least Favorite Things to Do on the Weekend

The largest share of teens hang out with friends on weekends, but they would rather go to a party.

(percent of teens responding when asked, "What do you usually do on a weekend night, and what would you most like to do on a weekend night?")

	actually do	most want to do
Hang out with friends	48%	34%
Be with family	43	11
Watch TV	35	9
Go to someone's house	32	20
Go to a movie	25	28
Watch rented movies	25	13
Hang out with boyfriend/girlfriend	24	37
Talk on phone	24	10
Go to/have a party	22	42
Play sports	22	14
Go to a restaurant	21	13
Sleep	21	13
Go on a date	17	37
Work	17	10
Do homework	14	5
Go downtown	13	18
Play home video games	13	9
Read	13	8
Play on computer	12	10
Go skating	11	14
Stay home alone	11	7
Do something illegal	9	11
Go to a dance club	8	22
Go to a video arcade	7	11

Source: The TRU Study, Teenage Research Unlimited, Inc.

As social as they are, teens want to spend even more time with their friends away from home. Their favorite venue for socializing is—no surprise here—a party. In focus groups, when we ask teens, "What's going on this weekend?" a typical response is simply, "Don't know . . . but gonna check to see if there's a party." When asked what they most would like to do on a weekend night, teens in our quantitative study say they want to go to a party. As discussed in Chapter 7, parties combine teens' favorite social activities in an unstructured and comfortable environment—friends, the opposite sex, music, dancing, food, games, and—for some—drinking and drugs. Teens' favorite parties (especially among older teens) are devoid of parental supervision. In qualitative research, we often use the party theme for getting teens to describe brand imagery. For example, we might say, "If Brand X were to have a party, what would it be like? Who would be there? What kind of music would be played? What would everybody be doing? Would parents be there?" By asking the same series of questions about Brand Y, a distinct brand personality begins to emerge.

Teens, of course, also want to be active on the romantic scene. A plurality of each gender wants to hang out with their boyfriend / girlfriend or go out on a "date." Other weekend activities teens say they would like to do include hanging out with friends, going to a movie, going to a club (mentioned by almost twice as many girls as boys), and going to someone's home.

Teens become more independent—both socially and financially—once they reach the age of 16, when many gain their driver's license and find an outside source of income. Significantly more older than younger teens hang out with their boyfriend / girlfriend, go to or have a party, work, and date. In fact, older teens participate in fewer activities than younger teens because they're so driven by a singular pursuit: socializing.

Television, sports, and video games are more appealing to boys than girls. As noted previously, significantly more boys play video games and would like to play them during a weekend night—whether at home or at an arcade. More boys also play sports and would like to participate in athletics on a weekend night. Further, more boys than girls list watching television on weekend nights as a priority.

Girls yearn for more social contact than guys do. More girls talk on the phone, instant message each other, hang out with their boyfriend, and go to restaurants. Girls are also more interested in going to dance clubs.

Plotting what teens actually do on weekend nights against what they want to do yields four quadrants (see chart) showing the popularity and aspirational qualities of various weekend activities. Evaluating the activities that fall into each quadrant shows the ones marketers can use to develop and place advertising, as well as the ones marketers should avoid.

Quadrant I (Do and want to). Quadrant I shows activities that teens both want to do and actually do on a weekend night. Because teens both like and participate in them, these popular activities offer realistic, highly relateable scenarios for teen-targeted advertising. These activities also suggest venues through which to reach teens with place-based media.

Quadrant II (Don't do but want to). We call this the "aspirational" quadrant. Although few teens date, go to the city, or go clubbing on weekend nights, many teens want to do these things. These are the weekend nights teens long for and which excite them when depicted in advertising.

Quadrant III (Don't do and don't want to). These are the weekend activities that few teens do or want to do. Because these activities are less popular, they might be suitable for use in humorous advertising scenarios, such as showing a teen being freed from spending a weekend night alone doing homework.

Quadrant IV (Do but don't want to). Although many teens watch TV, talk on the phone and spend time with their family on weekend nights, they would much rather do other, more social and exciting things. These activities, then, are teens' "last resorts"—those they opt for only when they

"Like to Do"
Versus "Actually Do"

The quadrant map shows at a glance what teens do,
and what they want to do.

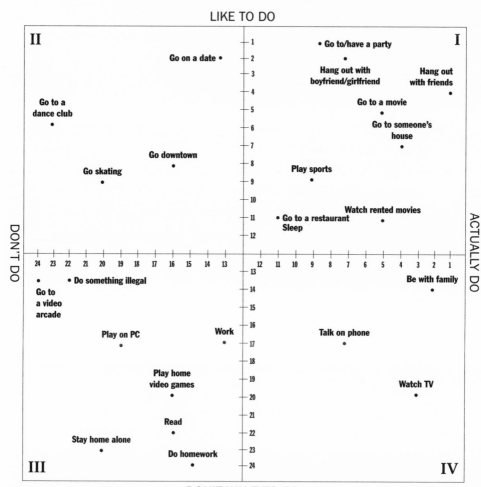

Source: The TRU Study, Teenage Research Unlimited, Inc.

have nothing better to do. Additionally, these activities are especially common for younger teens, who tell us they blame their sorry state of affairs on the fact that they are "parentally challenged."

Bonus Hours

Here's a fantasy for teens and adults alike: the magical appearance of two "bonus" hours during the busy weekday in which to do whatever they want. Understanding not only what teens do—but what they want to do— can point to opportunities. This time, we concentrated on the weekday (school days, in particular). We posed this question, "If you had two bonus weekday hours, how would you spend them?"

Teens' penchant for socializing—for being with friends—is revealed in the answer to the question. The number-one answer, by far, was simply "hanging out with friends." The number-two and number-three answers, being with boyfriend/girlfriend and partying, emphasize teens' outgoing nature and desire to have fun. No wonder nine out of ten teens in a recent TRU Study said they like being a teenager!

Interestingly, teens would choose to spend their two bonus hours in face-to-face rather than "virtual" communication (hanging out with friends was clearly preferred to talking on the phone or going online). Studying and spending more time at school were, not surprisingly, last on teens' wish lists.

With such busy, scheduled lives, teens often tell us they would like to add a few hours to their days just to keep themselves sane. Understanding teens' fantasies (in this case, nothing terribly exotic!) can be as insightful as getting a grip on their reality. By knowing the allure of bonus hours—and how teens would spend them—marketers can determine which activities and events to portray in advertising, on Web sites, and in promotions. Give teens what they want: show them in control, spending time on their own terms (socializing, partying, sleeping, playing, and simply chilling).

What Teens Would Do
With Bonus Hours

Most teens would use bonus hours to hang out with friends, but one in four would spend them sleeping.

(percent of teens responding when asked, "If you could add two 'bonus hours' into your next weekday to enjoy any way you'd like, how would you spend the extra time?" by gender)

	total	female	male
Hanging out with friends	52%	56%	48%
Being with boyfriend/girlfriend	34	36	32
Partying	29	33	25
Sleeping	25	25	25
Playing sports	22	14	30
Going to/watching a movie	19	19	19
Relaxing	17	20	14
Working out	17	16	17
Listening to music	15	14	16
Going to the mall	14	22	7
Spending time with family	13	15	11
Watching TV	10	7	13
Just being by yourself	9	9	9
Driving around	9	7	10
Reading	8	10	7
Playing video games	8	2	14
Talking on the phone	7	11	3
Going online	6	6	7
Eating	5	4	6
Studying	2	0	1
More time at school	1	0	1

Source: The TRU Study, Teenage Research Unlimited, Inc.

Sports

One of the simplest and most effective warm-ups in teen focus groups is to ask respondents what they like to do for fun. I wish that I'd started keeping a tally years ago when I began asking this question, because the answer (while still qualitative no matter how many times asked) would be quite revealing. I'd estimate that about half the responses to this question are sports-related. What's particularly interesting is the changing nature of the sports teens play. For example, although we still hear a lot about football, basketball, and baseball, we are getting many more mentions of individual sports, including skating, surfing, snowboarding, hiking, and bicycle racing.

Probably the biggest change is the number of girls who name a sport. Our focus group findings are validated by national statistics, which show the effectiveness of Title IX in expanding girls' sports participation and opportunities. Since Title IX's passage in 1972, the number of girls participating in high school sports has increased by more than 800 percent, from 300,000 in 1972 to 2.7 million today.

For teens, sports have always been larger than the games themselves. Sports represent a canvas on which to express their developing personalities. Traditionally, guys have used sports as an outlet for their aggressive and competitive natures, while girls' participation in sports—although more competitive and physical than ever—emphasizes friendship and sociability. Today, teens of both genders often sign up for interscholastic sports simply to be part of a team. My oldest son, for example, was a successful sprinter during his recently completed high school career. Despite his success, he adamantly maintained that it wasn't the love of his sport that kept him on the track team for four years. After all, he argued, running is used as punishment for those in other (more fun) sports! He insisted that what he really loved about track was simply being part of a team. Still, I never fully bought his argument, because I could see the competitive fire that burned within both him and his teammates during meets. But, then again, I was never there to witness the rather grueling practices—six days a week, two seasons a school year.

There's something unique about being on a team—especially during high school. This is something I've heard from many of our teen respondents through the years, as well as observing it first-hand in all three of my kids, regardless of the sport they played. My daughter is a tennis player, and in Illinois, where we live, girls high school tennis is a fall sport, which means tryouts and the first week or two of team practice occur before the start of school. I remember how wonderful it was for her as an incoming freshman to walk into her first day of high school already part of a group—a special, tightly knit group with a common mission and the budding friendships that go along with it.

Just as boys are discovering the camaraderie of sports, girls are discovering the benefits of competition. For example, my daughter has now seen her second teammate in as many years get a full scholarship to a Big Ten school. Not only has Title IX increased girls' participation in sports, it has also opened the door to athletic scholarships. In fact, because collegiate football commands so much attention (fans, budget, and revenue), it awards a disproportionate number of scholarships, creating bigger opportunities for girls (thanks to Title IX) in other sports, including tennis.

Teamwork and camaraderie are excellent fringe benefits, but to many guys the basic premise behind sports is still to showcase athletic prowess. My youngest son, who's the biggest jock in the family, makes the case for guys being more athletically competitive and aggressive overall, which is where I began a few paragraphs ago. Whether he's playing his own sport (basketball) or any other, he's all about winning—and doing whatever it takes to get there. Although he's not quite the tennis player his older sister is, he'll dive for a shot on a hard court—even if no one's keeping score.

What are the big sports with teens? The easy answer, based on TRU participation data, is basketball and swimming. More than half of teens

Sports Participation and Favorite Sports

Swimming is girls' favorite sport, while boys like basketball the best.

(percent of teens responding when asked, "Which of the following activities and sports have you participated in outside of school gym or PE class during the last 12 months? Now, which are your three favorites?" by gender)

FEMALES

Participated in during last 12 months	One of three favorites
1. Swimming	1. Swimming
2. Exercise/aerobics	2. Basketball
3. Basketball	3. Volleyball
4. Jogging/running	4. Baseball/softball
5. Bowling	5. Exercise/aerobics
6. Volleyball	6. Soccer
7. Bicycling	7. Cheerleading/poms
8. Baseball/softball	8. Bowling
9. Billiards/pool	9. Jogging/running
10. Soccer	10. Billiards/pool

MALES

Participated in during last 12 months	One of three favorites
1. Basketball	1. Basketball
2. Football	2. Football
3. Swimming	3. Baseball/softball
4. Baseball/softball	4. Weight training
5. Weight training	5. Swimming
6. Bowling	6. Billiards/pool
7. Bicycling	7. Soccer
8. Billiards/pool	8. Fishing
9. Jogging/running	9. Skateboarding
10. Fishing	10. Bicycling

Source: The TRU Study, Teenage Research Unlimited, Inc.

participate in both during a given year, which make them number one in participation. But these sports are also teens' overall favorites.

The more complete answer to the question of which sports are big with teens is that teens are interested in a variety of sports. In fact, the athletic fragmentation of teens offers marketers opportunities to tie into the sport that matches the lifestyle and/or aspired image of their brand's teen users. Clearly, one dividing line is team vs. individual sports. But within individual sports there is an additional division between more traditional solo sports (wrestling, track, swimming) and more modern, aggressively individualistic sports such as skateboarding, surfing, and other activities included under the "extreme" umbrella.

Among organized sports basketball is dominant. Two factors no doubt contribute to the sport's popularity with teens—the marquee status of the National Basketball Association and the relative ease and spontaneity of basketball (minimal equipment, one-on-one games, year-round play, plenty of public courts). In fact, twice as many teens name basketball as their favorite sport to play than either football or baseball/softball.

Whereas guys have traditionally gravitated toward team sports, six of guys' top-ten favorites today—weight training, swimming, pool, fishing, skateboarding, and bicycling—are nonorganized, individual sports. Girls' top-ten list is evenly split among team and individual sports.

One recent trend in teen sports is weight training, which now ranks as guys' fourth most-favorite sport. This is especially good news for the weight-training industry, as this recent spike in participation stops an eight-year slide. Weight training's rise in popularity may be attributed to teen guys increased concern about developing a more toned physique. TRU qualitative research and anecdotal evidence reveal that guys are increasingly focused on their outward appearance and, like their female counterparts, want to use their bodies to project their own brand of sexuality. Though they wouldn't admit it, teen guys appear to be taking cues from the gay community (reflected by an increased interest in tighter, form-fitting clothes) and even body shaving (though in the past year, we've seen this curious trend trail off a bit). Teens themselves point to recent debates over steroids and ephedra in Major League Baseball and the body-baring Abercrombie & Fitch quarterly catalog as factors that may have raised their awareness of, and interest in, the social ramifications of bulking up.

Tony Hawk's iconlike status vividly demonstrates teens' broad interpretation of what it is to be an athlete. After all, the thirtysomething skateboarding legend can't pull off a jump-shot like Michael Jordan (not even contemporary Michael Jordan), and he's probably too scrawny to play football. But he's got an astonishing 13 "X Games" medals on his mantle, as well as a line of products and product endorsements even Allen Iverson would envy.

This success proves that while mass marketers would do well to continue to tie their brands to high-profile sports, they should also consider a wider variety of sports. By sponsoring niche sports at the local level, integrating them into promotions, or simply portraying them in advertising, you can earn the coveted "they get me!" response from teens.

After marketers decide to leverage sports in marketing to teens, the next question is, "Which sports?" Most marketers—equipped with TRU or industry data—are aware of the sports teens play. But this cursory knowledge can be misleading, because it's key (not to mention tricky) to distinguish between the sports teens play and the sports for which they have a passion. For example, both bowling and running make guys' top-ten list for participation, but both sports plummet in the list of favorites.

To help marketers make this distinction—to reveal the sports that garner exceptional enthusiasm—TRU developed the Sports Affinity Index, which ranks sports based not upon how many teens play them, but upon how much the sport is enjoyed by those who do participate. This analysis allows marketers to see beyond the participation figures and zero in on the sports with perhaps fewer (but more passionate) participants. The index reveals the sports that marketers should consider as attractive options. Some may be less well known, but they are often so popular with their adherents that their appeal will likely spread to teens who have not yet participated in them.

Which sports rank highest on the Affinity Index? Cheerleading, basketball, martial arts, and football top the list, with some notable differences by gender. (See the accompanying table for the complete list.) Clearly, the board sports as well as a handful of outdoor activities (among guys, motocross, dirt biking, and hunting; among girls, horseback riding, water skiing, and kick boxing) are highly ranked on Affinity, especially in comparison to their participation numbers.

While some brands have successfully appropriated high-affinity sports in attempting to get closer to teens, savvy brand managers know that tying their products to the latest cutting-edge sport comes with risks. Sports that grab teens' fickle attention may be relevant one moment but "been there, done that" the next. The decision comes down to whether your involvement is short-term, such as a promotion, or a long-term brand-building relationship. Therefore, it's important to be sure you're targeting the right teen audience (the one with the greatest likelihood of identifying with and, ideally, embracing your brand) with the right sport.

Pro Sports

Teens love to watch sports as well. This is especially true for boys, whose media preferences alone tell a big story. For example, sports is typically the first section guys turn to when reading a newspaper; *Sports Illustrated* and *ESPN the Magazine* are their two most regularly read magazines; *SportsCenter* is one of their favorite TV shows; and ESPN.com is one of their most-visited Web sites.

When it comes to attending a sports event, girls are almost as involved as guys: nearly one-third of girls and 40 percent of boys attend a sporting

Sports Affinity Index

Sixty percent of boys involved in marital arts name it as one of their three favorite sports. For girls, the top honor goes to cheerleading.

(Sports Affinity Index by gender)

FEMALE	Sports Affinity Index	MALE	Sports Affinity Index
Cheerleading/poms	63	Martial arts	60
Basketball	53	Basketball	58
Baseball/softball	51	Football	52
Soccer	50	Baseball/softball	44
Horseback riding	49	Skateboarding	41
Swimming	49	Ice hockey	39
Volleyball	48	Motocross	38
Gymnastics	47	Soccer	37
Snowboarding	35	Hunting	36
Track and field	34	Weight training	36
Downhill skiing	32	Snowboarding	35
Water skiing	31	Fishing	32
Kick boxing	31	Billiards/pool	31
Football	31	Wrestling	30
Exercise/aerobics	29	Golf	27
Tennis	29	Track and field	27
Jet skiing	26	Downhill skiing	26
Inline skating	26	Swimming	26
Yoga	26	Dirt biking	26

Note: The Sports Affinity Index is the percentage of teens participating in a sport in the past year who also name the sport as one of their three "favorites."
Source: The TRU Study, Teenage Research Unlimited, Inc.

285

event during a given week. For many teens, this means supporting their high school team. As teens will tell you, going to the school game is as much (if not more) about socializing as it is about sports.

Pro sports, on the other hand, are a completely different ball game. Catching a game on TV—or better yet, in person—is a great diversion for many teens (and, with escalating ticket prices, a rare treat). For teen boys, pro sports are an easy conversation starter, and they provide a comfortable, low-pressure venue for those living in bigger cities to take a date (hey, if it doesn't work out—and, depending on the girl, it might not—at least they caught a game!). For the true fan, though, sports can be much more than a conversation-starter. Occasionally, sports become all consuming: *the* topic of conversation for many guys. These are the teens who know the stats, who visit NBA.com or NFL.com daily, who never miss an episode of *The Best Damn Sports Show ... Period* on Fox, and who play fantasy leagues online (and often make draft day a big, organized event). These teens are also more prone to wager money on their game-day picks.

Certainly, what drives much of sports' appeal are the athletes themselves. The celebrity of sports stars puts them on par with the biggest names in movies, music, and TV. Many teens, of course, aspire to emulate their favorite sports star beyond the court or the field, including how they dress, talk, and even walk.

For nearly 20 years, TRU has been tracking teens' favorite athletes in a measure known as TRU*Scores, which is a calculation of a celebrity's popularity based upon familiarity. If there's been one constant in this study over the past many years, it's Michael Jordan. Jordan has no equal as a celebrity—even when he was playing minor-league ball and during his first retirement, teens named him their most familiar and favorite athlete.

Recently, for the first time, a football player topped the list of teens' favorite athletes. But Michael Jordan also was still at the top, matching Atlanta quarterback Michael Vick's score. Although the National Football

TRU*Scores: Athletes

Michael Jordan remains high on the list of teens' favorite athletes.

*(athletes with the ten highest TRU*Scores, by gender)*

TOTAL	TRU*Score	FEMALES	TRU*Score	MALES	TRU*Score
Michael Jordan	47	Allen Iverson	46	Michael Vick	52
Michael Vick	47	Kobe Bryant	44	Michael Jordan	50
Tony Hawk	45	Serena Williams	44	Tracy McGrady	49
Tracy McGrady	43	Michael Jordan	43	Tony Hawk	46
Vince Carter	43	Tony Hawk	43	Warren Sapp	46
Warren Sapp	42	Venus Williams	43	Vince Carter	45
Allen Iverson	42	Mia Hamm	42	Anna Kournikova	43
Kobe Bryant	41	Lisa Leslie	42	Donovan McNabb	42
Donovan McNabb	38	Sheryl Swoopes	40	Marshall Faulk	42
Sammy Sosa	37	Vince Carter	39	Eddie George	41

*Note: The TRU*Score is derived by dividing the percentage of respondents who say they like an athlete "very much" by the percentage who are familiar with the athlete.*
Source: The TRU Study, Teenage Research Unlimited, Inc.

League is teens' highest-rated pro league (discussed below), five NBA stars fill the ranks of teens' top eight athletes. Historically, pro-basketball players have dominated this list.

What's so special about Michael Vick that puts him on equal grounds (at least in one study) with Michael Jordan? Think Barry Sanders meets Troy Aikman—a quarterback who could be a star running back. Teens appreciate athletic versatility. In fact, their current favorite NBA stars—Jordan, Tracy McGrady, Vince Carter, Allen Iverson, and Kobe Bryant—are all known for their well-roundedness as basketball players, being able to take it hard to the hoop and hit the outside shot with equal fervor. Teens love the NBA's high-flyers, as well as athletes (from any sport) frequently featured in ESPN's "SportsCenter Play of the Day." To teens today, growing up with round-the-clock sports on TV and the 'Net, it's all about the highlight reel.

Along with Vick, teens gave high scores to four other NFL players in the recent study: Warren Sapp, the trash-talking defensive tackle whom teens love to hate; Donovan McNabb, another athletic quarterback; and two great running backs, Marshall Faulk and Eddie George, who gained teens' respect through strong, consistent performances and making the occasional highlight reel.

Tony Hawk, the famous skateboarder mentioned earlier, remains in the upper echelons of teen favor, showing that the age group enjoys diversity almost as much as versatility in athletes. And Hawk is universally loved—his high rating is consistent across gender, age, and ethnic lines. As the star of the "Tony Hawk Pro Skater" video games, he's especially popular with game-playing African-American guys, who are by far the most ardent sports fans.

Serena and Venus Williams, Mia Hamm, Lisa Leslie, and Sheryl Swoopes all received high TRU*Scores not only in the most recent study, but in the few preceding it, cementing their positions as strong role models for teen girls. These athletes equaled the high scores girls gave to Jordan, Hawk, Iverson, and Bryant.

Just before publication of this book, TRU's Omnibuzz online survey measured Kobe Bryant (and a few "control" athlete-celebrities) to determine whether (and the degree to which) Bryant's legal problems would affect his TRU*Score rating. The findings: Bryant's score precipitously declined; in fact, of the seven fairly popular athletes measured, Kobe was the highest on "don't like." This turn of events shows the risk to marketers of tying into a celebrity from any field. What's most striking from a marketing perspective is that Bryant was uniformly considered as low a risk as could be found in professional sports.

That said, the excitement and potential payoff that a brand gains by appropriately associating itself with a sports star remains alluring. Look no farther than the $90 million contract Nike awarded high-school graduate LeBron James, before he ever played an NBA game. In fact, James (along with other up-and-coming NBAers including Carmelo Anthony and Yao Ming) is likely to benefit from Bryant's woes; though many marketers are understandably more gun-shy than ever, the value of celebrity in attracting teens is too high to pass up.

Pro sports offer an opportunity to reach teens, and the multitude of leagues have created sponsorship opportunities at various levels and for various budgets. Because of such strong involvement in pro sports (both by teens and marketers), TRU measures teens' interest in some of the top leagues.

The NFL, over the past several years, has been the pro-sports league in which teens are most interested. Pro football has even surpassed the NBA, which led on this measure when Michael Jordan was with the Chicago Bulls. Without question, the NBA is more conducive to breeding mega-stars than the NFL—basketball is designed to spotlight high-fliers and showboaters, while football players are concealed by protective gear and obscured by a confusing cluster of bodies on the field. So why does the NFL beat the more star-studded NBA? It's the game! Teens tell us there's simply more excitement on the gridiron; to guys, pro football means raw contact. The NFL also benefits from its shorter season and regular timetable. Sixteen regular-season games make the sport feel special. And, since the great majority of games are held on Sunday afternoons—teens' traditional down day—it's easier to tune in. The NBA, in contrast, is bogged down with two seasons: an interminably long 82-game regular season, followed by another long postseason (which the league just made longer by lengthening the first-round match-ups to best-of-seven).

The NBA still boasts more of teens' favorite athletes; a disproportionate number of athletes atop our TRU*Scores are pro basketball players. But, despite having the star power, the NBA trails (albeit quite closely) the NFL in teen interest (53 percent vs. 49 percent). Pro basketball's star appeal is especially telling among girls, who profess—by the slightest of margins—a greater interest in the NBA than the NFL. Among girls, basketball has several inherent advantages. First, only 10 players are on the court at any one time, compared to 22 in football. So, for girls in particular, the NBA is easier to get to know—both the players and the game (many girls tell us that they just "don't get" the rules of football). Second, girls like to see more of the athletes; in this regard, the NBA's jerseys and shorts better show off its athletes than the NFL uniforms. In fact, the NFL penalizes teams when players remove their helmets on the field. Talk about a marketing disadvantage! How can the NFL leverage its athletes when they're hidden behind their helmets?

TRU data show that the NBA has been gaining fans among Hispanic teens. Latino teens like the easy access to urban courts and one-on-one pick-up games as opposed to baseball's or soccer's more demanding player quota. We've also found (as has other research) that many Hispanic teens aspire to be part of mainstream culture, and they see basketball as one

Interest in Pro-Sports Leagues

Both guys and girls are most interested in the NFL, followed by the NBA.

(percent of teens saying they are "very" or "somewhat"
interested in the pro-sports league, by gender)

	females	males
Major League Baseball (MLB)	22%	42%
Major League Soccer (MLS)	12	16
NASCAR (stock car racing)	14	19
National Basketball Association (NBA)	40	57
National Football League (NFL)	44	73
National Hockey League (NHL)	16	25
Women's National Basketball Association (WNBA)	28	12
World Wrestling Entertainment (WWE)	12	24

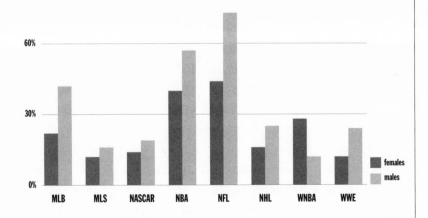

Source: The TRU Study, Teenage Research Unlimited, Inc.

bridge to greater assimilation. (Their strong interest in both rap and rock music is another example.)

When it comes to teens' interest in the various pro leagues, it's a two-horse race: teen interest in Major League Baseball trails the NFL and NBA badly. This is not surprising: the game's pace has been called "deliberate" or "deadening," depending on whether you're a fan or not. Either way, a plodding game is not a formula for capturing teens. And if an 82-game season is disadvantageous to the NBA, consider that baseball has nearly twice that many games—162! But it's not just the long season; even the homerun races of recent years have failed to spark teens' interest. With the exception of a few athletes (Sammy Sosa and Derek Jeter, in particular), baseball has been unable to compete with the star-power of basketball and football.

In contrast to the highly energized action of the NFL, the NBA, extreme sports, and even many video games, Major League Baseball's slower pace may make it ever more difficult to generate teen interest, particularly among African-American teens, whose interest in the league has declined for the past few years. Whereas football and basketball culture celebrates (or at least tolerates) brief displays of individuality (victory dances, trash talking) by its athletes (a theme that resonates strongly with teens), the culture of baseball discourages this flamboyance.

The National Hockey League trails even further behind—with an interest rating among teens about 10 points below that of Major League Baseball and 20 or more points behind the NBA and NFL. In many ways, the NHL remains the niche sport among the mass-marketed leagues. We believe, however, that if we had the data to calculate an Affinity measure, the NHL would probably do quite well. In other words, teens interested in hockey are typically huge fans. Also of note is that the NHL is Edge teens' favorite pro league; not surprisingly, teens who are skaters (the largest and most mainstream faction of the Edge Teen/Type) are most drawn to the sport.

The redubbed WWE pro-wrestling league garners notable teen interest, with one-fourth of total teens—and one-third of the boys—claiming interest. And, as with hockey, guys who are WWE fans live and breathe the sport. When we include some of the current big-name pro wrestlers (The Rock and Stone Cold Steve Austin, for example) in our TRU*Score ratings, they score highly. In fact, even the NBA might be envious of how much of these athletes is shown off in uniform (although we doubt many NBA stars would be willing to trade uniforms—they may not want to show off *that* much!).

The WNBA finds a modicum of teen interest—more so from girls than guys. Unfortunately, the sport is hampered by its greater appeal to girls, who are not as avid about sports as guys. Still, big-name WNBA players like Lisa Leslie and Sheryl Swoopes score highly among girls who are fans.

Teen Complaints About Everyday Life

Many of our first-time clients hold the opinion that it's difficult (or nearly impossible) to get teens to talk to you. Of course, we know that's not true— we employ a number of strategies and techniques to get teens to open up. One technique is to ask teens a question for which they have an easy answer—or, even better, an answer that they're eager to share with someone. One such question is, "What are your complaints about everyday life?" Because we've had so much success—meaning, we've learned a lot!—by asking this question in face-to-face research with teens, we thought it might be enlightening to quantify the results. So, we included the question in a recent wave of The TRU Study.

Clearly, teens lead busy lives. Their schedules are demanding and often overstuffed with academics, sports, and social, family, work, and extracurricular activities. As teens learn to juggle these demands, the frenetic pace takes its toll: almost one-third of survey respondents cite stress as their biggest everyday complaint, making it the most common response to this question.

Perhaps resulting from overscheduling, 30 percent of teens—like many adults!—claim they don't have enough time during the day to do everything they would like to do. Digging deeper in qualitative research, we've learned that what teens feel they miss the most is unstructured hangout time—time to be with their friends or simply do nothing at all.

The next most mentioned complaint is one that has immediate marketing implications: not having enough money. But I suggest taking a deep breath before blaming advertisers for this teen curse. After all, if a similar question were asked of adults, it's likely they would complain even more loudly about lack of enough money. Teens always want more money (who doesn't?). Although teens typically have greater discretionary spending power than many adults, they are voracious consumers. At any given time, they lack the funds to buy or do whatever's the latest and greatest.

As teens try to fit everything into their busy schedules, from fun to homework, something has to give. For many teens, it's sleep: a full one-fourth complain about "not getting enough sleep," making this teens' fourth-most cited daily complaint.

Then there are the nagging complaints, the things that bug teens but don't cause them enormous grief. Twelve percent say their parents' and teachers' expectations are too high. The same percentage complains about their parents in general, a surprisingly small figure—showing that teens and parents get along pretty well these days. Peer pressure, the perennial complaint of younger teens, garners 10 percent of the mentions. Only 5 percent of teens claim they have too many responsibilities.

Between the ages of 12 and 15, most teens transition from elementary school into middle school, and from middle school into high school. Each transition is accompanied by more freedom and also more demands on their time and emotions. As they get older, teens have more schoolwork, more choices in extracurricular activities, and must cope with a changing

Teens' Biggest Complaints About Everyday Life

Among teens, stress is the number-one complaint.

(percent of teens responding when asked, "Of only the following, which two are your two biggest complaints about your daily life?")

Stress	31%
Not enough money	30
Not having enough time in the day	29
Not enough sleep	25
School	21
Parents	12
Too high expectations of us	12
Too many rules	11
Peer pressure	10
Too many responsibilities	5

Source: The TRU Study, Teenage Research Unlimited, Inc.

social scene. It's no surprise that this age group has more complaints about both school and home life. Young teens are especially anxious about their responsibilities, others' high expectations of them, restrictive rules for people their age, and peer pressure.

Although teens must cope with packed schedules, they generally love their busy lifestyle; being crazy-busy, after all, is part of the thrill of teen life (it sure beats being bored). Like adult consumers, teens appreciate marketing and advertising messages that don't waste their time.

Prom

After nearly two decades of shelter and security, graduating high school seniors are on the cusp of adulthood. Many will go to college; others will go to work. Not surprisingly, graduating seniors—ready to take the next big step in their life—are in the mood to party. And they get the opportunity to do it with the prom. Prom, as discussed earlier, has become institutionalized in American culture as the coming-of-age night. The spring formal combines equal parts excitement, elegance, and enthusiasm for a future teens don't yet know. It's a big deal.

It's also big business. TRU projects that teens spent nearly $300 million on the prom and prom-related activities last year. In a nationally representative survey conducted online through TRU's Omnibuzz service, we discovered that more than half of those aged 16 and older go to prom. The number rises sharply for those in their senior year (many schools restrict prom to seniors and their dates). Other TRU data show how anticipated prom night is, with girls reading the special prom issues of their favorite magazines and dreaming about the big event before they even reach high school!

Prom-goers pull out all the stops. The average teen will spend $265 on clothing, entertainment, transportation, the after-party, and other prom items. Girls spend more than guys, and teens in the Eastern U.S. spend the most. In fact, the average Easterner spends $296 on prom-related expenses—that's almost $600 per couple! Teens in the Midwest place second, followed by those in the West and the South.

It's no big surprise that guys and girls have differing opinions about prom night's highlight. Both agree that it's not the prom itself that's so important. The dance ranks second on both genders' lists.

Girls love the build-up to the big night: many grab their friends and head to an expensive salon to get their hair, nails, and makeup done. "You get all that attention and then, when you're done, you're the prettiest you've ever been," one of our Trendwatch panelists shared with us. "It's heaven!"

Many guys, on the other hand, would just as soon skip the fussier parts of the evening—including the dressing up and the dancing—and go directly to the after-prom party. Make no mistake, guys believe prom night will be every bit as memorable as girls do. But while young women often hope for an evening of unparalleled romance, guys anticipate *getting romantic.*

Prom night is often a night of firsts for young consumers: first tuxedo, first limousine ride, first experience with a florist, first parentally sanctioned mixed-gender overnighter (perhaps in their first personally rented hotel room, made possible by their first really big lie to mom and dad). And, to many teens, prom marks the last, best chance for that ultimate first (maybe with their first love) before they graduate.

Other potential prom night firsts include drinking and recreational drug use, although many of the teens open to this behavior start experimenting long before the end of their senior year. Still, many schools hold their own after-prom lockdowns on school grounds, hoping to ensure that teens will be able to recall the memories they made that night.

The opportunities to tie into prom are abundant for marketers. First, it's an editorial heaven for the girl mags, with most having special issues. But that's just the beginning. Retailers, too, are in a special position to leverage this night by providing all sorts of special prom-related services and making shopping for the prom dress an event. Other marketers can get in on the action in a variety of ways, such as sponsoring pre- and post-prom parties, offering discounts for prom couples, and depicting prom in advertising.

Summer Vacation

Ah, the trials of youth. Prom is behind them, school is over, but there's a notable pause before "next year." From June until August, teens face a daunting dilemma: how to fill up those sultry summer days (and nights) now that school's out. At first, the season may seem daunting to marketers as well: how to sort through the countless diversions that tempt teens? In an effort to narrow the field, we recently asked our Trendwatch panelists, "What did you do last summer?" We were impressed by the variety of summer activities in which teens participate.

Travel. Most of our panelists say they traveled last summer or plan some sort of trip this summer. Often, it's an ambitious, meticulously planned family vacation. Sometimes it's a quick out-of-state jaunt to visit friends. The trip may even serve a practical purpose, such as an internship, college orientation, or summer camp. And although air travel may be an increasingly popular choice among teens, nothing screams "freedom" to a teen like a good, old-fashioned road trip. That being the case, promotions at gas stations or popular roadside attractions prove irresistible to teen travelers. Offers of free gas or discounts on amusement park tickets or other teen travel destinations are another possibility. And everyone knows that no road trip is complete without a cooler full of snacks and soft drinks— make sure teens choose yours!

Fun in the sun. Even if some teens aren't planning to hit the road this summer, chances are they'll hit the beach. With more than 100,000 miles of winding coastline in America, there's more than enough room for most teens to plant a towel, socialize with friends, and check out the local *Baywatch* wannabes. In fact, teens consider the beach to be the ultimate party mecca: they'll gladly drive hundreds of miles to be where the action is. Once they finally get to the shore, they'll likely stay a while, which means they'll be enthusiastic about trying out free samples of food, drinks, sunscreen, music, sunglasses, and other summer-friendly products. (TRU's experience indicates you rarely need to ask twice to get a teen to take free samples!)

Movies. It's 104 degrees outside, and the air feels like a used tea bag. Frankly, it almost doesn't matter what movies are showing—the theaters are going to be packed. Luckily for teens, Hollywood has discovered them in a big way, offering them plenty of teen fare headlined by their favorite young actors. And luckily for marketers, most of the movie-goers will show up early to make sure they can get good seats with their friends—which gives them time to socialize, to play arcade games, and to buy plenty of concession stand items. Teens who arrive early also are an attentive (mostly) audience for pre-movie commercials, which are actually a hit with teens (while most adults detest them, teens view them as "bonus" entertainment). Contests or instant-win promotions (perhaps on popcorn or soft-drink containers) are always popular with teens, who crave instant gratification. And new movie releases are a perfect way to target Influencers, who want to see movies when they first come out so they can be the first to "review" them (teens are some of the most eager proponents of viral marketing!).

Reaching On-the-Go Teens

This chapter paints a picture of teens as busy, even frenetic. But don't let this fact frighten you into thinking teens are too busy to pay attention to you. In fact, the opposite is true. Teens want to know what's going on with your brands; you've just got to do it on their terms by reaching them where they are and when they're ready to listen.

To evaluate where and how to reach teens, it's important to hone in on your particular teen target. For example, when it comes to reaching teens at play, think about not just the places where your teen segment spends a lot of time, but also the ones that are important to your target. Vans, the skate-shoe brand, has done an impressive job in this area, supporting its skating segment with a variety of promotions and events, including branded skate parks.

Chapter 6 described ways to reach teens at home (mostly through traditional or mass media) and at school (through sponsorship programs and a growing roster of in-school media). Reaching teens where they play is the third leg of the stool in your teen pervasiveness strategy. Think about all the typical teen lifestyle destinations—malls, sporting events, concerts, amusement parks, skate parks, beaches, neighborhood parks, and more—

and how best to become a part of those places. These are venues teens frequent with friends, putting them in a mood conducive to receiving your messages (assuming, of course, that your messages are presented in an appropriately engaging way). In fact, when you sponsor events or support the places teens love, you buy into a lifestyle. Not only are you getting your name out there (increasing brand awareness), you're also shaping your brand by associating it with what's important to your teen target.

Chapter 9

Teens and Brands

The good news for marketers is that teens have a penchant for new brands. Adults often develop strong ties to their established, comfortable, and familiar brands—a fact that can put new brands at a marked disadvantage. Teens, on the other hand, have relatively little long-term brand loyalty. As a group, they are innately attracted to brands based on their newness—although newness alone only gets you so far.

The bad news for marketers is that teens bore easily. This makes you vulnerable to even newer brands that catch teens' attention. But the brand that stole your thunder is likely to have just as hard a time trying to stay on top!

Arguably, when it comes to the totality of teen marketing, there's no area as fascinating as branding—understanding what it takes for a brand to interest teens, to be adopted by them, and to become ingrained in their culture. There's also no area as challenging.

Much of what we do at TRU involves understanding what brands mean to teens. Some of the work centers on the essence of branding: what brands stand for or could stand for. But probably much more touches on the periphery of branding—the strategies and tactics that determine how a brand is perceived and how it evolves, including advertising, packaging, promotions, partnerships, new-product launches, etc. What's particularly notable is that it's the latter area of our work (brand strategies and tactics) that primarily dictates the former (how a brand is perceived and how—or whether—it appropriately evolves).

Are teens distinct from other age groups in how they interact with brands and in how brands motivate them? The answer, like so many in the art of marketing, is both "yes" and "no." Brands serve teens in much the same way as they serve adults or children: they stand for something greater than the products they represent, forging an emotional and (hopefully) enduring connection. Teens interact with brands differently from other age groups, however. They look for a number of distinct attributes in a brand. Chapter 2 on "Teen Psyche" and Chapter 3 on "Teen Attitudes" collectively lay out the personality traits that draw teens to brands. These attributes fulfill, address, complement, and/or compensate for teens' fundamental psychological needs. Brands that enhance teens' self-expression and those that stand for something teens want to emulate—or affiliate with—are the brands toward which they gravitate. Brands that are strategically rooted in meeting teens' psychological needs are best positioned for enduring success.

Brand success with teens can be short-term—even for big brands with big marketing budgets. Not only do teens naturally seek out brands that are ahead of the curve from a cultural perspective, the teen population itself is forever evolving—emotionally, physically, and chronologically. Most brands with a teen target tend to zero in on ages 12 to 17, and many have a "bull's eye" target of 14 to 16. Think about it: in only two years, a third of the larger 12-to-17 population and two-thirds of the finer 14-to-16 target have moved on (or, as we refer to this phenomenon, "aged out"). The individuals now making up the ranks of the teen target are likely to be different in meaningful ways from those they replace.

TRU's Coolest Brand Meter

About 20 years ago, we began conducting regular, exploratory focus groups with teens to uncover how they differentiate among brands. And even at that time—without the more sophisticated approaches and analytical measures we've devised in the ensuing years—we learned that teens don't categorize products the way marketers do. This has not changed. A candy marketer might think its competitive set (i.e., the alternatives to its brand of candy bar) is other chocolate candy bars, for example, or even something more specific such as "enrobed" chocolate candy bars with peanuts.

To teens, the competitive set might include salty snacks, cookies, ice cream, or even pizza or power bars. Why? Instead of reaching for a candy bar, they could just as easily reach for an alternative snack that satisfies their hunger.

We also discovered many years ago that teens have a unique way of evaluating brands. The relationships teens have with brands—and the attributes they look for in brands—are much broader than simple product characteristics. So, brand research that works with adults may not be as relevant for teen branding wants and needs.

We have developed a unique measure, known as TRU's Coolest Brand Meter, which over the past many years has become widely accept by youth marketers as being the ultimate barometer of brands in the teen market. Many of our 150 subscribing companies anxiously await the twice-yearly release of the Meter results, which assesses how much a brand has moved (and, of course, in what direction) in the past six months. In The TRU Study, we ask teens to write in (with no list provided) the names of the three brands from any product category, service, or retailer which they think are the "coolest," applying whatever definition of "cool" they choose. Typically, teens write in a huge range of brands—from H&M to Hot Topic, from Ford to BMW, and (unfortunately but not surprisingly) from Bud Ice to Marlboro.

Which brands typically populate the upper echelons of the Meter? At the top are the brands teens wear—or the stores where teens buy what they wear. Clothes are literally the brands in which teens wrap themselves, so fashion brands (clothes, shoes, accessories) have an almost unfair advantage on this measure. As much as teens love their favorite brand of breakfast cereal, how can it compete on a measure of "coolest" with the latest jeans brand that has captured teen attention? Still, this measure distinguishes the brands that have been most successful at winning teen favor.

Advertising is a key criterion of what constitutes a cool brand to teens. It's no surprise, then, that teens' favorite television commercials correlate

The Coolest Brands to Teens

Apparel brands are most likely to rank among the cool, and Nike is still the coolest brand to teens.

(percent of teens citing brand as one of the top three cool brands, by gender)

	total	female	male
Nike	24%	19%	28%
Sony	16	6	26
Abercrombie & Fitch	11	13	8
Adidas	11	11	10
Pepsi	9	8	9
American Eagle	8	9	6
Old Navy	7	9	6
Coca-Cola	7	5	8
Chevrolet	6	4	8
Tommy Hilfiger	6	6	5
Ford	5	5	6
Nintendo	5	2	8
Gap	5	7	3
Cover Girl	4	8	0
Mudd	4	7	0
Honda	3	3	4
FUBU	3	2	5
L.E.I.	3	6	0
Mountain Dew	3	3	4

Source: The TRU Study, Teenage Research Unlimited, Inc.

with their favorite brands. When we ask teens in qualitative research about their favorite ads, they frequently mention ads from companies at or near the top of the cool brand list—Nike, for one, not only resides atop the Meter, its ads are often mentioned by teens as their favorites

Because "cool" is such a subjective term, respondents write in hundreds of brand names in each TRU Study wave, including many up-and-coming smaller or "micro" brands. Not surprisingly, then, the brands that rise to the top of this pool of cool are the tried-and-true brands that have reached long-term, widespread acclaim. What are their commonalties, besides mainstream appeal and wide distribution? Celebrity endorsements, enviable advertising budgets, a well-known name, regular new-product releases (again, the importance of new), and a winning design. Plus, most of these brands are just plain big. We've found that many teens—especially mainstream Conformers—are less interested than their edgier peers in supporting the underdog and less intent on pursuing the new and different. Consequently, there's not as much movement among the top 10 or 20 brands as might be expected among an audience so known for fickleness. There's more action among the brands that make up the lower ranks of the Meter—those that make the list for the first time, hoping to climb to the upper tier. So, not only are our bigger-brand clients carefully monitoring their latest Meter score, so do newer and relaunched brands that hope to grab teen attention. The goal is to move up the ladder by becoming more than a flash on teens' radar screen. That happens when a brand stands for something meaningful to teens, making teens want to adopt it.

At TRU, we've been fortunate to work with many of the most successful youth brand managers. They understand that the last thing their brand should do is rest on its laurels. Brands must continue to evolve to remain fresh with teens. There's no question that one of the greatest challenges for any successful brand is maintaining long-term relevance for a restless teen public. In fact, popular youth brands face the same dilemma as popular musical performers, whose high visibility makes them case

Other Brands Teens Think Are Cool

While not the coolest of brands, these names at least earned an honorable mention.

(brands mentioned by 1 to 3 percent of respondents)

Vans	Mitsubishi
Dr. Pepper	Roxy
Aeropostale	Bath & Body Works
Microsoft	Levi's
Reebok	Maybelline
K-Swiss	Toyota
Clinique	Mercedes-Benz
Skechers	Wet Seal
New Balance	Steve Madden
Dodge	Jordan
Express	Cadillac
Polo/Ralph Lauren	Lucky
BMW	Mac Makeup
Phat Farm	Converse
Volkswagen	Ecko
Sprite	Limited

Source: The TRU Study, Teenage Research Unlimited, Inc.

studies in how to stay popular. After all, today's brands are in the same competitive environment as other figures in pop culture. With brands working more closely with entertainment partners, they find themselves in the same predicament as music acts who continually need to prove their relevance to each new group of teens. We think brands can learn and benefit from what's gone right (and not so right) with their counterparts in music.

Branding Lessons from the Music Industry

Back in 1993, an alternative band called the Crash Test Dummies emerged seemingly out of nowhere (Canada, actually) to take the country by storm. The band vaulted to international stardom thanks to the hit song, "Mmm Mmm Mmm Mmm." Remember, this was the grunge era: crunchy guitar riffs and angst-ridden lyrics were the order of the day. Many listeners were intrigued by the novelty of the lead singer's deep baritone and the group's pared-down, almost folksy sound.

At the same time, the newly released U2 album, *Zooropa*, was less successful than expected. U2 went on extended hiatus until 1997, when it released *Pop*. That album saw the group experiment with a distinctly disco-influenced sound that alienated some fans. Worse, some observers believed the accompanying PopMart tour (billed as the most expensive tour ever and featuring a 12-foot wide stuffed olive on a 100-foot toothpick) was bizarre and self-indulgent. At the end of the troublesome PopMart tour, U2 again went on hiatus.

But with musical groups as well as brands, neither giddy successes nor costly disappointments are irreversible. In the months following their initial success, the Crash Test Dummies followed up their hit single with a couple of lesser tunes, including "God Shuffled His Feet" and "Afternoons and Coffee Spoons." Not quite as catchy as the original, these songs failed to resonate with a young public that was by now familiar with the band's sound. Reaction was muted, and by the time the Crash Test Dummies released their follow-up album in 1996, interest had dried up entirely.

Whether knowingly or not, the band had made a promise it couldn't keep. The offbeat nature of the first song suggested to fans that they would be able to count on the group for catchy music that would break new ground. When the public burned out on the original song, the Crash Test Dummies couldn't offer anything of interest to take its place. The audience moved on.

Conversely, when U2 released another new album in 2000, they needed a hit. They turned to the basics that had originally made the group a household name—the giant toothpicks were gone, replaced by the kind of anthemic, socially aware music that symbolized the band's early years. U2 recognized its strengths, and capitalized on them in a way that recaptured the public's imagination. They were well rewarded: *Rolling Stone* magazine hailed the album as "a triumphant return for the band and its rock 'n roll roots." Well beyond simply resuscitating the band's career, U2 won numerous awards—including arguably the biggest award of all: huge album sales.

It's often said that teens are fickle and unpredictable. That's only half right: if there's anything you can safely predict, it's that teens will be fickle. In this respect, popularity can be a double-edged sword. Any product (be it a song or otherwise) that lingers in the public's consciousness for an extended period of time becomes so familiar that it may become tiresome. The phenomenon of burnout may be more familiar in music, but it's no less important in marketing. Show a teen a hit product, and you'll likely hear, "That's cool. What's next?" Teens want to be captivated and, if your product isn't up to the task or your brand isn't as interesting as it once was, they will look elsewhere.

Still, as U2 handily demonstrated during the last decade, straying too far from your brand's original premise may well confuse or alienate your target. The lesson from Bono and the boys is to update without creating upheaval. Now lets apply this finding to the world of marketing by examining a much more mundane category. The dental hygiene product category can serve as an example because it's experienced a great deal of creative updating. It's hard to imagine a more straightforward product than toothpaste: everyone needs it, so the market's assured. And for years, that's pretty much all the category had—plain, white, fresh-smelling goo. But in recent years, companies began to realize minty-fresh might just yield a mint. In addition to the gels, polishes, and various permutations of toothpaste, the market now includes all manner of gums, strips, whiteners, brighteners, and even cobranded mints. The lesson is clear: make sure your brand always does what's expected of it in unexpected ways. If marketers can breathe life into oral care, surely there are similar opportunities in any product category.

Nike's Success

So, who is the teen-branding equivalent of U2? One brand has dominated TRU's Coolest Brand Meter since its inception ten years ago: Nike, the behemoth athletic-shoe and apparel marketer. Nike has done so many things well for so long that it eventually became vulnerable to teen desertion. In the summer of 1997, 52 percent of teens listed Nike as one of their three coolest brands—a truly incredible number (especially considering this is a write-in question with a nearly unlimited number of possible answers). Nike not only competes with the likes of Adidas, Reebok, Converse, and Puma (although 52 percent would still be a strong number even in the confines of its own product category), it is also up against every relevant, new, cool, and interesting brand from any product category.

How did Nike surge ahead of everyone else—and stay ahead? How did that one brand attract so much teen attention and favor? The easy answer is that Nike did almost everything it could—reaching teens from every angle—and did it well. The fuller answer is that Nike hit a deep emotional chord with its consumers—strategically, the brand hit its mark with teens like no other brand before or since.

Certainly Nike owes much of its allure to the strong relationships it has forged with athletes over the years and to artfully conveying the magic of those relationships to consumers. But Nike did not achieve this level of success simply by leveraging celebrity; its success rose from carefully managing these brand endorsements so that they fit and furthered Nike's primary brand position of excellence, performance, and inspiration. There may not be another corporate slogan that so succinctly captures a company's positioning as Nike's "Just Do It." And the swoosh! In short order, that simple symbol stood for "Just Do It" and Nike itself.

The athletes Nike has worked with—starting, of course, with Michael Jordan—put a face to the brand, one that is equal parts aspirational and inspirational. It's the combination of these two emotional components that most deeply resonates with teens. Nike's success is due to an important consumer insight—that its brand could both inspire and enhance individual performance. It then executed it flawlessly through endorsements, advertising, sponsorships, events, partnerships, and, of course, product. The fact that teens line up around the block or down the mall corridor at their neighborhood retailer in order to get the latest Air Jordans did as much to make the brand a teen must-have as Nike's well-executed branding techniques. And the brand hasn't made a critical misstep (at least not yet)—it has been careful not to take itself too seriously. Its advertising, through the wonderful work of its primary agency, Wieden and Kennedy, shows that Nike understands that its consumers need to see the brand as human—that it has an approachable, personable, entertaining side. Nike's Bo Jackson/Bo Diddley ads, along with its Lil' Penny series, made teens laugh while—at the same time—giving the brand greater license to hit consumers even more emotionally in other work. Its lighthearted ads made its more passionate, brand-defining advertising all the more powerful.

Still, Nike has recently found it difficult to sustain the stratospheric popularity numbers it posted back in the late 1990s. Why did Nike begin to decline? First, there's only one direction to go when you're at the pinnacle.

Where, after all, did U2 go after *Joshua Tree*? But, Nike's mainstream success was in some ways its own worst enemy. Teens are not only drawn to that which is new, they also feel most connected with brands that are aimed particularly at them.

When Nike became mainstream-fashionable, everybody (including moms, little kids, and even geriatric mall-walkers) started sporting the swoosh. Nike's brand proposition no longer seemed so new—not only because of the brand's massive ad budget but also because its competitors wanted in on the action. Planet Reebok produced Nike-looking ads, and Gatorade leveraged Michael Jordan effectively, as well, even producing a hit "Be Like Mike" jingle. As Nike began to look to other demographic segments, teens also began to look elsewhere, and Nike's score—though always remaining the highest on the Brand Meter—went into a steady decline. Allegations of paying Asian factory workers starvation wages didn't help either, and some teens told us they wanted a smaller, gentler brand. Perhaps most threatening of all, teens started to diss Nike products, claiming its designers had gone astray, trying too hard to please too many contingents and not doing particularly well with any of them.

But, just as U2 recognized that it needed to get in touch with its roots and deliver on the initial promise that so captivated consumers, Nike also got back in touch with its core proposition and audience. The company has begun to focus on teens once again, creating product and advertising that more intimately targets this age group. Fortunately for the brand, it never became irrelevant and never came close to hitting rock bottom. Nike has been able to maintain loyalty among its key demographic segment: African-American male teen athletes. Many of these teens fall into TRU's Influencer Teen/Type, and they hold a particularly vaunted spot in the teen hierarchy. This is key because, as many once-proud brands know, it's much harder to make advances when you're fighting an uphill battle!

The lesson in brief is that teens can be a volatile and unforgiving bunch, but you *can* work your way back into their favor. Find out where you went wrong and adjust. Figure out what you were doing right and update it. Reach teens in new and surprising ways, but always err on the side of being true to your brand.

Now for the example of a brand gone wrong (and stayed wrong). Who has been following a career path similar to the Crash Test Dummies? Staying within the Nike category, the case could be made that Fila is going the way of the alternative rockers. During the heyday of the sneaker wars, Fila found itself in an unexpected position—that of an urban, street shoe adopted by, and associated with, gangbangers. This imagery was diametrically opposed to Fila's heritage. The Italian designer brand was traditionally a favorite of American country clubbers who appreciated its high-priced, colorful ski and tennis lines.

Still, teens represented a new frontier for Fila, and the company worked out an endorsement deal with the young, affable NBA rookie phenom, Grant Hill, who supplanted Bjorn Borg as the most recognizable Fila endorser. To Fila's credit, the brand had no baggage: teens viewed the brand as new, unaware that some tennis playing Swede had modeled its tight-fitting shirts and shorts on Wimbledon's Centre Court. The Hill shoe was a hit; so was the Hill 2. But that was it. Whereas Nike saw its core target begin to dissipate because of the brand's mainstream appeal, Fila was handcuffed by an almost too-fine, too-targeted street image. Yes, it had street cred (before this term was widely used), but too much of its appeal ended there.

As much as Fila appreciated African-American youths' adoption of its product, it wanted to increase volume by reaching beyond this segment. TRU undertook some qualitative research on Fila's behalf following the release of the Hill 2. The goal was to help the brand team understand how far Fila could push its allure to non-African-American teens. We conducted research in several mid-America markets, including Denver, where we set out to recruit Caucasian teens who had purchased Fila in the past six months. The extent of the brand's problems became evident when I received a phone call one day from the focus group facility assigned to recruit the teen respondents. The facility owner told me this was the toughest recruit he had been assigned since the IRS commissioned him to do a qualitative study. In that case, every prospective respondent declined, fearing it was a sting operation. In this case, however, the facility found that fewer than 1 percent of non-African-American Fila buyers in Denver were within the target age group. This, in itself, was a huge finding.

Because of the big budgets required, Fila found itself hard-pressed to compete with Nike and Reebok in what was becoming an increasingly aggressive arena of signing young, rich athletes. Being financially tied to Hill proved costly as well. Although he became one of the truly great and well-liked NBA stars, Hill also became one of the most injury-prone, and—because of cost—Fila had to pass on other young athletes. Like the Crash Test Dummies, Fila appeared unlikely to have more than its one or two hits—at least among teens.

Should Fila return to its roots as an exclusive country-club brand (buoyed by endorsements from tennis players Jennifer Capriatti, Mark Philippoussis, and Jelena Dokic)? Or should it explore how best to re-connect with the young urban audience with which it had so much success that it saw its stock rising to $90 per share before plummeting to the single digits? Or, alternately, can Fila become something new and exciting to another consumer segment? These are issues Fila is likely debating.

What Teens Want from Brands

TRU continues to consult with teens when it comes to matters of brand-ing—no surprise here. Perhaps just as predictably, we learn more by read-ing between the lines than by simply accepting what teens say at face value. Although understanding brand dynamics and how teens view brands is anything but simple, we seldom walk away from research feeling as though checking with teens was fruitless.

One avenue we explored recently was within the confines of our national syndicated study. Based on what we learned, we went back to teens in a qualitative setting to help us make sense of the quantitative data. We found this follow-up insightful, which validated the importance of reading between the lines.

The particular question we posed to the national sample was, in many ways, the million-dollar question: "Think about those brands that used to be your favorites but no longer are. And, think about those brands that are currently your favorites. What could the brands you used to like have done so they would have continued to be your favorites?" Talk about a broad, theoretical question! Still, we think it worked, yielding insights—but only after prudent follow-up and careful analysis.

In fact, the results of this measure provide a lesson in reading between the lines: teens immediately say brands should lower their price—not a surprising piece of advice from any consumer, especially those who don't have the income of a full-time job. But upon further probing we found that teens weren't guided by price so much after all. Today, we warn clients not to be misled when teens tell them they want lower prices; they simply can't resist! When teens are probed about whether their favorite brands are those that offer low prices, they waver. Yes, teens reluctantly admit that a favorite brand can become more accessible if it goes on sale. But can a brand really be cool if it's sold at a low price? Not necessarily. By the very act of becoming accessible to more teens, a brand may lose its elite caché. Complicated? You bet. But so are the decisions teens must make when facing so many competitive brands vying for their dollars.

The bigger learning from this question is the validation of teens' attraction to that which is new. The fact that teens desire newness is, well, nothing new. In fact, the vast majority of respondents suggested that the brand in question do something new! Nearly half the sample (47 percent) maintain that a key ingredient in making a brand their favorite is to continually offer them new products; another 22 percent say brands should

How to Maintain Brand Loyalty

Teens say lowering prices and developing new products are the top ways to maintain their brand loyalty.

(percent of teens responding when asked, "Think about some of your favorite current brands of all types of products. Now think about some of the brands you used to really like but don't anymore. Which three of the following do you think are the most important things for brands to do so that they'll continue to be your favorite?")

	total
Lower price	67%
New product	47
Improved quality	35
Sell product in your favorite store	31
New advertising	22
Do something surprising	20
Sponsor events	18
New contests and promotions	17
Get a celebrity to use or wear the brand	13
Donate money to a cause you care about	11
Come out with another brand	6
Sell the product on a really great Web site	2

Source: The TRU Study, Teenage Research Unlimited, Inc.

produce lots of new advertising; nearly the same number (17 percent) advise brands to develop innovative contests and promotions.

As TRU has continually found among teens, image isn't everything. As much as they appreciate and are attracted to brands that offer a constant stream of newness, if those brands don't deliver on quality, teens will turn away. In this measure, more than a third of respondents (35 percent) advocated for quality—suggesting that they turned away from their previously favored brands because they saw product quality decline. Interestingly, teens tell TRU that quality means different things in different product categories. For food, quality means great taste. For footwear it's durability and style. For fashion it's style above all else. (We warned that you would have to read between the lines.)

The importance of retail is also key to shaping teens' attitudes about a brand; nearly a third (31 percent) say look no further than their favorite stores to find their favorite brands. There's a strong association—among all consumer groups—with what's sold and the store that sells it. The image of the brand and the image of the retailer rub off on each other; so, each must choose its partners carefully.

In the retail-brand equation, teens are becoming increasingly open-minded, appreciating the value and relevance of mass-merchandisers like Target and Kohl's. Levi's is perhaps the prime example of a brand that has been hurt by—and is now aggressively fixing—its retail associations. Several years ago, after Gap made the decision to stop selling non-Gap brands in its stores, Levi's found its base brand being sold primarily in outlets not deemed to be all that teen-cool, including JC Penney and Sears (despite teens shopping at both these stores—especially Penney's—in big numbers). The Levi's brand decline has been well documented, including how the company was slow to catch on to the wider silhouettes preferred by teen guys some years back. Levi's, in time, offered these styles—but the damage had been done; teens didn't realize the company actually was making the jeans they wanted. Levi's simply wasn't in many of the stores that teens favor (especially the stores in which Edge and Influencer teens, who lead the trends, shop). Levi's is currently working on closing this perceptual gap (no pun intended) by developing more upscale lines and getting them placed in specialty retailers, such as Urban Outfitters, which teens not only frequent but also find aspirational. This association will do more than sell what's in stock; it should also boost Levi's overall brand image. The power of the right retailer!

Other teen suggestions for how brands can remain in teens' favor include hooking up with celebrity endorsers (13 percent), donating money to their favorite causes (11 percent), launching subbrands (6 percent), and selling the product on a "really great" Web site (2 percent).

Because the competition is formidable—with teens constantly exposed in new ways to new ideas, new messages, and new brands—it's incumbent upon you to surprise them with innovative ideas that stand out. Don't worry if your brand is not new. Some of teens' favorite brands, such as Adidas, Abercrombie & Fitch, and, yes, 7 Up, have been repositioned, relaunched, or even resurrected from the near dead. An updated image, a fresh message, and innovative delivery can bring a brand a long way.

One way to surprise teens with your brand's versatility is to show up where least expected—or to extend your brand to other channels teens view as appropriate and different. To this end, several well-known lifestyle brands are charting a new course. Rather than leave their brand image totally at the mercy of transient ad campaigns and promotions, brand managers are creating entirely new services, showing a keen grasp of consumer wants and needs. Not quite a brand extension, not quite a promotion, these offerings complement a company's core business.

Perhaps one of the most striking examples is *Seventeen* magazine, which has opened a nightclub and retail store in Los Angeles. As discussed in Chapter 8, the *Seventeen* store allows the fashion-conscious to find the fashions featured in the magazine each month in one convenient location. Next door, at an under-21 dance club called "One Seven," the magazine promotes itself as a key purveyor of style and fun even as it allows editors to observe the latest trends among what it hopes are the trend-leading members of its target. What's more, the magazine is launching a combination salon, studio, and spa without the snootiness that tends to intimidate young first-time spa customers. The spa/salon is a natural springboard for the magazine's steady stream of health and beauty tips— talk about a surprising but appropriate brand extension! Helpfully for *Seventeen*'s purposes, girls in a recent qualitative session told us that if they had some extra cash, they'd head straight to a spa to be pampered and destressed. It's a sign of the times that teens have enough cash to make such a concept viable and enough stress (or at least enough interest in adult aspirations) that they feel they need the full spa treatment. And, *Seventeen* recognized the need to offer a spa experience that's both age-appropriate and brand building at the same time.

Although *Seventeen* is aggressively pursuing this brand-extension strategy, a male-oriented lifestyle brand furthered the concept years ago. When West Coast skate-shoe manufacturer Vans began building eponymous skate parks across the country, it did so in areas with eager but underserved skateboarding communities. In addition to encouraging demand for Vans' products, the skate parks also foster goodwill among boarders—reaching them at perhaps the most relevant contact point: where they skate. Since then, Vans has had a hand in all manner of lifestyle marketing, from the Vans Warped Tour to production assistance for the recent film documentary *Dogtown and the Z-Boys*. The company even has its own "indie" record label.

Though ambitious, such attempts don't necessarily spell sure success. Vans recently closed one of its skate parks and admitted that most of them have "significantly under-performed" lately.

Recent data from Omnibuzz, TRU's online omnibus survey, suggests that teens are willing to give these kinds of "branding extensions" a shot— but only if they already like the brand's core product. Some 71 percent of teen girls who read *Seventeen* reported they are "very" or "somewhat" interested in a *Seventeen*-branded spa, compared to 52 percent of non-readers. And 73 percent of teen guys who reported liking Vans products expressed interest in the skate parks, compared to only 29 percent of teens who didn't like Vans. As teens themselves assert, these extensions need to make sense. They must be easily recognizable as enhancing the base brand.

Teens appreciate brands when they support their lifestyle. For years, TRU has advised clients that the best way to stay in a consumer's life is to become almost indistinguishable from it. But, as the Omnibuzz data suggest, choose your opportunities carefully. Though you'll undoubtedly gain greater notice from your target by extending your brand into other areas of their life, make sure the attention leads to positive associations. Teens may reject you if they feel you're playing too far afield—trying too hard is the absolute antithesis of cool.

In addition to recognizing the importance of evolving your brand through new marketing tactics (including appropriately extending your brand to new areas), it's equally important to assess these efforts regularly. To this end, TRU regularly conducts quantitative "brand-equity" or "brand-value" tracking studies that measure brands on a host of relevant attributes ("is interesting," "surprised me at times," "has great advertising," "is for someone like me," "is a quality product," "is cool," etc). Thanks to our syndicated study, we've been able to get a handle not only on the attributes that should be included in this type of customized research, but also those that teens use to assess the personal relevance of brands.

How do teens know a brand is cool? What are the elusive qualities that shoes, beverages, clothes, and other products share that bring them a halo of coolness? The answer, according to the results of another recent measure in The TRU Study, is style. Teens' number-one answer (offered by 43 percent of the sample) is that it's cool if it looks cool. In other words, they know it when they see it! Pretty simple. But there's more: for a brand to be really cool, teens say that other teens have to think it looks cool, too. Anyone who has passed Teen 101 isn't surprised by this answer, but the

What Makes a Brand "Cool"

Design, popularity, and quality make a brand "cool."

(percent of teens responding when asked, "Thinking about all sort of different products, how can you tell if a brand is 'cool'?")

It looks cool	43%
Friends want it or like it	41
It's a great quality product	40
It has great advertising	25
Everyone's talking about it	21
Everyone has it	19
It's especially for someone your age	16
It's the newest thing	16
It's sold at cool stores	15
Popular people want or like it	14
You found out about it in an unexpected way	11
It's been around a long time	10
A celebrity you like uses it	8
It's expensive	8

Source: The TRU Study, Teenage Research Unlimited, Inc.

finding is a reminder about how word of mouth can make or break you. Forty-two percent of teens admit that their friends' good opinion of a brand influences its coolness.

Of course, as discussed above, teens are rational, savvy shoppers, and they consistently maintain that quality is an important element of cool brands. Forty-one percent of teens claim that quality products make a brand cool. But remember what "quality" really means to teens—particularly in the fashion category! Quality equals style.

There are important differences by demographic segment. For example, younger teens are particularly conscious of their peers' role in defining cool brands. More younger than older teens report that a brand is cool if their friends want it, if everyone has it, and if "popular people" like it. African-American teens, who are perhaps most influenced by oral communications, emphasize that a cool brand is one that everyone's talking about.

From teens' point of view, brands can play a key role in shaping one's reputation—especially within the hypersensitive social spheres of younger teens. Brand choice is an infinitely personal decision for teens—an important point for marketers and advertisers to remember when thinking about their brand in the context of teen life.

Brand Loyalty

Today's teens are tomorrow's adults. The simplicity of this statement tempts many to ignore its fuller implications. However, as teens gain experience as consumers, they are establishing preferences that brand managers hope they will carry with them as adults. This is a big reason why more companies than ever are reaching out to teens, hoping to develop a long-lasting relationship. But do teens return the favor? Just how loyal are they as consumers?

Several times during the past few years, we have been asked to submit proposals for a research study that would determine teens' brand loyalty across a range of product categories. Undertaking such an endeavor would be extremely complex and expensive, however. To get a proper sense of brand behavior, the ultimate study would have to be longitudinal, carefully tracking the same group of individuals over time, beginning in their early teens and continuing into adulthood. (Because of expected attrition, the sample size would need to be large, and—because of the quality and quantity of the learning—the questionnaire would have to be extensive, probably requiring a diary-type reporting form.) The study would monitor whether current purchases and brand perceptions influence future purchase behavior and attitudes, and whether and how brand choices and preferences change over time. Although we have yet to execute this type of longitudinal study, the fact that every few years a client requests such a proposal shows how important the issue of brand loyalty is to businesses in the teen market. Someday, a client may spring for such research. Due to the survey's duration and expense, however, the company that commissions it will likely be a long-term player already at the top of its field—and expecting to stay there.

It is possible to persuade teens to abandon trusted brands even in categories where brand names are most important. Even among brand-conscious teens, for example, private-label clothing lines are making inroads. Arizona, which is JC Penney's store-brand jeans, is finding strong success in the teen market: 14 percent of teens purchased the brand in the past year. Penney's has been smart in not tying the brand to its own corporate image, which may be less than relevant to teens. In fact, when we ask teens in qualitative research where Arizona jeans are sold, they typically not only answer JC Penney, but also list other popular retailers.

Contributing to the erosion of brand loyalty is the fact that today's teens have far more product and brand choices available to them than ever before. Teenagers are willing to experiment rather than buy a brand because that's what their parents buy or that's what they've always bought. The jeans category is a strong example based not only on the proliferation of store brands, but also small, regional brands. So many upstart competitors have fragmented the jeans category that the biggest jean brands—including Levi's, Lee, Mudd, and L.E.I.—are feeling the pinch. Not too many years ago, teens (especially guys) owned Levi's and maybe one or two other brands of jeans. Now, with brand choice growing and changing rapidly, teens can choose from a number of smaller brands, making a statement about their own personal style.

To determine the product categories to which teens are most loyal (i.e., the categories from which teens repeatedly purchase the same brand), we gave The TRU Study's national sample of respondents a list of 20 categories and asked: "Thinking about the last three times you bought (or your parents bought for you) this product, how many times did you or they buy the same brand for you?"

With the exception of camera film, the top-ten categories are all health and beauty aids. The more intimate the category, the less teens are willing to experiment. After all, there's a greater risk to self-confidence when trying a new brand if a consumer is already (to some degree) satisfied with his or her current brand. Brand switching in some of these categories (i.e., feminine-care products, shampoo, acne medication, antiperspirant/deodorant) is, therefore, considered risky. Teens are justifiably concerned that switching brands within these intimate categories might jeopardize their appearance or image. And, for teens especially, how they look is tied to how they feel within their greater peer group. The link to social belonging is great and, as a consequence, it's one that marketers of these products appeal to when advertising to teens. Though most teens enjoy at least a modicum of risk, when it comes to the high stakes of appearance and social status, they become quite risk-adverse.

Of all the health, beauty, and personal-care products, feminine-hygiene products enjoy the greatest loyalty among teens. Mothers typically introduce their daughters to brands in this category, deciding the form and brand their daughters will use; there's little experimentation after that.

Arguably, there's no category as intimate as this one; therefore, convincing girls to switch brands is especially challenging.

Not all health and beauty-aid products fall into this "intimate" category, and some face significant battles when it comes to brand switching. In fact, some health and beauty aid products attain loyalty for almost the reverse reason. Take bar soap and toothpaste, for example. Many teens use the same brands of these products over and over again. It's not because brand choice is important to them; instead, it's because they are content with whatever brand is purchased for them. They would neither choose to spend their own money on these items nor go through the "trouble" of requesting specific brands. After all, teens understand trade-offs: campaigning for a specific brand in these categories would likely hurt their chances of getting a special request in a category they care about more.

By the time children reach their teen years, they have experimented with a tremendous number of brands. Teenagers have a sense of which brands work best for them, based on efficacy, comfort, or a variety of social or psychological needs of which they may be unaware. So, when teens feel secure with how a brand performs, particularly health and beauty aids, they regard changing brands as risky or unnecessary. This was our hypothesis about teen brand choice. Intrigued, we decided to investigate further.

What always struck us about our brand-loyalty data (which, incidentally, have been extremely stable over the years) is that fashion categories rank relatively low in loyalty. On the surface, this finding appears to contradict our qualitative research, which shows that clothes, jeans, and shoes are the categories in which brand choice is most important to teens.

We call such products "badge" items—items that offer signals to the peer group about their users/wearers. Brand loyalty in badge categories typically is low because of factors such as the fluctuating popularity of "in" brands, current styles and colors, availability, and price. This is not to say that brand name is less important in these categories. On the contrary, we believe it's more important. Supporting this assertion are the findings of the Coolest Brand Meter, which shows that fashion brands regularly rank at the top.

So, we have an apparent contradiction: some of the categories in which teens are the most loyal behaviorally (i.e., they buy the same brand repeatedly) are those in which brand choice (i.e., caring about which brand is purchased) is relatively unimportant. Therefore, investigating the importance of brand choice, both independently and in combination with brand loyalty, is a prerequisite to more fully understanding the teen–brand relationship.

Based on our research over the years, we believe that teens' willingness to buy or campaign for certain brands is directly related to the importance of brand choice in those categories. But there are categories in which brand choice is extremely important to teens, yet because the set of desired brands within these categories is constantly changing, the brands enjoy less loyalty.

To test the relationship between brand choice and brand importance, we added a brand-importance measure to The TRU Study. We presented respondents with the same categories listed in the brand-loyalty question and asked them to choose those that best fit the statement: "Getting the brand of my choice is most important when buying (or when someone buys for me)." This question examines brand relationships on an attitudinal basis, while the previous loyalty measure was behavioral. The findings identify the product categories in which getting the brand of choice is most important to teens, regardless of their loyalty (i.e., how often they use or buy the same brand).

The rank order of this list is strikingly different from the behavioral brand-loyalty measure. The fact that two of the top-three are fashion categories supports our hypothesis about the distinction between brand loyalty versus brand choice. This distinction is also supported by our finding that teens regard brands within the fashion category as the coolest. Again, these are the brands in which teens physically wrap themselves—those that send signals to others about what brands (and, by extension, what lifestyle) the teen wants to associate. Athletic shoes and jeans, for example, are badge items (the former, particularly, for teen guys). Their importance to teens transcends their use as consumer products. Expensive items signal affluence, for example, and some teens (like many adults!) want to be perceived as affluent—or at least having the means with which to purchase such items.

Tampons and sanitary pads rank first and second, respectively, in brand loyalty. But they rank eighth and first, respectively, in brand importance. In other words, girls are likely to use the same tampon brand, yet choice of brand is less important than it is when buying sanitary pads. This difference may be explained by the fact that there are simply more pad brands than tampon brands. Only one health and beauty aid (antiperspirant/deodorant) appears in boys' top-five list, compared to four in girls' top five, reflecting guys' and girls' different purchasing priorities.

Mapping the Findings: Brand Loyalty vs. Brand Importance

How do brand loyalty (buying the same brand within a given category at least two of the last three times) and brand choice (the importance of brand choice within a category) interact? To find out, we rank-ordered the 20 categories in each of the two measures and plotted them on a quadrant map.

Quadrant I shows the product categories toward which teens feel most brand loyal and for which brand choice is most important to them. Teens care about buying certain brands within these categories and repeatedly purchase the same brands.

Quadrant II shows the product categories toward which teens are not brand loyal but brand selective. Although teens find it important to buy specific brands within these categories, their brand of choice frequently changes.

Quadrant III shows the product categories toward which teens are not brand loyal or brand selective. Teens do not purchase the same brands, nor do they consider it important to purchase specific brands in these categories.

Quadrant IV shows the product categories toward which teens are brand loyal but brand indifferent. Teens repeatedly use the same brands within these categories, yet the choice of brand is not particularly important to them.

Note not only into which quadrant a product category falls, but also where in the quadrant it lies. Location within a quadrant indicates the degree of loyalty and the importance of brand choice relative to other categories in the quadrant. Sanitary pads and acne remedy, for example, both fall within Quadrant I, yet sanitary pads enjoy greater brand loyalty and brand importance than acne remedy.

Categories in Quadrants I and II offer marketers the greatest opportunity for developing a long-lasting relationship with teens. A brand-switching strategy would be particularly challenging for Quadrant I categories, while gaining brand loyalty is a challenge for Quadrant II categories. The big implication for marketers of Quadrant I products is to grab consumers early, understanding their "point of entry" (i.e., at what age they enter the category) and reaching them then. If you're late, you may be too late.

Notably, all the categories in Quadrant I are health and beauty aids (sanitary pads, tampons, antiperspirant/deodorant, shampoo, and acne remedies). These are all products for which brand switching could present a social risk. Once teens feel comfortable with a certain brand in one of these categories, they don't want to risk switching brands.

Some of the Quadrant II categories are composed of relatively large sets of acceptable brands. Teens rotate their brand of choice depending upon price, availability, and advertising. Because brand choice is important

Brand Loyalty and
Brand Importance

The quadrant map shows at a glance how brand loyalty and brand importance interact for teens.

(Loyalty and Importance: Combining the findings)

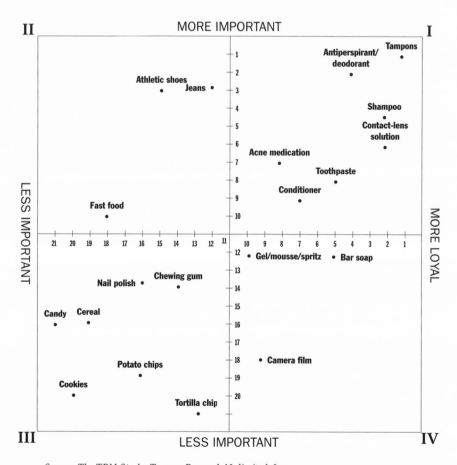

Source: The TRU Study, Teenage Research Unlimited, Inc.

to teens when buying products in Quadrant II, marketers of these products are presented with an opportunity to convert less-loyal category enthusiasts to loyal brand users. To exploit this opportunity, marketers should explore the unique attributes and perceptions of their brands to properly frame and develop strategies for encouraging loyalty.

Quadrant II categories are image-oriented and heavily advertised. Several are badge items teens use for positioning themselves socially. If a similar analysis were performed among adults, beer and automobiles would almost certainly fall into this quadrant. Cigarettes are an intriguing category here, especially considering the average age of initiation is approximately 12. As a teen first begins to smoke, cigarettes likely take a place somewhere in Quadrant II. Imagery strongly sways young people and cigarettes are marketed as having distinct personalities. Think about the Marlboro Man as independence, Joe Camel as the partier, and Newport as preppy all-American. There's an image for every teen so inclined to emulate. Not coincidentally, these happen to be teens' three most-used cigarette brands. But because of the unique physical properties of tobacco—namely, nicotine's addictiveness—once teens get hooked, cigarettes as a category move over to Quadrant I. That's the power of addiction.

Product categories plotted in Quadrant III (low loyalty and low importance) face the most difficult challenge of all. Teens neither care strongly about brand choice nor do they, even out of habit, use the same brand frequently. Four of the six products plotted in this quadrant are foods, each with many competitive brands vying for teen attention: candy, chewing gum, tortilla chips, and potato chips. Teens are less loyal to brands in these categories because there are so many interchangeable options and because low price points make it less risky to experiment. Further, purchase cycles are short. Still, it is important to remember that teens have favorite brands in snack and candy categories. Most likely, their favorite sets include several brands, suggesting that pricing and value strategies may be particularly effective in these categories. Doritos is an example of a brand pushing upwards toward Quadrants II and I, although category dynamics place most snack foods in Quadrant III. Through carefully crafted advertising, promotion, and packaging (as well as its inherent product appeal to teens), it's defined itself as the teen-appropriate, fun, party snack brand (more on Doritos soon).

Four product categories fall into Quadrant IV: toothpaste, contact-lens solution, bar soap, and camera film (which, thanks to highly sought-after digital cameras, is declining as a relevant teen category). Teens use the same brands repeatedly in these categories, but they do not regard brand as particularly important. Most likely, Mom is choosing the brand and the teen is content to use whatever brand is available. Marketers of these products need to appeal to teens directly, so that teens begin to request certain brands. Another approach would be more long-term: develop a strong relationship with young consumers, recognizing that they typically are neither the purchasers nor active requesters now, but will be when they are adults.

Summing It Up: Teen Branding Guidelines

Now you have a handle on the importance of branding to teens—what brands mean to them emotionally, psychologically, and physically, as well as which brands have developed the type of emotional connection with teens that set them apart. I've also shared a host of qualitative experience, quantitative data, and secondary research to show the relationship between teens and brands. This chapter's final pages seem to call for both a workable definition of what a brand is from a teen perspective and what it takes to become a strong brand from a marketing perspective.

First, a brand is who you are. It's that simple—a brand is an identity. As brand managers, you need to understand what consumers expect of you and what you can rightly deliver. Similarly, you need to know what you aren't and where you can't go. In other words, understand your boundaries! Teens might respect you today, but understand that it's a contextualized respect. If you stray outside the realms of where teens feel you belong with new products and/or marketing, you're vulnerable to being dismissed.

Think about Doritos. As mentioned earlier, much of its advertising has positioned it as the party snack chip brand. But through conducting research with teens, its brand managers learned that being the party brand wasn't enough. More so, they learned that simply being relevant to teens wasn't enough. The Doritos brand team learned that teens wanted and expected product variety from Doritos. Consequently, in keeping with the brand personality, Doritos launched irreverent new-flavor introductions, coming out with a host of crazy, anything-but-ordinary flavors. Go to a grocery store today and take a look at all the flavors, sizes, and variations, including four cheese, salsa verde, taco, toasted corn, ranchero, and Doritos 3Ds (an extension that itself comes in different flavors).

So, a brand is first and foremost your identity. But, it's much more than just who you are. It's what you stand for—it's your core, and it's the underpinnings of your identity. Truth, the antitobacco campaign, is a prime example of a brand whose identity transcends a symbol or a current marketing campaign. And Truth clearly transcends product—after all, it's a product-less brand. What most distinguishes Truth is what it stands for and—in this case—what it stands against. Truth is, well, for truth—it fights against the deceptions and lies that historically have been the hallmark of tobacco-industry marketing. Sounds boring from a teen perspective? Truth is all about tonality and execution. Its ads are anything but preachy and pedantic; instead, they're irreverent, edgy, and—at times—funny. In fact, since the American Legacy Foundation launched the campaign, Truth ads— created by Arnold Advertising in Boston and Crispin Porter + Bogusky in Miami—have garnered a good share of mentions in each wave of TRU's favorite commercial measure, in which our quantitative teen sample is asked to write in their three favorite commercials. So, teens rate Truth's ads on the same level as those from Nike, Pepsi, and other traditonal youth advertising heavyweights.

A brand's image is also an important cue that helps teens determine what you're about and whether they want to affiliate with you. Teens should feel in good company with your brand. For the roughly 88 percent of teens who aren't of the Edge Teen/Type, it is vital who else is wearing or using your brand, and this association extends beyond user imagery. For an apparel brand, the company you keep includes the stores that sell your brands. Brands that are themselves retailers—Abercrombie & Fitch, American Eagle, Old Navy, Gap, and others—benefit from having total control of their retail environment. From displays to the full realm of merchandise to the store aesthetic (layout, lighting, music, signage) and sales clerks, these retail brands are able to craft the environment to complement, enhance, and convey their brand message and overriding identity. Nonretail apparel brands, in contrast, must rely on their retail partners for these tactics; as discussed earlier, Levi's move into stores like Urban Outfitters will undoubtedly benefit the brand through positive, aspirational association.

In addition to your end users and retailers, your brand is also noted for the company it keeps with promotional partners. Clearly, the idea of partnering with other brands at events—in particular entertainment events—presents opportunities to be associated with fun. You will also be able to borrow (or perhaps add) a halo of cool from the association with compelling brands and properties.

Mountain Dew is an example of a large brand that's still nimble enough to move quickly to maintain teen interest, yet has been careful not to drift too far from its essence. Ask teens what they associate with Mountain Dew, and their typical response is extreme sports. Not bad. But, take a good look at what Mountain Dew has done with "extreme"—in many ways, the most overused recent youth positioning. Fortunately for the brand, Mountain Dew got there first and—in many ways—owns extreme. But Mountain Dew very smartly is more than extreme sports—it's about extreme humor and an extreme sensibility that's relateable to teens and continually engaging to them.

Enduring brands surprise teens by growing and moving in unexpected but acceptable ways. MTV is a prime example of a brand that's maintained enduring relevance through evolution. At its onset the network was revolutionary; today, it's evolutionary. MTV, after all, is no longer a teen itself—having been launched more than 20 years ago. Clearly, it has moved away from its namesake identity of being exclusively a music channel. But that original premise gave it the license to extend its brand into other areas of teen culture, which in turn made it the cultural touchstone it is today. And, MTV continues to push the boundaries of its programming; in fact, at any given time, MTV offers more than 50 shows, many of which are new. MTV has had an amazing string of hit TV shows, including *House Party, Real World, Beavis and Butt-head, Road Rules, Singled Out, TRL, The Tom Green Show, Jackass, The Osbournes,* and *Punk'd.* But the network never rests on its laurels. In addition to this regular lineup, the network's omnipresent Spring Break specials have done more to shape the nature of this teen rite of passage than any other factor. Its various award shows bestow the MTV seal of approval on everything from music videos to movies, allowing the network to crown itself the entertainment authority for a generation. And a constant stream of timely specials, including those that delve into politics and social issues, elevate what would otherwise be a fluffy programming roster to a concerned media citizen. Clearly, MTV is a living, moving, evolving brand. Beyond its programming, MTV simply looks and feels different than the MTV of even five years ago—edgier, grittier, less studio-based, less pop. It's these changes—in both programming and aesthetics—that are responsible for MTV being such a relevant brand 20 years after its launch. The network has succeeded in staying true to its roots while continuing to surprise and engage its audience (many of whom weren't born when MTV launched as a music-video cable channel).

Successful teen brands inherently respect teens. In fact, part of being relateable to teens is demonstrating to teens that you respect them (and, more specifically, your particular teen segment). Teens' marketing radar is finely attuned; they can easily separate the sincere from the cynical. The WB television network decided early on to use programming to talk to teens about the tough issues they're facing and thinking about. But instead of using a tired, manufactured, *Saved-by-the-Bell* approach, the WB employs relateable characters and compelling storylines to make the communication dramatic and appealing. Teen girls could instinctively tell the WB took them seriously, and they responded by making the network one of their favorites.

Part of evolving your brand is not being afraid to take risks. Standing out from the crowd is not only key for established brands, but also for new brands that need to gain notice. Jones Soda, up against the marketing and distribution muscle of Coke and Pepsi as well as the established brand portfolio of the Dr Pepper/Seven-Up Company, knew its greatest challenge was to be heard despite the plentitude of louder, stronger voices. Clearly, Jones Soda wasn't going to make great inroads when it came to shelf space in the big guys' key distribution channels. So, early on, the brand team decided to sell its product only in surf and skate shops; through such alternative distribution and great-looking, innovative packaging, the brand built awareness and imagery despite the notable lack of any real ad budget. Just imagine the risk Jones Soda's brand managers took trying to sell investors on the idea of marketing a soft drink without selling the product at convenience stores and supermarkets! But it worked—consumers took notice, aided by the brand's unusual flavors and its practice of allowing customers to go to its Web site to create their own bottle labels. After gaining attention and trial through nontraditional distribution outlets (and gaining a cult following), the brand has since gone mainstream, getting its products placed in more traditional, accessible channels. Coke, Pepsi, and Dr Pepper/Seven-Up don't yet have to worry about keeping up with Jones, but at least Jones is figuring out a way to keep up with them!

A brand is more than the sum of your products. In fact, most brands that successfully engage teens over a period of time do so because their product line is not static. Each season brings with it new product lines for apparel marketers, for example. Where's the continuity when you need to constantly shake things up? It's the core essence of your brand; it's what you stand for.

Similarly, a brand is more than a single message or marketing program. It's more than a symbol, word, phrase, or overarching theme. In the same way that it can be tempting to live on your last product line, your latest ad campaign should be viewed as just one communication from your brand. If you're fortunate at present to have a hit ad campaign, enjoy it while it lasts and push your agency to plan the next one—or, at the very least (and if your budget allows), develop fresh executions within your current campaign. And if you happen to misstep with advertising that doesn't work, take comfort in the fact that teens' fickleness can benefit you as well. We believe teens are more forgiving than they used to be. But, you're now obligated to surprise teens by coming up with different, memorable, new advertising and products that put you back in their competitive set.

A brand is about affiliation. Do teens want to be a part of you? Do they want to join you? Do they want to hang out with you? Ultimately, the answers to those questions reflect your brand's success with teens. All truly successful teen brands are relevant, engaging, and enduring. To be relevant to teens, a brand must be grounded in their world. Your brand becomes important to them only if it understands them and provides continuing evidence of that understanding. A successful brand connects emotionally. It resides in the heart and springs from the gut. It's visceral and emotional. An engaging brand interests teens—and keeps their interest. It gains their attention, gets them to think, and encourages them to wonder about you. An enduring brand is one that has evolved, yet done so without departing from that for which it stands.

Chapter 10

Teens and Media

Never before has a generation grown up so completely immersed in the media. At home, teens' TVs are rarely turned off. At school, their computers are wired to the Internet. Radio follows them everywhere they go, from the car to the gym to teen-friendly stores at the mall. Their downtime, when they can find any, is often filled with reading magazines and surfing the Web via Internet-enabled mobile phones.

Remarkably, this constant media bombardment only seems to make teens hungrier—and savvier—media consumers. They're quite accustomed to multitasking with multimedia: it's not rare to find teens simultaneously talking on the phone, researching their homework assignments on the Web, sending Instant Messages to friends, and watching TV or listening to the radio. This level of sensory input would be enough to stun and bewilder many adults, but young people frequently find complete silence more distracting than anything else. Even the oldest teens can't remember life without MTV and AOL. The proliferation of media is such a familiar part of their existence that many tell us they can't concentrate without background noise from a TV or radio.

Nevertheless, we frequently answer calls from clients and the press asking how best to reach the "elusive" teen market. Twenty years ago, we understood the question. But today, this puzzles us. Teens may be a lot of things, but media-shy they aren't! Given that the teen population will continue to increase until the end of the decade, it's clear that anyone who's having an unusually difficult time reaching teens through the media is probably doing something wrong.

Clearly, teens and the media coexist in a symbiotic relationship—each party has an exceptionally strong interest in the other. That said, though, teens differentiate among mediums, recognizing that each serves a specific purpose and excels in its own particular way. For that reason, teens look to different media for different purposes. In this chapter, we'll take a closer look at some of the biggest players in the teen-media world. First, though, let's outline the roles different mediums play in teen life.

To help paint a more definitive picture of teens' attitudes toward the media, we asked teens in our national syndicated study to assess the strengths and weaknesses of the major media: TV, radio, the Internet, magazines, and newspapers. Among the objectives of these questions: to find out which medium teens find most entertaining, trustworthy, and informative; to determine the media teens spend the most time using; to find out what medium boasts the most effective advertising; and—arguably most telling—what medium teens couldn't live without.

The results are clear: television stands out as teens' favorite medium. Thirty-eight percent say television is the one medium they can't imagine living without. Television's dominance owes mostly to the fact that 62 percent of teens claim it is the most entertaining. TV's closest competition, the Internet, garners only 15 percent of votes. And, understanding that teens mostly use media for entertainment, television's rating on this attribute is all the more striking.

These days we often hear that consumers want to interact directly with the media. In some respects this is true about teens: many, for example, love video games, and if they're looking for information they want to cut through the clutter and find it as quickly as possible. Still, teens tell us that one of the attributes that makes TV so appealing is its passive nature. There's no need to flip pages or click on links. Unlike radio, in which the nature of the entertainment may fluctuate wildly every four minutes or so, TV offers regular programming blocks that lessen the temptation to channel-surf. Teens can kick back and take a break from their harried academic, family, and social lives. What's more, there's something for every taste. With the growth of so many niche cable networks, girls can watch *Trading Spaces* on TLC, while guys can tune into ESPN's *SportsCenter*.

Teens Rate the Media

Teens say television is the most entertaining and informative medium, but they trust newspapers more than TV.

(percent of teens responding when asked, "For each of the following statements, what one source [newspaper, magazine, etc.] best applies?")

Most entertaining

TV	62%
Internet	15
Radio	12
Magazines	9
Newspapers	0

Can't live without

TV	38%
Radio	30
Internet	23
Newspapers	2
Magazines	2

Spend most time using

TV	41
Internet	29
Radio	24
Magazines	3
Newspapers	1

Most informative

TV	33
Newspapers	20
Internet	24
Magazines	7
Radio	5

Most trusted

Newspapers	45
TV	33
Internet	7
Radio	7
Magazines	6

Pay attention to ads

TV	54
Magazines	19
Radio	11
Newspapers	7
Internet	6

Source: The TRU Study, Teenage Research Unlimited, Inc.

It's a testament to TV's influence that the medium dominated all our questions except "most trusted," in which it came in second only to newspapers. Teens tell us that, despite the plethora of news shows and news cable networks, TV is largely about entertainment. The medium's credibility as a trustworthy news source falls 12 points behind that of newspapers. As they noted, TV is "easy," with information readily attained and digested.

Interestingly, prior to the September 11, 2001, terrorist attacks, newspapers also reigned as the most informative media. However, in the days following the terrorist attacks, ever-changing events led teens to depend on television's immediacy—an attribute that newspapers simply can't match. Notably, not a single teen from the more than 2,000 who participated in the study ranked newspapers as the most entertaining medium. Ironically, teens' favorite newspaper sections are those that are entertainment-related.

Radio may not hold TV's popular mandate with teens, but it does have a unique place in the teen psyche. Most individual assessments of radio suggest young listeners consider the medium engaging but wholly untrustworthy. Just 15 percent judged it "most entertaining," 7 percent said it is "most trusted," and a mere 5 percent say it's "most informative." Still, nearly one-third said it was the one medium they can't live without—putting it within striking distance of TV. What's going on here?

Teens tell us radio has a lot of annoying commercials, the deejays often are idiots, the news broadcasts are a joke, and the play lists tend to be unimaginative and repetitive. In recent years, the pace of consolidation within the radio broadcasting industry has been staggering, and teens seem increasingly frustrated by the changes resulting from this concentration of ownership. Complaints about local radio are similar in major markets across the country: stations all sound alike, computerized networks mean there's no way to tell where the signal is coming from, and little attention is paid to local artists or local news, despite teens' natural affinity for a local focus. In fact, whereas cable and satellite TV present viewers with a huge and diverse selection of programming choices, broadcast radio is heading in the other direction—toward ever-increasing homogenization.

Does all this mean the end of radio is near? No. For most teens, it's the devil they know, and they can't imagine life without it. Further, this age group is perhaps less concerned about radio's increasing homogeneity because the teen experience tends to encourage conformity. If a teen on vacation in New York hears the same music she normally hears back home in Toledo, Ohio, she'll likely consider it validation that the music she listens to is really on-trend. To some extent, radio—and other media—nationalizes the teen experience.

Beyond this, however, radio may be on the verge of a revolution similar to the one that rocked television 20 years ago. Satellite radio, still in its infancy, is of keen interest to TRU. Although awareness is low among teens right now, TRU is monitoring how the public reacts to an ad-free, subscription-based format with a huge variety of broadcasting choices. How ironic if the loosened federal media ownership rules supported by the huge conglomerates actually set the stage for a satellite competitor that could steal away listeners!

The Internet continues to gain importance as an information source. The Web is the runner-up (behind TV) for both most-entertaining medium and the medium teens spend the most time using. Still, there's a sizable gap between the number of teens who say the Internet is the most informative (24 percent) and the number who say it's the most credible (just 7 percent). Clearly, teens believe the Web's strength—allowing anyone to have a site and share content—is also one of its great weaknesses. The consensus seems to be that the Internet's democracy of ideas leaves room for anyone to hammer away on his or her pet issues, casting doubt upon much of the information a Web search might yield.

When it comes to advertising, purveyors of online pop-up and banner ads should take note: teens say these tactics don't work. Respondents judge 'Net advertising the least noticed of any media source. Even newspaper ads get more attention from teens than these online annoyances.

Conversely, teens actually enjoy some TV ads. Fifty-four percent of teens rate TV as the strongest medium for showcasing attention-getting advertising, compared to 11 percent for radio, 7 percent for newspapers, and 6 percent for the Internet. Teens consistently tell TRU that humorous advertising is the best way to reach them, and few other media can match the humor possible on television. Just as TV programming entertains them, many teens tell us they consider their favorite ad campaigns a "bonus" form of entertainment; they look forward to seeing new installments, and they enjoy watching "reruns" of their favorites. Note that this affection extends only to the best of the best, and teens repeatedly remind us that a bad TV ad is a truly awful experience.

Notably, in TRU's qualitative research teens also consistently praise magazine advertising, a runner-up here (behind television) with 19 percent claiming to pay attention to magazine ads. This form of advertising is popular mainly because teens can browse at their own speed, stopping to investigate anything that catches their eye. It helps that magazines frequently combine strong visuals with specific product information that's hard to come by in other forms of advertising.

To properly understand both teen culture and teen buying behavior, it's imperative to understand teen media. What follows are overviews of some of the most important forms of media, including TV, movies, the Internet, magazines, and newspapers. Radio and music are rich enough subjects that they were fully covered in Chapter 4.

Television

In the past, when TRU compiled measured teen network viewership, we put cable and broadcast networks in separate lists, as is the industry standard. Eventually, we came to realize that this is not how teens watch TV. Most teens have never lived in a world without pay-TV, and they draw little distinction between cable and broadcast because, for the most part, their broadcast channels arrive via cable or satellite anyway. (As one panelist memorably told us, "It all comes out of the same box!") To teens, the traditional broadcasters are simply the channels at the bottom of the cable guide's channel listings.

Realizing this, we decided to put broadcast and pay-TV networks on the same list in our syndicated study. We now ask teens to tell us how many hours they spend watching each network, and which one they consider their favorite. Not surprisingly, MTV is the hands-down winner on both counts.

Though the network occasionally likes to promote itself as the scrappy rebel valiantly fighting conformity in an adult-dominated world, the truth is, MTV's days as an underdog are well behind it. The channel predates even the oldest of today's teens, and this cohort can no more imagine the pre-MTV era than the rest of us can visualize the world before commercial air travel. It owes its success mainly to its ability to gauge, and act upon, cultural changes barely perceptible to the larger audience or its competition. (Not coincidentally, the modern musical performer who probably best embodies this chameleon like skill is Madonna, one of the first performers to reach superstar status thanks to MTV.)

The modern-day MTV not only plays the artists who set the trends, it helps set trends itself by lending automatic legitimacy to those artists it chooses to feature. It routinely creates top-40 sensations with the flick of a wrist and the change of a play list. It produces a raft of TV programs featuring a trademark mix of choppy editing, popular music, and attractive people. MTV Films has produced teen favorites including *Jackass, the Movie*, *Orange County*, and *Save the Last Dance*. It is, in short, an American icon.

That's not to say that MTV is invulnerable to challenges. History is quite clear on this point: nothing attracts challengers like an established

Teen Television Viewership

Teens spend more time watching MTV than any other channel.

(average number of hours teens spent watching each television channel in the last seven days)

	hours/week
MTV	4.54
Fox	3.43
Disney Channel	3.11
WB	2.68
Nickelodeon/Nick at Nite	2.62
ESPN	2.45
HBO	2.45
Comedy Central	2.39
ABC	2.30
The Cartoon Network	2.18
BET	2.05
NBC	2.02
TNT	1.89
ESPN 2	1.84
CBS	1.83
USA	1.54
UPN	1.49
VH-1	1.44
TBS	1.38
ABC Family	1.22
Showtime	1.16
Fox Sports	1.13
The Movie Channel	1.05
PBS	0.59
The Box	0.20

Source: The TRU Study, Teenage Research Unlimited, Inc.

success. The network's nearest competitor, BET, is in a respectable fourth place on teens' list of favorite networks thanks in great part to the wildly popular show *106 & Park*. And BET is number one for the highly sought-after African-American teen segment. But for now MTV remains above the fray; 16 percent of teens—significantly more girls—list MTV as their favorite network compared to 9 percent who name BET. Teens spend an average of four-and-a-half hours per week watching MTV compared to an average of two hours per week for BET.

Teens' second-favorite network is surprising to most of our clients: the Disney Channel. This entry skews both heavily young and heavily female—16 percent of girls rate Disney as their favorite channel compared to only 4 percent of guys. Tied with Disney is the WB (also wildly popular with girls), which has done an admirable job of supplying the relationship-driven television shows—such as *7th Heaven* and *Gilmore Girls*—that teen girls crave.

Fox garners 9 percent of the "favorite network" votes, but the Simpsons' television home still falls below BET, demonstrating just how big a bite cable networks have taken out of free TV's dominance. On the other hand, teens watch an average of three-and-a-half hours of Fox programming per week—placing the network second only to MTV—which likely takes some of the sting out of the "favorites" results. Fox does especially well with guys, who frequent the network on Sundays for NFL games and are drawn to the irreverence of Fox Sports' *Best Damn Sports Show … Period*.

As a rule, girls tend to be more engaged and enthusiastic about a variety of mainstream brands, including many television networks. There are, however, a few networks that appeal to guys more than girls. These include the Cartoon Network, Comedy Central, and—most notably—ESPN, the overall favorite of teen boys and a testament to the importance of sports in young guys' lives. As a brand, ESPN also stands out: *ESPN the Magazine*

Favorite TV Channels

**Disney Channel is one of teen girls' five favorites.
ESPN is the number-one favorite of teen guys.**

*(percent of teens responding when asked, "Which one
TV channel is your favorite?" by gender)*

Total teens		Females		Males	
MTV	16%	MTV	22%	ESPN	16%
Disney Channel	10	Disney Channel	16	Comedy Central	12
WB	10	WB	14	MTV	11
BET	9	BET	10	Fox	10
Fox	9	Fox	7	BET	8

Source: The TRU Study, Teenage Research Unlimited, Inc.

has quickly become teen guys' second-favorite title (after *Sports Illustrated*); ESPN.com is one of this segment's favorite Web sites; and, of course, now in eight cities, ESPN Zone has become a sought-after vacation stop.

Sensing an untapped market for male-targeted TV, another cable network is rebranding itself in an effort to appeal to young male viewers. Ever since it abandoned its country-music focus in 2001, TNN has courted young men with guy-friendly programming such as World Wrestling Entertainment and *Star Trek*. Notably, retention of the TNN moniker (formerly an acronym for The Nashville Network) confused potential viewers and muddled the network's brand image. In August 2003, after much legal wrangling, the cable network formally adopted the manly moniker *Spike TV*.

Spike's new branding efforts don't stop at its new name, however. The channel also embarked on a fresh lineup of testosterone-fueled programming and partnerships with popular men's magazines such as *Stuff* and *Men's Health*. It's an ambitious plan: women already have a host of channels (including Lifetime and Women's Entertainment) devoted solely to their interests, but traditional "guys' channels" are mostly devoted to a specific niche, such as sports, cartoons, or music. From *The Man Show* to *Maxim*, programmers and editors are figuring out how to cater to young men, recognizing that such a large media audience is—in some ways—a niche find.

Our research on TV has revealed a seismic shift in viewing behavior over the last decade or so. The Big Three aren't that big anymore—at least to teens. Who would have thought just a few short years ago that the top TV networks for a prized demographic such as teens would lack even one token appearance by ABC, CBS, or NBC? The big broadcasters' famine is a marketer's feast, however. Advertising time on teens' favored TV networks is often less expensive than on the traditional industry giants. And, not only is a teen-targeted network media buy relatively more affordable these days, it also affords greater selectivity. The spectrum of specialized cable channels allows marketers to pick and choose from a wide variety of demographic possibilities, from ESPN to MTV, from BET to Fox's new action-sports channel, Fuel.

So, now we know which networks are hot from the teen perspective. But a network is only as strong as its programming, so let's take a closer look at some of teens' favorite TV shows. The findings of our most recent data on teens' favorite programs will surely be familiar to anyone who's seen a copy of The TRU Study in the last several years. That's because, to the average teen, two shows are killer, the rest are mostly filler.

Although networks often seem to put a premium on pretty faces (sometimes at the expense of acting and writing talent), it's interesting to note that only 9 percent of teens report "an attractive cast" as a main reason they watch programming. Don't get us wrong, we're not claiming pretty people don't help a successful show's popularity. We're just saying *V.I.P.*, Pamela Anderson's low-budget silicon cavalcade, doesn't rank with teens.

When it comes to teens' favorite television shows, there's *The Simpsons* and *Friends*—and then there's everything else. The fact that these two juggernauts have stood, unchallenged, at the top of the teen charts for eight consecutive waves of The TRU Study proves that it may be difficult to attract teens of both genders and all age ranges to the same show, but it's not impossible.

Television is rarely short on sitcoms, but few have the power to compete with these two teen powerhouses. What do *The Simpsons* and *Friends* have that the competition doesn't? For starters, each boasts smart writing and a well-chosen cast. Teens tell us there's simply no way to achieve top-notch humor without both of those ingredients. But it doesn't hurt that each program skirts the traditional sitcom formula in its own respect. *Friends* rejects the obvious sitcom setup ("Look at my crazy family!"), instead opting to follow the lives of a handful of young (okay, youngish) New York hipsters. They have good jobs, cool clothes, wildly aspirational apartments, and an interesting social circle. What's not to like?

The Simpsons, on the other hand, takes a completely different tack. It embraces the crazy-family formula with an almost-pathological fervor. The fact that the program is animated means that it's exempt from many traditional Hollywood limitations, including the high costs associated with casting and set design, not to mention the laws of physics. This freedom gives *The Simpsons* the opportunity to mix outlandish storylines with sitcom gags so well worn that simply referencing them sounds like parody. The result is a show with something for everyone—younger teens appreciate the program's more obvious, cartoonesque qualities, while older teens respect the biting social commentary.

Favorite TV Shows

**_Friends_ is far and away the favorite TV show of teen girls, while
The Simpsons ranks number-one among guys.**

*(percent of teens responding when asked, "What are
your three favorite TV shows?" by gender)*

Females		Males	
Friends	24%	The Simpsons	31%
7th Heaven	11	Sportscenter	12
Gilmore Girls	9	Friends	9
Real World	8	South Park	9
The Simpsons	8	SpongeBob SquarePants	7
Lizzie McGuire	7	Dragon Ball Z	6
Will and Grace	7	CSI	5
SpongeBob SquarePants	7	106 & Park	5
Boy Meets World	6	That 70's Show	5
CSI	6	Seinfeld	5

Source: The TRU Study, Teenage Research Unlimited, Inc.

Following these two big hits are numerous, smaller programming successes that, while popular, can't boast such enormous success because they tend to cater to narrower, gender-based teen viewing preferences. Significantly more girls find themselves drawn to the relationship-driven fare that shows like *7th Heaven*, *The Real World*, *Gilmore Girls*, and the sitcom *Boy Meets World* provide. In contrast, significantly more guys prefer comedy and sports, selecting shows such as *SportsCenter*, *South Park*, and *Saturday Night Live* as favorites.

Given teens' interest in the "latest and greatest," it may come as something of a surprise that most of teens' top-10 shows are in syndication. This begs the question, why would ordinarily fickle teens want to watch something they've already seen? TRU's Trendwatch panelists explain it's because they really like the added perspective they get from being well acquainted with a show's cast. Knowing the quirks and nuances of each character gives an added sense of perspective that helps teens catch the minutiae they might have missed the first time around. Plus, watching older episodes lets them see how their favorite shows have evolved over time. There's also the matter of scheduling. Teens rarely have the luxury of watching "appointment TV"—they say non-prime-time airings fit into their lives better. Finally, some purists contend that early episodes of their favorite shows are simply fresher and funnier. Whatever the reason, reruns, re-broadcasts and episode marathons have no doubt helped endear shows such as *The Simpsons*, *Friends*, *Boy Meets World*, *South Park*, *SNL*, and MTV's *The Real World* to teens.

But where does reality television fit into the equation? Teens were invested in this genre before most adults had even heard the phrase, "reality TV." As with many things on television, MTV was the forerunner here—the groundbreaking *Real World* is now in its 13th season! And while relatively few teens claim such TV shows as their absolute favorites, programs such as *American Idol* remain of great teen interest.

Reality programs are cheap to produce and turnaround time is usually quick, allowing for multiple variations on similar themes. This constant evolution has thus far kept a genre that would seem to have a short shelf life fresh and engaging. Notably, because producers save on paying real actors' salaries, networks have a vested interest in flogging this particular mule until it's dead. After all, *The Bachelor* may never be as popular with teens as *Friends*, but the producers don't have to pay six cast members $1 million each—per episode—either! As a result, such programs will continue to proliferate as long as the public is willing to tolerate them. And, at least thus far, teens still seem to enjoy discussing the most shocking, shameful points of such programs with their friends the morning after.

If you're looking for prime TV real estate in which to plant your marketing message, we suggest you can't go wrong with a teen-favored comedy. Our 20 years of data point to teen-focused or teen-relevant comedies as standing the test of time in teen popularity. If you're interested in one gender over another, consider something action-packed or touchy-feely, depending upon your target. And, if you're looking at a "reality show," do your homework first. The genre's not dead yet, but it's aging. Before you make a commitment, you should make sure your prospective advertising vehicle isn't just a worn-out retread.

But it's important to look beyond GRPs ("girps," as media people sometimes pronounce the acronym for Gross Rating Points, which quantify audience size over the course of a media buy). Even if your plan gets you the numbers you need (or, even better, cost-efficient numbers), make sure the programming and the network are such that teens will want to keep company with it—after all, teens are all about affiliation. The nature of the programming that wraps around your ads also should work to further your brand message. Remember, every touchpoint your brand has with your consumer is an opportunity for both positive and negative associations. So, of course, take a hard look at GRPs and their economics, but also consider the more qualitative aspects of what your sponsorship says about you.

Movies

When we began asking teens about their favorite movies of all time, we thought they might reminisce about the movies with which they grew up—especially in light of the prevalence of VCRs and DVD players during this cohort's formative years. Instead, it's clear that teens either have a short memory or truly believe the art and science of moviemaking has progressed rapidly in recent years.

In Tolkien's writing, it's "one ring to rule them all," and *Lord of the Rings* does in fact rule this measure. Among guys in particular, the films are favorites they say they'll watch over and over. *The Rings* franchise, with its mix of epic fantastical adventure, cutting-edge special effects, and bloody fighting, catapulted the film past other favorites such as *The Matrix* and the *Dumb and Dumber* movies.

Guys' other all-time favorite is *The Fast and the Furious*, a fearsome combination of cool cars, fast races, beautiful women, and a high-intensity soundtrack to match. To a lesser extent, girls are into the film too—likely for Vin Diesel and Paul Walker. Not surprisingly, this popular film has also undergone the sequel treatment.

For girls, though, the current all-time favorite movie is much more sentimental—no drag races or dismemberments. *A Walk to Remember*, starring candy-pop princess Mandy Moore as a minister's daughter swept away by the popular bad boy sentenced to community service, is tops among girls. Sure, the plot is the oldest story in the book (i.e., a love story), but the movie is recent. Also popular among girls is *Save the Last Dance* (also a love story, but thanks to hip-hop-dancing girl-power diva Julia Styles, a more modern one). *Dirty Dancing* is one of the few older films in evidence at the top of either gender's list. It is the very definition of a "classic" love story. In fact, teen girls for years have been telling us that *Dirty Dancing* is the ultimate sleepover movie; they watched it with friends when they were younger, and many still return to it occasionally on quiet, rainy Sunday

Favorite Movies

The favorite movies of teen girls are very different from the favorites of teen guys.

*(percent of teens responding when asked,
"What's your favorite movie of all time?" by gender)*

Females		Males	
A Walk to Remember	4%	The Fast and the Furious	5%
Dirty Dancing	2	The Matrix	3
The Fast and the Furious	2	Dumb and Dumber	2
Save the Last Dance	2	Lord of the Rings: The Two Towers	2
Lord of the Rings (nonspecific)	2	Lord of the Rings (nonspecific)	2
10 Things I Hate About You	2	Scarface	2
Legally Blonde	2	Austin Powers in Goldmember	2
Love and Basketball	2	Back to the Future	2
Drumline	2	Friday	2
Moulin Rouge	2	Shawshank Redemption	2

Source: The TRU Study, Teenage Research Unlimited, Inc.

354

afternoons. The theatrical re-release a few years ago also brought renewed attention to this oldie.

Of special note is *Drumline,* by far African-American teens' favorite movie and the sixth-favorite among teens overall. This 2002 release features a Brooklyn-born college freshman and snare-drummer extraordinaire— with a bad attitude and no ability to read music—rocketing through the marching band ranks, and taking on Orlando Jones (of "Make 7 Up Yours" ad fame). Clearly, the film's appeal is at least partly fueled by a strong, teen-appropriate soundtrack (no small feat for a teen movie that features a marching band!).

Celebrities and the Media

Obviously, the media can't survive without public interest, and it can't flourish unless the interest is substantial. In this respect, celebrities can be viewed as the media's greatest assets.

Teens are particularly enamored of celebrity culture. To their adoring young fans, musicians, athletes, actors, and models are more than just attractive strangers with lots of money. They're role models, icons, and the embodiment of a dream nearly all teens harbor. These people—through some cosmic good fortune—have managed to achieve fame, fortune, good looks, and the undivided attention of the nation. Even the coolest and most popular of their peers look up to celebrities; how could teens help but be a little star-struck?

Celebrities nationalize the teen experience, assuring that a teen from Chattanooga, Tennessee, will likely have at least something in common with a teen from San Francisco. Celebrities inspire trends in lifestyles, fashions, attitudes, and behavior that teens everywhere eagerly mimic. For this reason, marketers eye celebrities just as covetously as entertainment editors do. Celebrity endorsers can bring attention, authority, and added appeal to a brand—provided the celebrity is chosen wisely. (We'll talk more about how to choose the right celebrity endorser for your brand in Chapter 11).

Music is one of the dominant cultural influences in teen life, and modern celebrity status is often built on a star's crossover appeal. Musical artists jump into movie and TV careers—Eminem in *8 Mile* is a prime example. Athletes have for years tried (with varying degrees of success) to cross over to popular entertainment, including the seemingly unrelated world of hip-hop.

All of this makes the results of TRU's quantitative favorite-celebrities measure quite surprising: it turns out that eight of teens' top-10 celebrities in the most recent study are good old-fashioned movie stars—blockbuster draws without platinum records to their name or prominent tunes on movie soundtracks. Indeed, despite musical artists' increasing forays into acting, it's still action heroes, comedians, babes, and good-guy all-Americans who teens name as their favorite celebs.

By asking teens to write in their two favorite celebrities in each wave of The TRU Study, we have identified the characteristics that make celebrities particularly popular with certain teen segments. Girls' top choices were split between women they admire and men they desire. For many girls, first-place celebrity Julia Roberts combines all of the attributes they themselves would like to possess: grace, beauty, sweetness, and the barest hint of attitude. Other leading ladies who made the grade include strong-but-sweet Sandra Bullock and sexy siren Jennifer Lopez, who's successfully crossed over from music to movies and is parlaying her celebrity to marketing areas as well, including a J-Lo-branded line of apparel, accessories, and fragrances.

Interestingly, when it comes to heartthrobs, many girls seem particularly taken with Hollywood's freshest faces. Vin Diesel garnered a great deal of attention in *The Fast and the Furious*, and his subsequent second-place rank on girls' favorite celebrities list immediately after that movie's release is a particularly strong showing for girls, who generally react coolly to action heroes.

Favorite Celebrities

Julia Roberts is the most popular celebrity among teen girls, Adam Sandler among teen guys.

(percent of teens responding when asked, "Thinking about TV stars, movie stars, and models, write in your two favorite celebrities," by gender)

Females		Males	
Julia Roberts	11%	Adam Sandler	8%
Sandra Bullock	7	Jim Carrey	6
Vin Diesel	7	Vin Diesel	5
Jennifer Lopez	7	Tom Hanks	5
Josh Hartnett	6	Chris Tucker	5
Brad Pitt	5	Jennifer Lopez	5
Jennifer Aniston	5	Will Smith	4
Orlando Bloom	5	Halle Berry	4
Reese Witherspoon	4	Mel Gibson	4
Julia Stiles	4	Mike Meyers	3

Source: The TRU Study, Teenage Research Unlimited, Inc.

Other female obsessions as this book went to print include Hollywood relative newcomers Josh Hartnett and Orlando Bloom. With good roles and a bit of luck, these hot young stars might hope to become the next Brad Pitt—the only guy on teen girls' favorites list with a longstanding career to back up his looks. On the other hand, it's just as plausible they could become another flash in the pan along the lines of Luke Perry.

Guys seem to have used a different set of priorities when compiling their list of favorite celebrities. Fully half of guys' 10 best are comedians—not particularly surprising when you consider that they prefer to watch sitcoms, cartoons, and cable comedy specials. What's more, guys seem less interested in passing fads: their top two choices—Adam Sandler and Jim Carrey—are established performers whose acts never fail to deliver what they promise. Guys also rated Vin Diesel highly, though we presume the majority of guys had different motivations for their favorable score than girls did.

Surprisingly, only two of guys' top picks—Jennifer Lopez and Halle Berry—are sex symbols. Put bluntly, although guys enjoy all the exposure their favorite female stars receive, it appears they aren't as fanatically devoted to their favorites as girls are.

Indeed, celebrity endorsers can make a powerful statement to young people. That's why we find the recent trend of teen idols hawking adult products so troubling. After rap stars Busta Rhymes and P. Diddy released a hit single called "Pass the Courvoisier, Part 2," the company that manufactured the liquor named in the song noticed a small but significant sales spike. In 2002, spokesmen for fellow hip-hop star Jay-Z acknowledged that the rapper had formed a "strategic relationship" to market and promote Armadale Vodka, a spirit which he has subsequently mentioned in several of his songs. TRU believes such tactics are every bit as manipulative as the tobacco industry's attempts to influence teen opinion by advertising in youth-targeted magazines. Such tactics may be even less welcome in other countries than they are in the United States. As this book went to print, Finland was set to pick a fight with Hollywood over product placement in movies — especially alcohol and tobacco, which the country has barred from advertising since 1979. Logically enough (notwithstanding the very real censorship concerns), the Finnish government appears increasingly hostile toward films that accept money for alcohol and tobacco product-placement contracts. Officials say they're out to protect children and teens from messages that portray the use of these products as cool. One Finnish producer (who described the review process as akin to being "put through the grinder") said he finds it unlikely that many U.S.-produced films will be acceptable to government watchdogs.

The Internet

Anyone who doesn't consider the Internet part of the average teen's media panoply is making a grave miscalculation. Although some adults (especially those who don't use the 'Net at work) may consider the Web foreign and esoteric, it is just as important as TV, radio, and magazines to today's teens. To help illustrate this point, let's put things in perspective. Today's oldest teens were born in 1984, two years *after* the first production models of the Commodore 64 rolled off assembly lines. The Atari 2600 video-game system was already seven years old when today's oldest teens were born. And today's youngest teens were just undertaking potty training when a group of tech-heads hatched the idea for the Excite search engine in 1993. If teens seem more comfortable with technology than adults, it's because they are. Downplay the Internet's importance to young people at your brand's risk.

Considering these facts, it's somewhat less surprising (though still impressive) that 91 percent of teens tell us they have access to a home computer. Fully 82 percent of teens say they can connect to the Internet at home. And 29 percent of those who can get online report having a high-speed 'Net connection.

We've already illustrated that the 'Net is nothing new to teens, but TRU's numbers offer definitive proof. According to The TRU Study, 96 percent of teens say they've surfed the Web at one time or another. Clearly, teen 'Net use grew by leaps and bounds during the height of the Internet boom. The number of teens who reported they had been online climbed from 54 percent in 1996 to 81 percent in 1998. But this rapid growth proved self-limiting: it's hard to improve on near-universal participation numbers! Today, the Internet's growth rate is just barely inching upwards.

At present, 83 percent of teens report having gone online from home, 60 percent say they've accessed the 'Net from school, and a strong 50 percent report logging on from another location, whether a library, a friend's or family member's home, or an Internet café.

America Online and archrival MSN remain the dominant Internet service providers (ISPs) both among teens and the general population. AOL's wildly successful instant-messaging service continues to give the user-friendly portal the edge over MSN; some 65 percent of teens report using AOL, compared to MSN's still impressive 51 percent. It follows, then, that AOL is the ISP more teens use at home. It's also what they use when they go online "somewhere else" (not coincidentally, "somewhere else" is often another teen's house).

AOL is not invincible, however. Teens gave a chilly reception to MusicNet, the company's fee-based MP3 downloading feature intended to make AOL even more appealing to download-obsessed teens. As of press time, Real Networks (one of MusicNet's founding partners) had abandoned the service in favor of a competitor, and MusicNet was in the midst of significant staff cutbacks. Industry observers were grim about the service's ultimate prognosis.

What's more, teens are increasingly vocal about what they perceive as AOL's diminishing attention to content. This—along with persistent complaints about spam and pop-up ads on AOL—seems to be stripping the market-leader of young customers.

Teen Online Activities by Gender

Girls are more likely than guys to e-mail or instant-message online, while guys are more likely than girls to play games.

(percent of teens responding when asked, "Which of the following have you done online in the last 30 days?" by gender)

	total	female	male
E-mailed	70%	78%	64%
Sent an instant message	59	64	54
Listened to music	56	58	54
Played games	53	48	57
Surfed for hobbies or interests	49	44	55
Researched for school	46	52	41
Looked for stuff to buy	43	42	45
Downloaded music	41	38	42
Forwarded a link to a friend	27	33	22
Gone into a chat room	27	26	28
Downloaded movies or videos	22	19	25
Looked at videos	21	19	23
Found out about companies or products	20	17	23
Sent online cards or gifts	16	24	9
Made a purchase	16	14	17
Read online newsletter you subscribe to	14	16	11
Read a newspaper	13	12	14

Source: The TRU Study, Teenage Research Unlimited, Inc.

AOL provides two principal benefits for teens: a means of logging onto the 'Net, and AOL Instant Messenger. Increasingly, today's sophisticated teens are shunning high-priced service providers in favor of lower-price alternatives (many of which are not subject to AOL's irksome parental controls). And though AOL's easy-to-use Instant Messenger service helped introduce instant messaging to teens across the country, most young people are now comfortable enough with the procedure that they no longer need the "training wheels" AOL supplies.

These fearless young surfers, having learned the basics from AOL, are now looking to more freely explore the Internet without the restrictions the company installs to appeal to parents. Often, they're eager to find content on the 'Net that goes far beyond what AOL is willing to provide within the bounds of its community. Apparently sensing teens' unrest, AOL has begun to introduce features it hopes will help it better match teens' current online behavior (including customized welcome screens, spam filtering, and auto redial), but until the provider eliminates teens' arch-enemies (pop-up ads, slow connecting/downloading speeds, paying for minutes, etc.), other ISPs have more than a fighting chance to make headway among this fickle crowd.

And the competition has indeed jumped on the opportunity. While the dueling empires of AOL and MSN remain locked in a pitched battle for supremacy, smaller players are taking advantage of their distraction, carving out pieces of the two giants' turf. The biggest threat to the industry giants seems to come from smaller, regional broadband providers.

Schools—which have moved more quickly to broadband than individuals—may be a sign of what's to come. Teens report they generally use regional high-speed ISPs to access the 'Net at school, and they're becoming increasingly accustomed to the broadband experience. Because teens are often the computer and 'Net experts in their households—many parents can't even make the VCR stop blinking "12:00"—adults often heed their children's advice on tech matters. As the cost of broadband falls and

Teen Online Activities by Age

Younger teens are more likely than older teens to play games online, while older teens are more likely to buy things.

(percent of teens responding when asked, "Which of the following have you done online in the last 30 days?" by age)

	total	12 to 15	16 to 17	18 to 19
E-mailed	70%	64%	74%	80%
Sent an instant message	59	57	63	59
Listened to music	56	54	59	55
Played games	53	60	49	41
Surfed for hobbies or interests	49	44	53	56
Researched for school	46	43	55	44
Looked for stuff to buy	43	37	49	50
Downloaded music	41	34	46	47
Forwarded a link to a friend	27	26	30	28
Gone into a chat room	27	29	29	20
Downloaded movies or videos	22	19	25	26
Looked at videos	21	23	21	19
Found out about companies or products	20	16	24	25
Sent online cards or gifts	16	15	17	17
Made a purchase	16	11	19	21
Read online newsletter you subscribe to	14	12	15	15
Read a newspaper	13	10	15	18

Source: The TRU Study, Teenage Research Unlimited, Inc.

its distribution becomes more widespread, more parents will likely heed teens' advice and opt for high-speed service. The natural benefactors of this service will likely be regional broadband service providers.

Demographically, young teens are just as likely to have high-speed Internet connections as their older counterparts. This suggests that connection speed has more to do with family finances than with parents allowing their older teens to graduate to a faster connection as they age.

For now, most teens continue to languish in the purgatory of dial-up service. This fact calls into question the wisdom of overly "tricked-out" sites that employ graphic-intensive bells and whistles to lure teens. Many Web designers consider flashy animation and technological trickery a tempting way to lure savvy teens, but the reality is that, at this time, a minority of teens has the fast connection needed to take advantage of the animation. The rest are often frustrated by flash-intensive Web sites; many teens tell TRU they simply give up trying to access sites that take too long to load. Teens tell us Web animation isn't a high priority for them anyway. Most teens say they get all the rich graphics they need from other sources, namely console and PC games (and cell phones' games are becoming increasingly console-like as well). When it comes to the Web, they already feel shackled by their slow service. So, make it easy and quick for them to opt out of flash! Teens become frustrated when they don't arrive easily at your Web site, and considering that the majority of teens are dialing up on slow modems, marketers should keep the bells and whistles on their sites contained. TRU Trendwatch panelists say they prefer straightforward sites that take them where they want to go, and pronto. Perhaps reserve the more "tricked out" content of your site for the deeper-down pages. Teens might appreciate them more once they've made a time commitment to be there.

As much as Internet use has grown in recent years, the Web activities teens engage in have changed little. Communication and entertainment continue to top teens' online agendas. Seventy percent of teens use e-mail, and 59 percent trade instant messages with friends. TRU's qualitative research suggests that teens use e-mail for all kinds of communication, from the serious (breaking-up with a boyfriend or girlfriend, corresponding with an out-of-town aunt) to the lighthearted (routing jokes, e-mailing electronic greeting cards, spreading the word about a big party). On the other hand, instant messaging seems more appropriate for idle chit-chat and spontaneous exchanges about everyday life. Reflecting their more gregarious social natures, significantly more girls than guys send e-mail, instant messages, online cards and gifts, and links to Web sites.

Teens, of course, also flock to the Web for entertainment. Some 56 percent of respondents to the most recent TRU Study routinely listen to music online, and 53 percent say they play games online. Guys appear more interested in entertaining themselves online: significantly more guys than girls report playing online games, downloading music, downloading movies or videos, looking at videos, and general surfing than communication-focused girls do. The increasing penetration of high-speed 'Net access and the multitude of post-Napster peer-to-peer file-sharing sites (*Limewire, Kazaa, Morpheus*) should continue to drive interest in online gaming, music, and video.

After a slow start, e-commerce appears to be gaining momentum with teens. The percentage of teens who say they "look for stuff to buy" online gained six percentage points in the most recent wave of The TRU Study, and the number of teens who actually made a purchase online also increased six percentage points between 2002 and 2003, rising to 42 percent.

Age is a major factor in explaining e-commerce behavior. Significantly more older teens (aged 16 to 19) report using the 'Net to "look for stuff to buy," "find out about companies and their products," and "make a purchase online" than younger teens (aged 12 to 15). No doubt, much of this involvement stems from older teens' higher level of disposable income and greater access to either their parents' or their own credit cards.

The average teen spends almost seven hours online weekly, and nearly 25 percent log-on for 11 or more hours each week. So where exactly are teens going online? Teens mostly frequent what we term "utility sites"—those that they find useful either in providing connections to others, entertainment for themselves and others, or information—either to help them with schoolwork or to learn more about their hobbies. And, this is where the 'Net differs fundamentally in teen usage from other media. Teens flock to TV, radio, and certain magazines primarily for entertainment purposes. But the Internet provides teens more than entertainment and—in some ways—just can't compete with other media when it comes to pure entertainment.

A close look at recent TRU data suggests that many teens are in agreement about three sites: Google, Hotmail, and Yahoo. Google, a specialized search engine, is renowned as the first place to go in order to track down anything and everything online. Hotmail delivers free e-mail (although the accompanying mountains of unsolicited advertisements, ranging in nature from mild to wild, might make parents cringe). Yahoo combines the best of both worlds, throwing in games and fantasy sports leagues for good measure.

Still, as much as teens appreciate functional Web sites, the bulk of their favorites—including MSN, MTV, ESPN, Blackplanet, BET, and Nick (the offshoot of cable TV's Nickelodeon)—offer expansive content. These sites give teens information of all kinds, including news on favorite sports teams and athletes, musical acts and songs, celeb happenings, and gaming strategies.

Surprisingly, sites for downloading music (Audiogalaxy, Kazaa, Limewire, Winmix, etc.) didn't pull as much teen support as expected in our most recent wave of data. Although teens tell TRU in qualitative settings that downloading music is a favorite online activity (many go so far as to contend that they will never again buy music at retail), Kaaza—which received the most teen mentions of any site was named by fewer than 2 percent of teens as one of their three "most fun" or "most visited" sites. (Notably, these data were collected before the recent much-publicized decision of the record industry to sue individual consumers who share music online.)

When it comes to shopping online, Ebay is teens' favorite site, followed by Amazon, AE (American Eagle), Bestbuy, and Alloy. Ebay also scored high marks as a fun site. Teens love a bargain, and they seem especially attracted to the excitement and intrigue of an online auction where they can find deals on everything from concert tickets to stereo gear to hard-to-find memorabilia. Interestingly, the relatively low prevalence of credit cards with teen-aged consumers doesn't stop this cohort from participating on Ebay, nor does the fact that the site requires users to be age 18. Some teens use their parents' registrations and credit cards, while others pay by money order, a practice that Ebay encourages and that facilitates teen involvement.

Our Trendwatch panelists have also been buzzing about another auction site, Stealitback.com. Think of it as the police department's version of Ebay. It's where police unload the confiscated merchandise that goes unclaimed after a criminal investigation. Teens not only appreciate the cut-rate prices they pay for everything from stereo gear to cars, they also get a thrill out of buying something they know was stolen. In this case, police enable—and actually benefit from—teens' sense of rebellion!

Even though the Internet (with all of its flashy multimedia infotainment) remains a relatively new and groundbreaking medium, teens' online behavior has largely (and consistently) reflected their traditional gender-related affinities. As a result, when it comes to online activity, girls are more social while guys are more functional. Sound familiar? We agree. But marketers and their Web designers can turn this difference into an advantage by directly tailoring site content to best match the interests and behavior of its primary teen surfers. And if a site targets both genders, make sure it combines both the social (instant-messaging opportunities,

Teens' Favorite Web Sites

Yahoo.com ranks number one as teens' favorite Web site and the most fun Web site.

(percent of teens responding when asked, "Write in the names of the two Web sites you visit the most often overall, the most often for shopping, and the most often for fun")

Visit most often overall		Visit most often for shopping	
Yahoo.com	18%	Ebay.com	17%
Hotmail.com	10	Amazon.com	6
Google.com	7	AE.com	2
Ebay.com	4	Bestbuy.com	2
MSN.com	3	Alloy.com	2
MTV.com	3	OldNavy.com	2
ESPN.com	2	Delias.com	2
BlackPlanet.com	2	Abercrombie.com	2
Pogo.com	2	Eastbay.com	2
Candystand.com	2	Gap.com	2

Most fun website	
Yahoo.com	12%
Candystand.com	5
Bored.com	4
Ebay.com	3
Nick.com	3
MTV.com	3
Neopets.com	3
ESPN.com	3
Pogo.com	2
Shockwave.com	2

Source: The TRU Study, Teenage Research Unlimited, Inc.

link-sending capabilities, etc.) and functional (easily locatable information, media downloading options, etc.) sides of teens' interests.

By all means, review the list of teens' favorite sites; it should yield promising opportunities for your brand. But know that you'll have better luck using the sites you find on the list as marketing partners rather than as virtual real estate on which to plant your advertising. Consider teen-friendly sites as potential promotional partners that help associate brands with popular Web destinations. But perhaps the most effective use of the Web is neither forcing teens to look at your pitch, nor hoping they'll come snooping on their own. Rather, concentrate on creating a great, teen-appropriate Web site that attracts both first-time and repeat visitors. Stock it (as appropriate, based on where you are) with games, music, and other content that will make it a veritable destination for your target; once you've given them a reason to show up, they'll be much more receptive to your information. Remember, though, to make sure your site's been well tested. It must not only provide great content, it must be simple to navigate and uncluttered enough to allow easy access via dial-up service.

Magazines

Magazines have for decades been an invaluable media resource, especially for teen girls. More gregarious and social than most guys, girls actively seek out precisely the mix of information and entertainment that teen lifestyle magazines provide—from style and fun to dating and relating, with many focusing on the traditional big-three topics of fashion, beauty, and boys.

Bright colors, plenty of photos and graphics, and a great deal of latitude with layout and design keep the publications fresh and eye-catching, and articles are typically written in the friendly, approachable voice of a trusted friend or benevolent older sister. No wonder many girls consider their favorite magazines more than just a media option—they're fashion tools and guides that help ease teenagers through some of the most confusing, exciting, and challenging years of their lives.

Generally speaking, magazines are more popular with girls (in fact, almost anything in print seems to succeed better with teen girls than guys). What's more, female readers seem reluctant to shift allegiances once they've settled on a trusted title, although they're perfectly willing to sample more than one. Familiarity certainly plays a large role, but because most major magazines often trade cover models and story ideas from month to month, many girls know they won't have to wait long until a particular feature reaches the pages of their preferred title.

The teen-girl magazine market is a little crowded at present, despite the recent departure of the veteran *Teen* magazine as a regular (it's still hitting the newsstands from time to time with special issues). For good reason, publishers court teen girls—understanding both the power of the teen market and the fact that girls love to read magazines written especially for them.

Seventeen is still number one in circulation and readership, although it dropped in both areas during the time it was owned by Primedia. Perhaps *Seventeen*'s aggressive pursuit of brand extension took too much focus off the magazine. As mentioned previouslym, last year it opened a nightclub and retail store in Los Angeles. The *Seventeen* store allows fashion-conscious readers (and nonreaders, too) to find the innumerable outfits the magazine features each month in one convenient location. Next door, at an under-21 dance club called One Seven, the magazine promotes itself as a key purveyor of style and fun. And in Plano, Texas, the first *Seventeen* studio/spa/salon opened in the past year. This 8,700-square-foot location comprises a spa and salon, a retail store, and an Internet café. More are planned for Texas and other states. Time will tell if *Seventeen*'s new publisher, Hearst (which also owns *CosmoGirl*) will be able to reverse readership and circulation declines at the most famous of teen titles.

YM, on the other hand, has been able to reinvent itself and remains strong. When *YM* went the "initials" route, smartly leaving the outdated

Teens' Favorite Magazines

Seventeen is teen girls' favorite magazine, while Sports Illustrated is the favorite of teen guys.

(percent of teens responding when asked, "Which magazine do you consider to be among your favorites?" by gender)

Females		Males	
Seventeen	45%	Sports Illustrated	27%
Teen People	35	ESPN the Magazine	17
YM	32	Transworld Skateboard-	
CosmoGirl	22	ing/Snowboarding	11
Cosmopolitan	19	Nintendo Power	11
People	16	Gamepro	11
Glamour	9	Maxim	11
Vibe	8	Electronic Gaming	
Rolling Stone	7	Monthly	11
Vogue	6	Sports Illustrated	
		for Kids	9
		The Source	9
		PC Gamer	7

Source: The TRU Study, Teenage Research Unlimited, Inc.

Young Miss name behind, it subtitled itself "Young & Modern," which never seemed to resonate with teens. I think they've nailed it with "Your Magazine"; after all, teens of both genders appreciate ownership.

Teen People came on strong right from the start, leveraging the equity of its base brand, which also happens to enjoy strong readership among teens (girls in particular). The teen version cleverly emphasizes celebrities, a subject near and dear to teen girls' hearts and one that allows this magazine to differentiate itself.

CosmoGirl, perhaps buoyed by the brand-extension strategy that worked for *Teen People*, is also enjoying success owing in no small part to the open-door policy of its editor-in-chief Atoosa Rubenstein, who not only asks readers to e-mail her with personal commentary but also answers them. Despite the parent publication's tradition of providing guidance on nearly all things sexual to young-adult women, Atoosa stresses inner beauty and confidence for younger women, sharing with readers her own experience of being a somewhat gawky teenager. (That Atoosa could ever have suffered from teenage insecurity is hard to imagine, judging by the glamorous photos of her inside each magazine. But her generous willingness to share her high school pictures reveals that she, too, was a "normal" teen once.)

Not to be outdone by *People* and *Cosmopolitan*, *Elle* and *Vogue* have also launched teen titles—*Elle Girl* and *Teen Vogue*. Though each is also looking to separate itself from the pack (*Teen Vogue* has even gone to a handy digest size and a low $1.50 newsstand price prominently displayed on its cover), it's hard to imagine that all these new titles can survive. But for now, teen girls can make the ultimate consumer statement: they can sample the various titles and decide their eventual fate.

Guys' favorite magazines tend to be devoted to specific interests (such as video games, sports, and music), so while they may print similar stories from time to time, the overlap is less obvious than in girls' titles. So, whereas girls tend to read horizontal magazines (the teen-girl titles listed above are all lifestyle publications), guys are vertical readers—when they read anything at all. One of the reasons that a teen-guy version of *Seventeen* has never made it is that teen guys want a much racier magazine than would be appropriate for minors. Not surprisingly, aspirational teens are looking at *Maxim* and *Stance*, among others. But these titles, which are wading into the world of men's lifestyle magazines, need to be careful to maintain a distinct voice that can't be confused with that of the competition.

Generally, teen guys' favorite magazines focus on sports and games. Their top titles at present include *Sports Illustrated* (whose readership has declined somewhat over the past few years, despite remaining number-one with guys for at least as long as The TRU Study has been measuring magazine readership), *ESPN the Magazine*, *GamePro*, *Transworld Skate*, and *Nintendo Power*.

Scholastic, Inc. continues to publish several titles that comprise the widely distributed in-school Scholastic Teen Network. These titles reach an impressive one-third of all U.S. teens.

When deciding among the various titles vying for teens' attention, as with television, we again suggest that you look beyond the numbers. Of course do your reach-and-frequency analyses, but also think about (and explore) what each title can offer you. Does its brand match and enhance yours and does it offer added value? Are there special promotions, events, and partnerships that can be part of your buy? Do they connect you with other advertisers who further your branding objectives? Are special issues planned that make sense for your brand or your own upcoming promotions?

Newspapers

Known for their notoriously short attention spans, teens tend to shun newspapers in favor of more dynamic and interactive media. But while newspapers probably will continue to struggle to attract teens for years to come, the industry should take comfort in knowing that more teens consider newspapers their most-trusted source of news than any other medium. Unfortunately, when teens do pick up the paper, it's rarely to read the news, and trustworthiness is not what they're really looking for from the media.

The TRU Study quantifies teens' most-read newspaper sections. For teens in total (counting both genders together), the two most popular newspaper sections—comics and the entertainment section—are read by roughly half of teens. The sports section (with twice as many male as female readers) is the third most-read section, with 46 percent of teens (but 61 percent of guys) browsing its pages. Allowing teens to follow their favorite professional sports, the sports section also usually serves as many teen athletes' initial "15 minutes of fame" in high school highlight sections.

As with all things print, girls tend to be bigger readers of newspapers than guys. Our data show that significantly more girls read the entertainment, local and community news, clothing, and food advertising sections, as well as the horoscopes. Significantly more guys read the sports and national news sections.

Newspapers should—and likely will—continue efforts to entice teens by incorporating color pictures, bold graphics, and teen-specific content and features (such as teen-oriented event calendars, special sections on high school sports, etc.) into the entertainment, sports, and local and community news sections. Barring major national or world news events, teens' interests have traditionally been rooted in their own communities; newspapers should continue to leverage their expertise in reporting on local happenings and highlighting teens and teen lifestyles. In addition, we think newspapers should complement these initiatives by focusing on bringing their product to teens in a "captive" environment in schools (taking a page out of Scholastic's successful programs). Newspaper-based educational programs are not new, but few appear to effectively leverage the Internet to allow time-and-material-starved teachers the immediacy of downloading timely and relevant articles, as well as lesson plans, quizzes, and support material. In better understanding and tailoring their programs to the needs of teachers, newspapers would go a long way toward cultivating youth readership for the future.

Alternative Media Channels

As The TRU Study has repeatedly shown, teens have become increasingly sophisticated consumers. They're not only aware of the various ways marketers hope to reach them, they've become adept at sorting through marketing messages. Teens are well aware they're being marketed to, and they're not entirely averse to it. Through necessity, they have set up strong defenses against advertising, filtering the desirable from the unwanted. As such, most teens will give a marketing message a fighting chance (if a brief one) to make an impression. If the ad doesn't pass muster within the first few seconds, they tune out without a second thought. The volume of competition and clutter that chokes the traditional media channels is one reason why astute marketers are continuing to look for new, innovative methods of getting out their name, identity, message, or offer to young consumers.

It's an ironic fact of the business that successful marketing generally parallels an arms race. Marketers must constantly develop new, groundbreaking advancements in order to overcome the defenses their targets put into place. But consumers are every bit as assiduous in developing new counter-measures. As a result, marketing seems to be moving ever faster toward a new world order. Internet spyware programs monitor a Web surfer's online activity and, based upon that information, send messages designed to look like helpful editorial content. The line between catalogs and magazines continues to blur: magazines feature purchase information in their fashion spreads, while magazines' discretely marked "advertising supplements" are designed to lead the casual reader to believe the marketing message is a genuine news story. On the other hand, many catalogs now offer editorial content that's every bit as edgy as that found in traditional lifestyle magazines.

On TV, product placement has morphed from the occasional shot of a product in the background to starring roles for soft drinks and snack foods. Music videos, once simply marketing tools to increase music sales, now also serve as marketing tools for automobiles. It remains to be seen how the public will react to marketers' more unconventional efforts. Protecting the privacy of Internet users, for example, is already of great public interest and growing public unrest.

Chapter 11

Marketing and Advertising to Teens

Now comes the fun part . . . the time to put it all together and see how well you can apply your understanding of teens to the marketing of products, services, and brands. So far, this book has documented how teens operate as consumers—from spending their own and their family's dollars to actively and passively influencing household purchases and developing consumer behaviors and attitudes. This chapter tells you how to capitalize on it.

Many marketers fear they will fall victim to the industry's own zealous pursuit of teen consumers. This is hardly surprising, given that the average child sees an estimated 20,000 advertisements each year. Even if these messages don't begin to sink in until age five (and we believe basic corporate identities such as McDonald's or Toys R Us become recognizable at a much younger age), the average teen has taken in some 140,000 messages by age 12 and nearly 300,000 by age 19. This titanic figure, while it may result in increased brand awareness (or awareness of a greater number of brands), also results in decreased attention to advertising and a remarkable rise in market-savvy, media-saturated teens. At the very least, your message faces greater competition than ever before in getting through to teens. The good news, however, is that there are more channels and individual vehicles for reaching teens and more data—a greater understanding, really—of how to break through to today's teens.

As TRU's research has shown in years past, teens have become increasingly sophisticated consumers—they're not only aware of the various channels through which marketing messages reach them, they're also expecting them. About ten years ago, we explained this phenomenon to clients by saying that teens have a finely developed "B.S. meter"—they readily detect messages that are less than credible. Today, as their meter has evolved in sensitivity, we say that teens not only see "it" coming, they actively look for it. So, your messages (and the channels through which they're delivered) are judged by teens with greater scrutiny than ever before.

In our experience, most teens are not sick of mass marketing so much as they are profoundly accustomed to it. This familiarity (arguably caused by marketers) comes back to haunt marketers when teens tune their messages out. So, teens' marketing savvy has become more active than passive, often causing them to automatically shut out targeted messages before they even register. Gone are the days when a straightforward media buy in a teen magazine or teen-favorite TV show alone could boldly introduce a new product, service, or brand. And that's the key reason why astute marketers are continuing to look for ways to integrate new, nontraditional methods of getting their name, logo, message, or offer out to young consumers.

Nontraditional Marketing

In much of TRU's recent research, we've explored teens' perceptions of many nontraditional marketing channels. These include the non-mass-media, under-the-radar, grassroots marketing innovations that catch teens' attention thanks to their unusual, unexpected natures.

Marketing that draws no distinction between individual teens and the rest of their peers is probably no more effective than campaigns that target the mass market. In many cases teens have gone out of their way to prove their individualism—and they're hungry for communication that recognizes this fact.

In a recent wave of The TRU Study, we asked teens to rate a number of these non-mass-media marketing methods (including direct mail, posters, events, e-mail, etc.). TRU asked teens nationally to identify how they would most like to learn about a new product. The results were somewhat surprising. Let's take a look.

Alternative Marketing Channels

Teens recommend direct mail as the best way to reach them through "alternative" channels.

(percent of teens responding when asked, "If not through TV, magazines, newspaper, or radio, what are the two best ways for a company to tell you about a new product?")

Mail	44%
Posters (on walls, buildings, bus stops, etc.)	31
Events and sponsorships	24
Internet	24
Movie previews	22
E-mail	17
At school	10
Handing out information	9

Source: The TRU Study, Teenage Research Unlimited, Inc.

Snail-mail. Yes, that's right. Whereas marketers often assume that teens' attention spans wouldn't favor the printed word, we found teens highly open to receiving something slow and antiquated. As illustrated in the table above, teens suggest using good old-fashioned U.S. mail to introduce a new product. At first, this finding caught us by surprise, but the more we thought about it, the more sense it made for three reasons.

First, teens simply don't get much mail. Unlike their parents, whose mailboxes are stuffed with solicitations on a daily basis, teens' mail is more sporadic, yet highly anticipated. Because so much of teens' social correspondence takes place electronically (even party invites are phoned, instant-messaged, or e-mailed these days!), teens receive only the occasional retail coupon or catalog, a monthly magazine or two, an annual batch of birthday greetings, or—come high school graduation—pitches from colleges and the military.

Second, snail-mail can be highly personalized—unlike 99 percent of their household's mail, it's addressed to them. Plus, unlike e-mail, it feels real—especially when someone has taken the time to write his or her address (for girls, it better be cute handwriting!) and affix the stamp. And if it's a new product introduction, snail mail's smaller-scale feel can seem almost exclusive. There's almost nothing more exciting to teens than feeling they're among the first to know about a new (hopefully cool) product.

And third, teens see direct mail as a prelude to something else, such as free offers and discounts (more about these later). Teens tell us that if they receive a mailed offer that scores them something free (like a buy-one-get-one burger, a discount on athletic gear, or even free pizza delivery), they're all over it. Because they are tangible, snail-mail offers are often more readily activated by teens—they're akin to cash in hand, nothing to print out!

The Internet. OK, so what about e-mail? If snail-mail is received so well, what do teens think about its electronic counterpart? Roughly one-fourth of teens name browsing the 'Net as a preferred method for learning about new products. Teens like going online to hear about new products, but prefer it as an active, rather than passive, pursuit. Teens would rather discover new products on their own when online (by going to companies' Web sites or by happening upon new products or brands as they surf) than by being e-mailed directly from a company. Teens tell TRU that they detest unsolicited e-mails and—almost by rote—quickly hit the delete key when they spot an unfamiliar or commercial e-mail address in their inbox. When teens are doing their own thing online, however, they enjoy discovering information that interests them—on their own terms and in their own time—

whether it's music, sports, movies, fashion, or even new products, brands, events, and promotions.

What's a marketer to do? Ban the banner ad? Well, not exactly. Some teens will click on banners that interest them or give them something fun to do (quizzes, polls, contests, audio-visual clips, etc.). But don't lead teens down a black hole where they can't find their way back to the original content they were browsing—that's the kiss of death according to online teens. Instead, consider ways to seamlessly integrate your brand or product into teen-relevant content when it makes sense to do so. Link up with a teen-favored celebrity (more on celebs later in this chapter) or favorite TV program for endorsements and sponsorships. Or, think smartly about ways to publicize your product or brand via editorial placements in Web-based content. In conjunction with the launch of its Winterfresh Thin Ice breath-strip product, the Wm. Wrigley Jr. Company, together with Edelman, its public relations counsel, commissioned TRU to conduct a study among teens regarding first impressions and the role of fresh breath in meeting people. We designed an online survey that asked teens about the biggest turnoffs when meeting someone for the first time, and bad breath was prominently mentioned. We also gave members of our Trendwatch panel samples of the strips and asked them to tell us what they thought. The results were released to the press. Several teen-targeted Internet sites picked up the story, focusing on teens' insistence on having fresh breath when making a first impression. The Internet stories included anecdotes from the newly mint-flavored mouths of our Trendwatch panelists about why teens like the convenience, discretion, and portability of breath strips such as Winterfresh Thin Ice.

Grassroots. Going back to the nontraditional marketing list, teens also rate highly the concept of place-based or "grassroots" advertising. Teens have grown accustomed to and accept seeing corporate identities in a plethora of places, from sporting events and concerts to bus stops, local street fests, and street corners. Grassroots channels and place-based media allow marketers to come at teens from new directions, allowing their brands to evolve while simultaneously staying in the public eye.

In fact, being where teens are—at concerts, beaches, sporting events, malls, etc.—gets you closer to the target, not only in proximity but also in relevance. Looking at the chart on page 380 and netting together some of the top choices ("posters" on walls, buildings, etc., "events and sponsorships," and "handing out information") shows teens' predilection to be reached on the go.

If you feel your brand could benefit from a strategy of selective communication with a highly specific teen target (rather than carpet-bombing the entire teen population), congratulations: you've taken the first step to a successful grassroots marketing campaign! Your grassroots effort may consist of a wide variety of tactics, including event sponsorships, giveaways, viral marketing, local promotions, and street teams. The main goal, of course, is to create "buzz" within your particular teen target. Executed properly, this form of marketing imparts your brand with a halo of coolness, fosters goodwill, and generates brand and/or message awareness.

This kind of place-based marketing also boasts several important advantages over more traditional strategies. First, it can be much cheaper to execute. Grassroots marketing campaigns, by their nature, distinguish their brand from the mainstream. If you're truly a niche player, and you're able to find the right venue or method for honing in on your teen audience, you may be able to go grassroots exclusively without bigger-budget media buys. (Note that most brands—especially those larger or more mainstream—would be remiss to cut major media out of the picture. For these brands, the big numbers delivered by major media more than justify the cost.) Many marketers use grassroots marketing as a supplement to their overall marketing and advertising budgets, as a way to fill in gaps and to help build the brand by making closer consumer contacts. Again, much depends upon your specific target, the nature of your brand, and, of course, the size of your budget.

Further, grassroots campaigns tend to focus more precisely on the core target. In many cases—such as concerts or sporting-event sponsorships—the most interested (and, often, the most receptive to you) will self-select. In other cases, a street team preaching your message can frequent the spots most likely to be populated by your core consumers.

Our research repeatedly reinforces the fact that teens are much more interested in their immediate environs than in the nation or world at large, which they often feel powerless to influence. Grassroots marketing's town-by-town focus dovetails nicely with this preference.

Note that this strategy works best if you have an edgy brand (or at least wish you did). Mainstream giants like McDonald's might find street teams less than appropriate. And the efforts tend to work best in larger markets, where the population is great enough to make such promotions worthwhile.

Truth, the youth-targeted national antismoking campaign, has used grassroots marketing extensively to unveil the tobacco industry's lies and deceptions; in fact, Truth is an example of integrating grassroots marketing with mainstream advertising. Each summer for the past several years, Truth-logoed trucks have gone on a "Truth Tour"—typically to a number of major markets, showing up at teen-appropriate events and venues. Truth has done a good job of selecting events most populated by its at-risk target. Grassroots marketing has worked especially well for Truth because of the nature of its advertising, which has maintained a direct-from-teens feel (even at a national level). To teens, running into the Truth team at local events seems a logical extension of the brand's advertising.

Recently, the Dr Pepper/Seven-Up Company launched an extension of its 7 Up brand, a distinctly green-colored soda named dnL (turn a 7 Up logo upside down and it reads "dnL"). The original strategy for the brand,

Case Study: Gravity Games

TRU regularly attends teen-targeted grassroots events; the 2002 Gravity Games is a good example. Although some observers have suggested that attendees are becoming more mainstream, we found the majority of visitors young, inked, pierced, and athletic. (The parents accompanying the young fans, on the other hand, are another story.)

The Gravity Games, and events like them (including the better-known X Games), remain hugely successful because they are more than just a sporting competition. They combine action and attitude, energy and entertainment. Perhaps more than any other fans, extreme-sports enthusiasts embrace an entire lifestyle: music and fashion are more or less inseparable from the overall experience. This makes the experience alluring to young people. And as such, it becomes every bit as attractive to marketers.

It's usually right about here that terms such as "saturation" and "lost credibility" arise—especially since those attending these events are the closest thing today's society has to an actual counterculture. The fact that decidedly unathletic products, including fast food and puffed-cheese snacks, are co-opting the "extreme" label shouldn't help. Remarkably, though, the true believers—teens who not only appreciate but often participate in extreme sports—usually draw a clear distinction between misplaced marketing efforts (which they mock mercilessly) and the gatherings that allow them to join their brethren (which they love unreservedly). What's more, marketers who have a legitimate claim to the "extreme" mantle—or successfully convince the target that they do—find a loyal and devoted audience.

Notably, 2002 was Lee Dungarees' first year as a Gravity Games sponsor. At first blush, a century-old clothing company might not appear to have a direct link with the Gravity Games. But, thanks to a two-foot-tall octogenarian, the brand is readily accepted as a sponsor. Buddy Lee, the brand's indestructible action-figure icon, was originally created in the 1920s, then discontinued in the 1960s. Research showed that Buddy Lee deserved to be resurrected: he has a nearly iconic presence with guys, who associate him positively with the Lee brand.

So what does a doll have to do with the Gravity Games? It's the attitude: if you've ever seen a motocross rider perform a 90-foot jump while executing a mid-air back-flip, you'll understand why extreme athletes appreciate Buddy Lee's stoic indestructibility. It works, and Lee is happy for the opportunity to cater to a style-conscious group of consumers who greatly prize durable clothes. Lee's association with the Gravity Games says that sponsoring or partnering with this type of event need not be restricted to brands with a more literal connection (such as skateboard or skate-shoe manufacturers). In fact, brands like Mountain Dew own such events as a result of their deliberate extreme positioning. In other words, a mainstream, mass-merchandised brand of jeans has found a way to connect with an event that offers street cred and a halo of cool.

as reflected by the tagline on its packaging, is "turn your thirst upside down." Logically, then, the brand team felt dnL marketing efforts should not be ordinary—that everything associated with the brand should be nontraditional. Clearly, the upside-down label stands out, although some teens find it confusing because there is little adjustment of the well-known 7 Up logo). To spread the word and create buzz around the new product, the brand literally papered street corners and construction sites with arresting posters showcasing the logo. In fact, brand management was content with the idea that some of these posters would be ripped down—either by consumers (hopefully for the purpose of displaying them with pride at home) or by those in authority (the very act of which—if seen by the target—could feel nicely rebellious). Once 7 Up got the word out about its dnL brand—bolstered by highly sought-after distribution in school vending machines—the brand made the decision to invest in traditional media, in this case, national TV advertising.

At school. With a few notable exceptions, teens' classrooms have been off-bounds to marketers, as they are believed to be a safe haven from the material world. The United States is taking a page, however, from the European strategy of enlisting corporate aid to build new classrooms and pay teachers. Ideology aside, educators continually find themselves strapped for cash, and taxpayers are often unsympathetic (just try passing a school referendum these days!). Many administrators are eager for nontraditional sources of income to help pay for programs and materials districts might not otherwise be able to afford.

Many marketers have been reluctant to get involved in school-based campaigns, fearing such a link would tarnish their brand. Despite associations with lectures, tests, authority, and discipline, however, most teens enjoy the overall school experience, and, even more, rely on its ready-made social network. After all, school's the place to meet friends, display and take note of fashion trends, and plan weekend activities. As discussed in Chapter 6 on home and school, school is the ultimate social environment;

it's the place where teens get to strut their stuff, where Edge teens look downright edgy, where Influencers influence, and where Conformers soak it all in, anxious to adopt the fashions, styles, and behaviors of their trend-leading peers.

The public's reaction to in-school marketing is an important factor in your ultimate decision, and it usually depends on the nature of your program or campaign. Channel One, the in-school television network, provides high-quality programming and accompanying lesson plans. For many teens, the network is likely their only regular exposure to news, and Channel One does a nice job of making its newscasts teen-relevant and comprehensible. Therefore, most school districts welcome the program (Channel One reports that 12,000 schools participate), despite its commercial sponsorship. Each 12-minute daily newscast typically features two minutes of advertising, usually including a 30-second public-service announcement.

In-school marketing is not new. Scholastic, with its stable of widely distributed magazines, has been creating lesson plans for schools for years. Many of its magazines carry advertising. Campbell Soup also has been doing school marketing seemingly forever: its Labels for Education program has been ongoing for more than 30 years. Students and schools collect Campbell Soup can labels that are redeemable for a catalog of educational merchandise (check out the full list at www.labelsforeducation.com), including technology sets, art supplies, musical instruments, globes, maps, flags, sports equipment, educational videos, computers, and even a 15-passenger van. Campell's is a good example of how a marketer can appropriately support schools and, in turn, how schools support the brand.

Vending machines can also be a lucrative revenue source, and the big soda marketers have secured contracts with many school districts involving large lump-sum payments in exchange for exclusive distribution in school hallways and cafeterias. More and more schools, trying to provide cafeteria food that teens will actually enjoy, are inviting quick-service vendors onto school property. Schools with open campuses—for better or worse—figure that if teens are going to go off-campus for branded fast food, they might as well provide it on campus.

But as teen waistlines have ballooned, so has the public's scrutiny of the symbiotic relationship between schools and fast-food marketers. To appeal to often-wary school administrators, food and beverage marketers are looking at other approaches in addition to stocking vending machines with healthier offerings (water, juices, milk, sports drinks, yogurt, carrots, etc.). Such companies frequently sponsor reading contests, academic or athletic awards and scholarships, or even philanthropic service projects.

Our experience is that schools will cooperate if what you offer them has educational or community-based merit and the school is appropriately compensated. Although we do little in-school research, when we do (always for a client who already has a relationship with the school), we make an appropriate donation to the school and minimize any commercial component of the work we do.

A final thought on marketing in schools: do your homework before starting down this path. Make sure both your product or service and your promotional method will engage teens and be appropriate for the venue. Equally important, involve the community from the start, especially if your idea is likely to be met with any resistance or controversy. Take care to meet with school boards, parent groups, and school administrators. Remember that a bruising fight over the propriety of your marketing campaign could end up doing more harm than good for your brand's image.

Cause-Related Marketing

Teens view "cause" marketers in one of two ways—with compassion or suspicion. Teens skeptical of corporations that sponsor causes question companies' true intentions, wondering whether corporate America genuinely cares for the issues it sponsors or is simply aligning itself with a good cause to achieve goodwill or profit.

Other teens are a bit more trusting of companies that connect themselves to social issues, acknowledging that cause-related sponsorships can foster feelings of respect and empathy toward the sponsoring company. Importantly, though, teens stress that both the cause and its company-sponsor must relate thematically, or at least connect in some obvious fashion. Companies and causes that appear to have a good "fit" (such as Avon and breast-cancer prevention or Nike/Michael Jordan and the Make-a-Wish Foundation) seem more credible to teens than those that appear to be ill matched (such as Philip Morris and youth smoking "prevention").

Regardless of how teens perceive these companies or their intentions, our experience is that a company's charitable act alone will not drive purchases or establish a strong affinity to a company or brand. Although teens tell us that cause-related marketing is admirable—and may boost a company's image—they contend that it's rare for such marketing to change their consumer behavior or motivate a purchase. In fact, teens say causal marketing could backfire on a brand. In qualitative research, we consistently hear from teens that they would prefer if companies simply offered lower prices than earmark a percentage of proceeds to a cause, no matter how special.

As discussed in Chapter 5, if you're considering a cause-marketing effort, keep in mind the issues that hit close to home, such as child abuse, health, drinking and driving, literacy/education, disaster relief, etc. These are the issues about which teens are most concerned.

Promotions

In a recent wave of The TRU Study, we asked teens nationally about the kinds of promotions in which they have participated during the past three months. What we discovered reinforces what teens consistently tell us in qualitative research. They prefer promotions that play to their nature: teens love free stuff; they want instant gratification; and, they can be pretty lazy (as can adults!) when it comes to participating in promotions. One of our

Trendwatch panelists aptly put it this way: "I think kids my age get excited by anything that has the word 'free' in it. 'Free' is a good word."

Instant-wins. Free is key when it comes to teens, especially if what's free is awarded on the spot. Our quantitative data show that more than two-thirds of teens in the past three months had looked to see if they were instant winners, making instant wins the most popular type of promotion. In study after study, we've found that promotions that offer immediate gratification are teens' favorites. There's no risk and no work in instant-win promotions, yet there's the real possibility of reward (and sometimes, it's big). But even if they're not lucky enough to score a million bucks, teens really don't mind—especially if they were planning to buy the product anyway. Enough teens have instantly won a free soft drink or candy bar to make it worth looking "just to see" if they're a winner. And, even if they don't win, their friend sitting next to them might; therefore, instant wins typically are noticed and enjoyed by more than just the participant—a good thing for your brand. We believe instant wins motivate purchase. They don't necessarily increase a teen's affinity for your brand, but a promotion that gains trial not only goes to the bottom line, it also gives your brand an opportunity to gain teen favor. So although instant wins may not be the best loyalty builder because other brands are out there doing it too, teens expect your brand to do the same.

Free Samples. A member of TRU's Trendwatch panel raved about Jolly Rancher's Fruit Chew lollipops, which had just been introduced and which she discovered through a free sample at the Taste of Chicago summer festival. "I wouldn't have ever known about it except for the booth [at the festival]," she explained. "But they were handing out a bunch, so I gave some to all of my friends. Next time I'm in the mood for a sucker, that's the kind I'll get."

Teens can't say enough about free samples and gratis gifts-with-purchase. Much of our research shows that product sampling and gifts can increase brand equity, build goodwill, and—providing the product itself is strong—deliver new converts. In fact, this method of marketing is so dominant, teens often recommend it as the best way to reach people their age.

Teens are famously averse to risk. They don't want to spend money on something that will hurt their appearance or damage their reputation. Girls often tell us how much they appreciate cosmetic samples because if they don't like how the product looks on them, they don't feel cheated.

This doesn't mean teens are cheap by nature. Far from it—their expertise in obtaining the cash necessary to get what they want is well documented. Rather, a primary reason they appreciate free samples seems to be their innate aversion to waste. Once they've tried a product and deemed it acceptable for their own use, they have little problem buying it or convincing a parent to do so. They just can't stand to see a large bottle of skin cream or a new CD gathering dust—even if they hate the product.

As much as teens consistently demonstrate a real attraction to what's new, when it comes to putting their money where their curiosity is, they hesitate. Recently, during a qualitative-research project for a new soft-drink brand, respondents were nearly universal in expressing their interest in trying the drink. They felt that its unconventional name, color, and packaging were particularly alluring. Asked whether they would then buy one if they saw it at retail, many explained that they would first want to sample it to hedge their approximately $1.00 investment. Fortunately, marketers have an array of forums for sampling new products—especially beverages and food, from retail to in-school (get your product into vending machines and you can be sure that the buyer's friends will ask for a "taste"), street fests, skate parks, sporting events, concerts—you get the idea!

Sampling obviously works better with some products than with others. It's relatively simple to offer free hot-dog samples at the supermarket, and it's fairly inexpensive to send magazine subscribers a tester-sized container of fragrance. However, as many marketers are aware, giving away

Teen Participation in Promotions

Teens are most likely to have participated in "instant winner" promotions.

(percent of teens responding when asked, "Companies offer lots of different promotions. Which have you personally done in the last three months?")

Checked to see if you're an instant winner	68%
Got a free sample	56
Used coupons to lower purchase price	50
Entered contest or sweepstakes	33
Received free gift with purchase	30
Particpated in online/'Net promotion	25
Sent in a cash rebate	14

Source: The TRU Study, Teenage Research Unlimited, Inc.

large quantities of jeans, electronics, or athletic shoes requires a significantly larger budget. In these cases, consider selective sampling: make sure your bigger-ticket products get into the hands (or onto the bodies) of Influencer teens. Talk about grassroots marketing! The right teens (those older trendsetters whose cues are adopted by others) can be the best ambassadors of your new product or brand.

Given the limitations of product sampling, marketers may wish to take advantage of teens' liberal view of what constitutes a product sample. Many teens are drawn to discount coupons, which can be a form of product sampling for more expensive items. One advantage of coupons for marketers is that they ensure the recipient must spend at least some cash to enjoy the reward. One drawback of coupons for teens is that they lack the immediacy and no-strings generosity that make a product sample appealing. Teens also can't decide how they feel about a product through a coupon, and sometimes (well, a lot of the time!), they simply lose the coupon.

Teens also appreciate small giveaways unrelated to a brand's core offerings. Seasonal items that evoke the carefree nature of youth or items that would help them in school (or at least help their image) are good bets. Although cost is always an issue, it's important not to sacrifice quality and desirability in the name of economy. Giving away cheap, shoddy, or age-inappropriate trinkets will likely do more harm to a brand than doing nothing at all.

Contests and sweepstakes. Hoping to rake in their share of phenomenal prizes, one-third of teens entered a contest or sweepstakes in the past three months. Though teens tell us these kinds of promotions are the longest of long shots, they admit they simply can't resist. And because the 'Net makes it so easy to enter contests, teens are clicking away.

Teens generally like contests and sweepstakes, but with a few conditions. They put a lot of weight not so much on the quality of the prizes, but on their quantity and appropriateness. Of course teens are attracted to expensive items that are relevant to them—they're more interested in a new car than a new home, for example. And teens typically aren't fans of travel as a grand prize, since they would need parental accompaniment. Teens typically are more interested in a contest with a lot of smaller prizes than one grand prize. Not only do they recognize that their odds of winning increase as prize price points diminish, but they also love a lot of relatively inexpensive products—food, beverages, music, fashion accessories, to name just a few. Of course, in designing promotions, not only should the prizes be connected to either your brand or the nature of the contest itself, but the promotion should do something for your brand beyond simply driving purchase (although that's not a bad goal!). Teens often have more time than adults (and are more savvy than kids) to think seriously about your promotion. So, any communication (point-of-sale, advertising, etc.) that promotes your contest is in some way going to rub off on your brand.

Teens are adamant about the time period allowed for winning: the briefer the better. And finally, make it easy for teens to participate. If you complicate the process (tedious forms, mail-in rebates, etc.), don't expect teens to play.

Although contests and sweeps may generate product interest or even trial, there's no certainty that they will instill a sense of loyalty. Think hard about the bigger objectives of your brand; design promotions that not only offer short-term potential (i.e., sales), but longer-term brand building.

Online Promotions. In 2003, one-fourth of teens had participated in an online promotion. This number increases daily, with not only more teens going online but also with almost every teen-friendly Web site offering promotions or contests. Teens are somewhat hesitant to participate in online promotions. They consider their online time precious, and they say they don't have the time to slog through the overwhelming number of unsolicited (and often irrelevant) pop-up promos that regularly clog their browsers. Many teens rely on free e-mail services or AOL, which attract more spam than many adults receive at their work e-mail address. Two other reasons why some teens are hesitant to participate in online promotions are (1) most have been warned by their parents not to (especially when required to submit personal information, such as their home address), and (2) teens are leery that certain promotions are nothing more than scams. Given their suspicions, it's important to think beyond the typical online promotions and contests. Instead think about how—through appropriately targeted content and relevant partnerships—you can offer teens a more meaningful promotion that concurrently benefits your brand.

Rebates. Not surprisingly, sending in cash rebates is last on teens' list of the types of consumer promotions in which they participate. Unless their parents goad them into filling out rebate cards for school-supply or high-tech purchases, teens are loath to spend time working for cash they won't see for weeks.

Rules for Promotions

Based on our promotions-related research, TRU has compiled a simple list of "rules" for creating promotions that resonate with teens. In addition to remembering the importance of the basics—"free," "fun," "instant," and "easy"—consider the following:

Give teens options. Rather than offering winners specific prizes (which might not match their interests), think about providing winners with choices. Remember, teens are all about customization. So, if the prize awarded is a shopping spree, don't pigeonhole winners into a spree at one clothing store; instead, let them choose. Can you imagine an Edge teen wanting to win a shopping spree at an all-American apparel retailer? No chance. But if they could blow the bundle at Edgier stores such as Hot Topic or PacSun, they would be far more interested in your promotion.

Involve friends. As with most things in life, teens tell us they're more likely to enter promotions when they're able to participate with friends. For example, if the prize is a video-game system, throw in components that friends could use (extra game controllers, Blockbuster certificates for renting games, food for lots of hungry guys) or participate in (a makeover for you and your best friend, two backstage-pass tickets, dinner for a group of girls). Remember, teens are social animals—friends make their experiences more fun and memorable. Even more important, some teens just won't go it alone. The only way they will participate in almost anything voluntarily is with friends; so, make sure your promotions are friend-friendly.

Support your marketing message. It should go without saying that promotions should leverage and link to the brands' main message; this is key to ensuring the promotion is properly connected to your brand in consumers' minds. Why do so many teens tell us they can't remember the brand behind a promotion in which they participated? It failed because the brand did not link its message to the promotion in a meaningful way.

Honda let teens know that its Civic brand was all about customization by way of a clever, relevant entertainment-marketing partnership. The car brand enlisted two teen-favorite alternative bands (Everclear and Blink 182) to customize their own Honda Civics. After band members designed their Civics, the autos went "on tour" with the bands and were prominently parked near concert-venue entrances. Bold signage let concert fans know how the band customized its car, and, in a clever promotional twist, teens could sign up for a chance to win the car.

Keep it real. Teens are naturally skeptical of promotions that focus on an elusive grand prize. After all, most don't know anyone who's ever won a grand prize. It's up to you to keep this skepticism in check—in fact, you can use it to your advantage. Rather than awarding just a few once-in-a-lifetime megaprizes, offer scores of highly attainable smaller cash-value (but still desirable) prizes. Slim Jim and *American Pie II* did exactly that when they teamed up to promote the theater release of the much-awaited sequel. With its lower-budget print promotion, the beef-stick brand with the irreverent image leveraged the film's rebellious humor and offered thousands of smaller, easily winnable prizes plus an appropriately funny grand prize (the infamous flute from the film). Not only does the tactic of offering many inexpensive prizes help teens feel they have a better chance to win (or at least hearing about a "friend of a friend" who won), they may even feel better about your generous brand.

Partner, partner, partner! Forging promotional partnerships with like-minded brands is booming these days, and for good reason. Teaming up with another brand has several benefits: you can share promotional costs, gain exposure to different (or untapped) teen segments, and gain access to your partner's unique resources. The key here, though, is to make sure that the nature of the partnership (and who you're partnering with) makes sense for your brand. A promotion involving the hardcore-rock band Insane Clown Posse and wholesome-image Oreos probably would leave teens scratching their heads. Think before you link.

A recent example of a natural partnership paired automaker Toyota and Quiksilver's Roxy brand of surfer-girl apparel. In an effort to better target young female drivers, Toyota and Roxy launched a limited-edition promotional line of "Roxy Echo" vehicles. The cars were specially designed to appeal to surfer girls (and surfer girl wannabes), and came complete with Hawaiian-print fabric, tropical-colored paint, Roxy logos, and a special surf-board-toting luggage rack. Not only did the partnership cater effectively to teen girls, but it also gave girls a reason to think favorably about both brands in a new way.

A growing trend is entertainment-marketing partnerships (defined as partnering with entertainment properties in music, television, or film), creating a high-profile, multiplatform marketing vehicle for your brand. In such a venture not only does your brand reap the partnership benefits outlined above, it's also aligned with cutting-edge media vehicles—keeping your promotions (and therefore your brand image) trend-relevant and fresh. A recent example involves the entertainment-marketing partnership of teen-girl magazine *YM* and media mecca MTV. The two youth powerhouse brands teamed up in a broadly integrated campaign, offering teens free stuff (with a Watch 'n' Win component and the YM/MTV Party Paks of free advertiser samples at the MTV store) and behind-the-scenes peeks into MTV and *YM* (via weekly MTV segments featuring *YM* editors, and an MTV-themed issue of *YM*). Not only did the effort boost the MTV Store's sales by 52 percent during the promotion, but the YM/MTV issue was one of the biggest in the magazine's history.

Although the above example is a marriage between two high-exposure media vehicles, nonmedia brands (such as apparel or packaged goods) can also get into the act. Even as basic a product as a breakfast cereal can engage in an entertainment-marketing partnership. Honey Nut Cheerios, for one, recently aligned with similarly lettered boy-band O-Town via an online, print, and retail program offering free posters and inside looks at the band.

Advertising

Over the past 20-some years, TRU has experimented with almost every conceivable research design and has focused on almost every imaginable subject. Still, the type of research I enjoy moderating the most is one of the most basic: advertising research. Maybe it's because seeing the results of these studies (i.e., the produced commercials) on TV is as close to show business as most researchers get. But I think the real attraction is that although advertising is an enduring mystery, I think we gain more understanding with each project.

My mentor in this business, Dr. Burleigh Gardner, published a monograph at age 80 titled, *A Conceptual Framework to Advertising*. Dr. Gardner's premise for writing the book, which was excerpted on page 1 of *Advertising Age* at the same time we founded TRU (May 1982), was fairly straightforward: to provoke thought and dialog and, in doing so, get closer to understanding how advertising really affects consumers.

Ad research among teens is particularly fascinating. The process reveals how difficult it is to consistently communicate as intended with an audience as diverse as teens while concurrently entertaining, inspiring, and/ or motivating them. I've been fortunate to have worked on many groundbreaking campaigns for some of the world's most influential youth brands and to have collaborated with some of the smartest researchers, brand managers, account planners, and top creative talent. It's hard not to have been entranced with the experience. I've learned much from it.

It's important to understand advertising's role in teen culture. First and foremost, advertising is more than a means to sell a product or to shape feelings about a brand. It's ingrained in teens as a staple of their lifestyle. It's information on which they depend. And it's social currency. Just as teenagers discuss new movies, music videos, or plotlines of their favorite TV shows, they also talk to one another about advertising. Sometimes they praise it. Other times, they trash it. Teens can be a most unforgiving audience, but they can also be the most embracing.

The more work we do on advertising, the more I'm reminded that advertising is more art than science. No question, it would be easier to consistently produce winning advertising if it were a science—if there were a set of formulas to be followed for various strategies and audiences. Copy-testing services provide full ranges of normative data—both hard quantitative measures (such as recall and persuasion) and more diagnostic measures (such as personal relevance or age appropriateness). These quantitative measures are deceptive, however, because they give the impression that advertising is a science. Instead, the science is in researching advertising, not in creating it. The burden of developing effective advertising lies in the imaginations of those who create it, guided by advertising strategy, which is guided by (hopefully) compelling, accurate, rich, consumer insights.

In our syndicated study, we ask teenagers to list the dos and don'ts of creating effective teen-directed advertising. We developed this measure by first testing it qualitatively, talking to teens in-depth about advertising. We showed teens a broad range of youth-directed TV ads from a variety of product and service categories—some that we thought excellent and others poor. After showing them the ads, we got them talking and jotted down their thoughts on an easel pad. In market after market, the teens were so involved in the discussion that we literally papered the room with sheets from the pad. We combined, condensed, and modified the rules, creating a list that we quantified in our syndicated study. Since then, this list has undergone further revision, based on our continued qualitative experiences. Included on the following page are the original "rules for advertisers," according to teens. Listed below—titled "Teen Advertising Tenets"—are our general takeaways not only based on the quantitative measure but also our ongoing experience.

The Teen Advertising Tenets

Be entertaining (make 'em laugh!). No question about it, teens love funny advertising. Inevitably, when you ask teens to list their favorite commercials, they gravitate toward those that are humor-based. Additionally, in examining the results of our ongoing quantitative "favorite-commercial" measure, we find the list always populated with ads that are marked by their use of humor.

Nothing attracts teens (and adults as well) to advertising more than humor. Humor is especially convenient in advertising because, if done well, it can broaden an ad's appeal both within and outside the target. Whereas other executional elements, such as celebrities and music, may not appeal to all segments of teens and could alienate some (more on this later), humor has nearly universal appeal.

Keep in mind that although using humor in advertising can lead to high rewards, it's not without risks. I'm reminded of the advertising for the first generation of the Reebok pump shoe—the idea was to create a campaign around the humorous hook of tough NBA athletes and coaches bending down to pump up their high-tops to gain a customized tight fit, with the shoes emitting a funny sound as they did so. The problem was the use of humor (which some teens claimed wasn't all that funny) to sell a new technology to an inherently skeptical audience. In this case, teens (at least at first) didn't buy into the pump technology, in part because the advertising perhaps didn't treat the shoe as seriously as its high price warranted. Not only is humor tough to get right, it must be used judiciously. Still, when you do get it right, you can create memorable, entertaining advertising while concurrently broadening the potential audience for your ad.

An important benefit of humor is the license to be serious without ever taking yourself too seriously. The result is that you become likeable—an important goal for almost any brand.

TRU conducted both the formative and evaluative work on the current "Make 7 Up Yours" campaign. The strategy—from Dr Pepper/Seven-Up and Young & Rubicam—was to make 7 Up more likeable, to get it on teens' radar. What teens told us about 7 Up prior to our involvement with the brand was that they 1) drink it when they can't get Sprite, and 2) drink it when they're sick (it seems to be one of mom's first remedies). Obviously, 7 Up had some baggage to contend with. The solution was a campaign featuring the 7 Up Guy, a well-intended bungler who—in his zealous quest to sell his beloved 7 Up—wreaks plenty of humorous havoc.

Not only has the campaign won major advertising awards, it's also been successful in getting 7 Up back on the map. In fact, over the past four years, teens typically mention 7 Up as the soft-drink brand that produces their favorite ads. Through the use of humor, the advertising has met its serious goal of making the brand more likeable, visible, and relevant. The 7 Up Guy's exuberant enthusiasm for his brand has rubbed off on teens. In describing what the advertising's all about, teens—laughing as they recall their favorite ads in the campaign—explain that the character will do anything he can to sell 7 Up because he himself so loves the drink. Not a bad consumer takeaway!

Let's be clear, using humor isn't the only way to create advertising that entertains teens. If humor isn't the right approach for your brand, based on its strategic direction, you need to find other ways to entertain teens in your advertising. Advertisers know they need to set their brands and messages apart from those of others. Teens appreciate ads that do so—that are compelling, entertaining, or provocative in an original way. When we hear teens say, "Wow, that's different! I've never really seen a commercial like that before," we know our client is onto something (assuming, of course, that the ad is communicating as intended). If you're not going to leave them laughing, leave them thinking or feeling. And here's a bonus "tenet": work to get teens' attention quickly (i.e., immediately), Otherwise, you're apt to lose them either to itchy fingers on the remote control or to another diversion. Then, hold their attention throughout the 30 or 60 seconds. Although there are natural peaks and valleys in every ad—the valleys better not be too low or last too long.

Rules for Advertisers

When advertising to teens, honesty is the best policy. Most teens also say it is important to be funny.

(percent of teens responding when asked, "What are the most important rules that companies should follow when they advertise to teens?")

Be honest	65%
Use humor, make me laugh	52
Be clear	45
Show the product	43
Tell me something important about the product	37
Don't use sex to sell	31
Show situations that are realistic	25
Have a great slogan or jingle	24
Don't talk down to me	22
Don't try too hard to be cool	21
Use great music	21
Show "hot" guys/girls	21
Show people/scenes I can relate to	20
Show people about my age	19
Don't tell me what to do	19
Show me things I've never seen before	14
Don't butcher a song I like	14
Don't make fun of other ads	14
Show celebrities who use the product	8
Show cute animals or babies	6
Be sarcastic	5
Show situations that are "fantasy"	4

Source: The TRU Study, Teenage Research Unlimited, Inc.

Be clear. Just as teens want advertising to entertain them, they also expect it to inform and communicate clearly and succinctly. Teens get frustrated and tune out advertising that doesn't answer their basic questions about your product or brand. Growing up in a high-tech world, teens are adept at quickly processing information. And they're well aware if critical information is lacking. In much of the qualitative work we've done, teens complain that "so many ads never even show the product." Remember, teens' funds are precious to them. If you want them to part with their dollars, you must give them a clearly understood, compelling reason.

Many media planners, when struggling with an ad that doesn't communicate its message as immediately as the client would like, convince themselves (and sometimes their clients) that teens eventually will get the message through repeated exposures. After all, they talk in terms of the number (rather than quality) of impressions. But when exposed to a confusing ad, teens may say, "Yeah, that was cool. But what did it mean?" The point is, teens want to get the message, and they want to get it right away. Here's the key: to teens communication correlates with liking. Probably the converse is even truer: if teens don't understand the point of a commercial, they will dismiss it. Teens are literal and aren't going to "work too hard" to understand what you're saying. There's no reason they should because there's nothing in it for them. As simple as this sounds, our clients sometimes need to be reminded of this.

Recently, an advertising-agency client of ours developed a new campaign for its client's brand. With a limited budget, the agency did some informal qualitative research on its own to test the campaign idea. When I asked the planner at the agency about the research findings, she told me the campaign "scored" well. Although teens didn't immediately "get" the idea, they were intrigued by it. Her comment caught my interest. When asked to elaborate, she explained that the campaign idea was admittedly complex and, therefore, the agency designed the research to allow teen respondents to admit that they didn't get it. By confessing their confusion to fellow respondents, the teens had collectively figured it out. She seemed to believe that this was a sound strategy, facilitating a type of viral marketing—teens would be so intrigued/confused by the advertising that they would naturally talk about it with one another and together decipher the campaign. While I agree that if teens talk about your ads you'll benefit greatly, I disagree that the focus-group environment would be replicated in teens' real world. But more so, I simply do not accept the notion that confusing teens with your advertising is ever a good idea. No matter how interesting the client's brand or campaign, teens are too busy to devote that much mental energy to an advertising campaign.

We recommend you communicate so clearly that teens "get it" the first time. Remember, there are too many alternatives available at the push of a button to expect teens to sit through an ad again and again until the message sinks in, no matter how provocative, cool, or funny it may be. As important as it is to entertain, clear communication and product information must never take a backseat in advertising to teens.

Be credible. Be honest with teens. Almost as a rite of passage, teens develop thick skins regarding advertisers' messages. Teens have been burned enough times (as all consumers have) by overzealous advertising claims that promise one thing but deliver something else. Teen-targeted products have promised them everything from clearer skin to the ability to run faster and jump higher. Some products hold up their end of the deal, but others fail miserably. If there's a chance you can't back up your words, then don't say it! It's that simple. Teens (and particularly those who have been misled in the past) are too savvy, discerning, and unforgiving an audience to give you another chance.

Remember what we said earlier in this chapter about teens' highly developed B.S. meter: there's perhaps no area in which you're more vulnerable than when it comes to making exaggerated claims about your brand. And, in past quantitative work that we've done (see Rules for

Advertisers), you'll see that teens' number-one piece of advice to advertisers is simply "be honest." That's advice worth heeding.

Connect your brand to the ad. Teens today are so bombarded with marketing and advertising messages that their heads spin. As a result, teens easily get confused about who's saying what. In qualitative research, we can't even count the number of times we've heard teens praise a particular ad but are unable to identify the advertised brand. A typical comment is: "That's a really cool ad, but I have no idea who it's for!" And, guess what? Teens get frustrated with that type of advertising.

As mentioned under Tenet # 2 above, teens need you to connect the dots. And, arguably, there are no two bigger dots to connect than your brand and your ad. Even if your brand name registers with teens in advertising, it needs to do so in a relevant manner; "recall" alone isn't enough—it's the quality of the connection. Teens need a reason for your brand to be in the ad. If you're really successful, your brand will be the star of the ad.

Be age-appropriate, but don't try too hard. This is probably one of the toughest tenets to follow: striking the right balance between showing teens you understand them and not acting like you're trying to be a teen. It's like a 45-year-old dad wearing leather pants when his teenaged son invites friends over—frighteningly uncool. Teens want you to relate to their lives, empathize with them, and solve their teen problems more than they want you to try to be cool. Show teens that you get them; don't try to be them!

This is why TRU recommends avoiding the use of teen language when communicating with teens. If you're considering pinching teens' private lingo for your advertising, watch out. As stated previously, teen slang is purposefully designed to be obtuse. Adults generally don't understand it because that's the whole point—it's a highly guarded, ever-shifting, often region-specific collection of words and phrases that imparts a sense of belonging to a select group while excluding everyone else. Generally, when the early adopters suspect adults (or even more mainstream teens) are close to breaking the code, they will change it.

Teens are executionally sensitive. Teens pay close attention to the details in advertising, so much so that a single element can completely turn them off. Before running with a teen-targeted ad (or heaven forbid, a whole campaign) it is critical to test the elements with the intended teen target. That means everything from the concept, themes, and positioning down to the smallest details, including the talent, their clothing, the color palette, even the language used by the talent.

Because TRU conducts teen research, you could say we're slightly in favor of our clients' conducting teen research. But you'll get the same advice from other researchers and almost every successful advertiser out there. One of our favorite "Ogilvyisms" (included as a famous David Ogilvy quote on the agency's corporate Web site) is: "The most important word in the vocabulary of advertising is TEST. Test your promise. Test your media. Test your headlines and your illustrations. Test the size of your advertisements. Test your frequency. Test your level of expenditure. Test your commercials. Never stop testing, and your advertising will never stop improving."

Mr. Ogilvy always looked out for his client's pocketbook. The money spent on research pales in comparison to the amount it would take to fix advertising gone wrong or—worse yet—to undo the damage done to your brand by untested advertising.

When testing advertising, always ask: does the idea communicate its intended message? Is the message important and believable? Is the concept age-appropriate? Can teens (or the specific teen target) personally relate to the idea and its execution? Is the premise new or different? Does it wrongly try to be cool? And do the individual elements of your ad resonate with the teens you need to reach?

Talent and Spokespeople

A favorite advertising axiom is that when you're unsure of how to increase the consumer appeal of an ad, you should throw in a baby or a puppy. This theory seems to be broadly validated. Teens, in our syndicated study, gravitate to ads that feature either of these creatures (although they tend to appreciate animals more). In fact, not only will teens choose ads that include dogs as their favorite, they often list ads featuring almost any type of animal—real or animated, including the Blockbuster hamsters, the Aflac duck, and the Geico gecko among their favorites

It's evident that teens are fans of all creatures furry, fuzzy, and feathered, but what about human? To get a handle on the type of people teens like to see in advertising, we asked respondents to The TRU Study to play the role of advertising casting director. We found that although teens like the idea of seeing someone like themselves in TV ads (someone their age, who's particularly relateable), they're also highly attracted to celebrities. Although teens name "regular person" as the person they would most like to see cast in a TV commercial, the vast majority of teens name some type of celebrity.

We questioned members of our Trendwatch panel about the appeal of seeing a "regular person" in TV advertising and what "regular" person really means to them. They explained that an unknown actor (cast as a "real person") exudes genuineness, while a paid celebrity can be less than credible. But we also conducted an exercise in which teens drew and described the type of "regular" person they had in mind. Although they consistently had in mind a noncelebrity playing the role of a real person, they also envisioned someone who was especially attractive (with almost celebrity-good looks).

We also found our panelists to be quite sophisticated in expressing their personal preferences for celebrity endorsers. For one, they think celebrities are more appropriate for certain types of advertising (and perhaps types of product categories). If there's a serious message that needs to be conveyed, the teens maintained, then a noncelebrity might be more effective in the role—particularly one who's about their age.

Of the various celebrity types we asked teens to rate in the quantitative study, comedians fared the best. Why? Teens love funny advertising. In fact, we would have been surprised if teens didn't give a ringing endorsement to using comedians in advertising. When asked to define a comedian, our panelists think broadly: any actor who has appeared in a funny movie or television show will do—stand-ups are not the only ones who qualify.

When teens talk about casting "actors" in advertising, a hierarchy is evident. Movie stars are number-one with teens, followed by lead characters in well-regarded television shows. Ads benefit based on the stature of the featured celebrity. A commercial starring a secondary actor from a likeable sitcom is less likely to grab teens' attention than an ad starring a movie actor or even a lead from one of their favorite TV shows.

Models as advertising spokespeople are polarizing, but that's no big surprise. Guys, by a three-to-one ratio over girls, want to see models (female models, it would seem) in TV advertising. Girls, who are bombarded by models on the pages of their favorite magazines, often complain that the idea of emulating a model is either too farfetched or too stressful.

African-American teens are especially enamored of celebrity; fewer black than white teens say they want to see "regular" people, while more want to see athletes. This preference is consistent with the scores given by African-American teens to celebrity athletes in The TRU Study. African Americans are bigger sports fans and, more specifically, fans of celebrity athletes from the big-three sports of basketball, football, and baseball.

As with employing humor in advertising, hiring a celebrity spokesperson is not without risks. Because teens spend an enormous amount of time monitoring the media, they know who the real bad boys are, and they know who's posing. Employ a poseur and you wind up with a silly, harmless, ineffectual spokesperson who will kill any credibility you have. Employ a real bad boy, though, and you may get everything you expected—and more.

Allen Iverson is one of teens' favorite athletes and a confirmed bad boy. The Philadelphia 76ers' star plays by his own rules (and, occasionally, the NBA's), and his teen fans love him for it. Guys appreciate his skills, and many emulate his hip-hop persona, while girls are attracted to his rebellious image. Iverson has a sponsorship agreement with Reebok and his own line of basketball shoes. But he's also has had his share of legal skirmishes. Obviously, it's important to gauge your risk aversion. In the case of Reebok, the brand likely benefited by its association with an athlete who feels genuine and exudes real street cred.

The list of celebrities who have tangled with the law is long. Many marketers carefully avoid those with tough images, preferring safer bets such as Yao Ming or the Williams sisters. Still, humans are quirky—image and appearance don't allow you to predict with any real confidence who's going to wind up in trouble or as a liability to your brand or organization. (Proving the point, on final editing of this book, we needed to strike Kobe Bryant as an example of a "safe bet.")

The media spotlight can magnify even the tiniest of stories, and larger stories take on a life of their own. When partnering with a celebrity spokesperson, remember that most teens are intrigued by risk and rebellion. You need to carefully weigh the advantages of employing any celebrity—especially a renegade—against your brand's image.

If you find you've chosen your celebrity spokesperson poorly, take comfort in this knowledge: although suburban parents may find your association with alleged criminals distasteful, teens in urban markets will likely be much more forgiving. Many inner-city teens are deeply mistrustful of law enforcement in all its machinations, and they give the benefit of the

The Type of People Teens Would Like to See in Advertising

Teen guys and girls have different preferences for advertising spokespersons.

(percent of teens responding when asked, "Whom would you most like to see in a TV commercial?")

	total	female	male
Regular person	30%	37%	23%
Comedian	28	25	32
Musician	25	31	19
Athlete	22	16	26
Actor	18	23	14
Model	15	7	23

Source: The TRU Study, Teenage Research Unlimited, Inc.

doubt to their uncompromising hero rather than to the police or the district attorney. In fact, urban consumers seem to consider Iverson's legal troubles little more than the establishment's punishment for nonconformity. His line of shoes experienced sales increases in Eastern and Midwestern cities immediately after his most recent legal entanglements.

Although they may tell you otherwise, teens—especially those younger and African-American—are drawn to celebrity spokespeople. The trick, then, is in selecting which celebrities to use and using them properly. What's key, of course, is to make sure your brand at least costars with the featured celebrity. By not being overshadowed, your brand can receive the "halo" effect of being associated with a respected and/or intriguing person.

Are celebrities a "must have" in ads to break through the clutter and command teen attention? The answer, of course, is no. As stated earlier, teens themselves tell you that "regular" people (i.e., really good-looking, age-appropriate, unknown actors posing as teens or young adults) are effective in conveying advertising messages. But without celebrity, the onus is on you to grab teen attention through other means—typically, through clever or just plain funny ads.

The Role of Music in Advertising

The use of well-known musicians in advertising is polarizing to teens. Though rap and certain rock artists signal to teens that the advertising in question is specifically for people their age, many teen music aficionados detest the role of musicians in commerce. They want their artists to remain pure—they don't want them "selling out" by hawking commercial products.

It's been just over a decade since Nike rocked the advertising world by pairing John Lennon's "Instant Karma" with a TV commercial for what's arguably the ultimate in conspicuous male teen consumption, Air Jordans. It's a testament to how far marketing has encroached into artistic expression that 11 years later, all the fuss over Nike's commercial seems rather quaint.

The automotive industry is another major player in the marketing-with-music phenomenon. Automakers have traditionally built cars that appeal to the people who buy cars—specifically, older people. Younger, trendier consumers reject these products as stale and uninspired. Consequently, there's an unprecedented rush to market cars that appeal to teens and young adults, even if the median age of buyers is solidly in the mid-forties. As a result, the auto industry has started hawking its wares to a soundtrack comprising everyone from the Barenaked Ladies to Sting.

Volkswagen and Mitsubishi have been two of the savviest proponents of this strategy, using music to construct a cool brand image that stodgier nameplates likely view with envy. Volkswagen's use of the 1980s Trio song

411

"Da, Da, Da" seemed to jump-start the trend, and TRU's Coolest Brand Meter shows that teens responded almost immediately. Years later, Volkswagen still enjoys a healthy cool rating.

Although the German automaker appears to be moving away from music-driven advertising, Mitsubishi has taken up the baton. The brand has paired music tracks with brand-building imagery so successfully that the company offers its "Mitsubishi Music Mix" (a soundtrack of the songs used in its TV ads) as a premium.

There's an even more remarkable story here, however. Although the company began by using familiar songs by the likes of Iggy Pop and the New Radicals, Mitsubishi's smash hit, Dirty Vegas's "Days Go By," was virtually unknown until the TV commercial created a national sensation.

Mitsu's marketers further blurred the line between art and commerce when the "Days Go By" video began airing on MTV. The video itself cast the Mitsubishi Eclipse as the principal star. Casual observers may well have difficulty distinguishing between the Mitsubishi sales pitch and Dirty Vegas's artistic vision. Regardless of your opinion of such interindustry fraternization, the fact remains that teens often list Mitsubishi as one of the cooler car makes in TRU qualitative research.

Now, even staid old General Motors is getting in on the trend. After Cadillac's luxury land-yacht, Escalade, began to receive unanticipated shout-outs in rappers' songs, the stuffy brand noticed burgeoning sales among a heretofore untapped segment: young African Americans. And, GM's Hummer division released 30- and 60-second spots indistinguishable from a music video, for airplay on BET. No logo or tagline appears in the spots, and a URL guides consumers to a Web site with information about the song and a link to the Hummer Web site.

*   *   *

New product launches, sub-brands, brand extensions, advertising, promotions, events, grassroots and viral efforts, partnerships. Where should all these marketing strategies and tactics come from? Certainly it's the responsibility of brand management, their agencies, and consultants to pursue, decide upon, and implement branding and marketing initiatives. But what should be the genesis of those ideas? The short answer is: the consumer. The fuller, more youth-specific answer is: all teen marketing efforts should have at their underpinnings the objective of solving this age group's problems and/or addressing its needs.

That's where consumer research comes into play. Our role—as well as that of other researchers—is to include the consumer in the marketing process. We advocate for teens on a daily basis to assure that their voices are heard loudly and clearly before strategies are formulated, decisions are made, and tactics are put into place. After all, detecting a flawed concept in research certainly beats learning about it in the marketplace!

Every aspect of the marketing business is advancing at breakneck speed. It's paramount, then, that research, which is used to develop, evaluate, and measure marketing efforts, keeps up. At TRU, our methods for involving teens in the marketing process continue to rapidly evolve, from equipping respondents with the latest technology so they can communicate with us in real time to developing proprietary panels of teens with special qualifications (including our own Trendwatch panel of Edge and Influencer teens) to conducting more and more ethnographic-style projects with video reports.

Still, the more years I've spent in this business, the more I'm convinced that consumer research is more an art than a science—or, more specifically, an art that borrows greatly from the social sciences. Sure, we can literally produce tons of data, using a variety of impressive, sophisticated analytical techniques. But what it really comes down to is: does the research result in a relevant understanding of teens' psychology? Do the specific insights guide our clients toward making the best decisions?

Regardless of your methods and the particular researchers with whom you partner, what's key is that you recognize that the consumer must always be front and center in everything you do and plan to do. Marketing must be consumer-driven and marketing to teens must take into account their unique needs, desires, and worldview.

I suppose it's both fitting and not surprising (coming from a researcher) that the final recommendation of this chapter on marketing (in fact, the final sentence of entire book) is that all marketing efforts be based on real consumer insight. In other words, do your research!

Index